Black Southerners In Gray

Black Southerners In Gray

Essays On Afro-Americans In Confederate Armies

By

Arthur W. Bergeron, Jr., Thomas Cartwright, Ervin L. Jordan, Jr.,
Richard Rollins, Rudolph Young

With An Epilogue By Andrew Chandler Battaile

Edited by Richard Rollins

Rank and File Publications
1926 South Pacific Coast Highway Suite 228
Redondo Beach, California 90277

Rank and File Publications
1926 South Pacific Coast Highway Suite 228
Redondo Beach, California 90277

Cataloging-in-publication data.
Richard Rollins, Editor. Black Southerners In Gray: Essays On Afro-Americans In Confederate Armies.

ISBN Number: 0-9638993-9-2

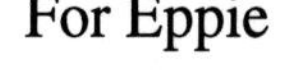

For Eppie

Contents

Part I. Essays

1. *Black Southerners In Gray*
by Richard Rollins.....1
2. *Louisiana's Free Men Of Color In Gray*
by Arthur W. Bergeron, Jr. 37
3. *Different Drummers: Afro-Virginians As Confederate Loyalists*
by Ervin L. Jordan, Jr. 57
4. *Servants and Soldiers: Tennessee's Black Southerners In Gray*
by Richard Rollins 75
5. *"Better Confederates Did Not Live:" Black Confederates In Nathan Bedford Forrest's Commands*
by Thomas Y. Cartwright 95
6. *Black Confederates In Lincoln County, North Carolina*
by Rudolph Young 121
7. *Black Confederates At Gettysburg*
by Richard Rollins 129

Part II. Reviews

1. *Clio's Forgotten Son: James Brewer and* The Confederate Negro
by Ervin L. Jordan, Jr. 145
2.. *Robert Durden's* The Gray and the Black: The Confederate Debate on Emancipation
by Arthur W. Bergeron, Jr. 163
3. *Glimpses of Invisible Men: Essays In Professional Journals and Popular Magazines*
by Richard Rollins 165
4. Epilogue: A Note on the Cover Photograph
by Andrew Chandler Battaile.....171

Preface

In 1990 I read Ed Smith's essay in *Civil War: The Magazine of the Civil War Society* entitled "Calico, Black and Gray." He described certain experiences of black Southerners in Confederate uniforms, and speculated about why they might have fought for the South. In his essay he included a quotation from the diary of Sanitary Commission Surgeon Lewis Steiner describing Confederate troops in Fredericksburg on their way to Antietam. Steiner estimated that about five per cent of them were black.

I was surprised and quite skeptical. I had been a reader of Civil War literature since the 1950s, but I could not recall having ever read about black Southerners in Confederate armies. I decided to track down the quote. Nothing unusual, just a typical Civil War diary. I then decided to do a bit of research to see if I could find more evidence of black participation in Confederate armies. To my surprise, I learned that, if one looked in the right places, there was much information, so much in fact that it became clear that there was a story waiting to be told.

I spent two years looking for more information, and along the way located several photographs of black Southerners in Confederate uniforms, including the one on the cover of this book. I wrote the essay included here entitled "Black Southerners In Gray," and sent it off to Dr. John McGlone, asking him to consider publishing it in *The Journal of Confederate History*.

In doing my research I became aware that there were other historians, both professional and amateur, who were interested in the same topic, though from slightly different perspectives. When Dr. McGlone accepted my essay for publication, I suggested that I contact the other writers and ask them if they would be interested in contributing to a special edition. You are now reading the end result of that conversation and much correspondence.

The essays appear here essentially as they were submitted to me. I decided early on that since each of us had come to this topic independently, in most cases without being cognizant of, or having read the work of the others, some overlap would occur. There are only so many sources. Thus a few of the citations are used by several of us. I have not changed any of the essays, with one exception. When I sent "Black Southerners In Gray" to Dr. McGlone, it included a lengthy summary of Arthur Bergeron's essay. I have removed that from my work, since the entire essay is included.

We thank Dr. John McGlone for his guidance and support. This collection has been nearly two years in development, and has gone through several changes. He has exhibited much patience.

Richard Rollins
June 13, 1994

About The Authors

Arthur W. Bergeron, Jr., is Historian for the Louisiana Office of State Parks and formerly served as Curator at the Port Hudson State Commemorative Area. A native of Louisiana, he received an M. A. and Ph. D. in American History from Louisiana State University. He is a member of several professional organizations and was the recipient of the Charles L. Dufour Award of the New Orleans Civil War Round Table in 1993.

Dr. Bergeron is the editor of *The Civil War Reminiscences of Major Silas T. Grisamore, C.S.A* (Baton Rouge: Louisiana State University Press, 1993), and author of *Confederate Mobile, 1861-1865* (Jackson: University of Mississippi Press, 1991) and *Guide to Louisiana Confederate Military Units, 1861-1865* (Baton Rouge: Louisiana State University Press, 1989). His essay originally appeared in *Civil War History* in 1986, and is reprinted here with some revisions, with their permission.

Thomas Y. Cartwright, a native Tennesseean, studied American history at Middle Tennessee State University and the University of Tennessee. He is co-owner of Battlefield Tours in Franklin, and Curator and Historian of the Carter House. He is a frequent lecturer and author on a variety of topics related to the Civil War in Tennessee.

Ervin L. Jordan, Jr., is the Associate Curator of Technical Services, Special Collections Department, University of Virginia Library. He specializes in Confederate history and is the author of *The 19th Virginia* (1987), *Charlottesville and the University of Virginia In The Civil War* (1988), and *Black Confederates, Afro-Yankees: The History of the African-American Experience in Civil War Virginia* (forthcoming). He earned a Bachelor of Arts *cum laude* from Norfolk State University and was a three-time recipient of the Floyd W. Crawford Award for Distinguished Historical Scholarship. He received a Master of Arts from Old Dominion University.

He would like to express his appreciation to Mrs. James Howard Brewer, Durham, North Carolina, and Professor Lucious Edwards, Jr., University Archivist, Virginia State University, Petersburg, for their assistance and cooperation in the preparation of the essay on James Brewer.

Richard Rollins is Vice-President of MidRange Software Solutions and Editor of Rank and File Publications, Redondo Beach, California. He received a Ph.D. in American Intellectual History from Michigan State University and taught at Michigan State, Ohio State University, Carroll College, and the University of Southern California. He is the author of *The Long Journey of Noah Webster*(1980) and *The Autobiographies of Noah Webster* (1989), and editor of *Pickett's Charge: Eyewitness Accounts* (1994) and *A Day With Mr. Lincoln: Essays in Honor of the Lincoln Exhibit at the Huntington Library* (1994). His essay on "Black Confederates at Gettysburg" originally appeared in *Gettysburg Magazine* in 1992. He would like to thank Bob Younger for permission to include it here. He would also like to thank Steve Madden and Jim Stanbery for their comments on various essays.

Rudolph Young is a genealogist specializing in African-American families in the counties along the Catawba River in western North Carolina. His interest in genealogy began in 1976 when he started research on his own family. He was born in Iron Station in Lincoln County, and now resides in Stanley, in Gaston County.

Black Southerners In Gray
Richard Rollins

One of the leading Southern historians of our time, C. Vann Woodward, remarked on the relationship between black and white in the South:

> The ironic thing about these two great hyphenate minorities, Southern-American and Afro-American, confronting each other on their native soil for three and a half centuries, is the degree to which they have shaped each other's destinies, determined each other's isolation, shared and molded a common culture. It is, in fact, impossible to imagine the one without the other and quite futile to try.[1]

Woodward's insight holds true for the Civil War era. We often imagine the armed forces of the Confederate States of America as all-white, but that is far from accurate. The South was a biracial, caste society, and the armies it fielded reflected that peculiar social reality. To imagine the Confederate armies without black Southerners in their ranks is to perpetuate the ahistorical myth of the South as a compartmentalized society. It ignores the real relationship between blacks and whites in the Old South, as well as the role and experiences of a small but significant portion of black Southerners in the Confederacy. The question then, is not *if* black Southerners played a role in Southern armies, but *what* and *how* they contributed to the war effort.

This essay will outline the process through which some black Southerners found their way into combat in Confederate armies. Black participation in Confederate armies can be divided into three categories. They served and bore arms as servants; as private individuals; and as units either predominately-black or made up of all black Southerners.

When the guns of Fort Sumter startled the nation in 1861, they released a great tension that had built up during the long years of controversy between the sections. Both North and South broke out into near-hysterical demonstrations of patriotism. In cities large and small, frenzied demonstrations of patriotism filled the streets with people pledging their lives and fortunes to the war effort. Volunteers signed on to put down the Rebellion or to defend their homeland against Northern aggression.

Black Southerners were also caught up in the emotion of the coming of war. While many awaited anxiously the "year of jubilo," some had a different response. As individuals and in groups, black Southerners across the South took actions that indicated their support for the South. Even before Sumter a group of free blacks in Charleston and Columbia, S.C. had sent messages to public officials, including Governor Pickens. "We are by birth citizens of South Carolina--In our veins flows the blood of the white race, in some half, in others much more than half white blood," said one. All indicated their support for the South. "Our attachments are with you, our hopes of safety & protection from you. Our allegiance is to So. Ca. and in her defense, we are willing to offer up our lives, and all that is dear to us." They offered themselves for "any service where we can be most useful." We are ready, they said, "whenever called upon to assist in preparing the State a defense, against any action which may be brought against her."[2] Another group of "able bodied free colored men" offered to work without pay on the breastworks being built on the coast.[3]

In Georgia another group published the following letter in the *Savannah Evening News*:

> To Brigadier General Lawton
> Commanding Military District
> The undersigned free men of color, residing in the city of Savannah and county of Chatham, fully impressed with the feeling of duty we owe to the State of Georgia as inhabitants thereof, which has for so long a period extended to ourselves and families its protection, and has been to us the source of many benefits-beg leave, respectfully, in this the hour of danger, to tender to yourself our services, to be employed in the defense of the state, at any place or point, at any time, or any length of time, and in any service for which you may consider us best fitted, and in which we can contribute to the public good.[4]

An observer in Charleston noted a "thousand Negroes who, so far from inclining to insurrections, were grinning from ear to ear at the prospect of shooting Yankees."[5] A group of black musicians in Richmond, calling themselves the "Confederate Ethiopian Serenaders" gave the returns of one of their concerts to help pay for gunboats and munitions.[6] Just after Sumter a company of armed blacks was seen passing through Charleston.[7] In Nashville a company of free blacks offered their services to the Confederate government and in June the state legislature authorized Governor Harris to accept into Tennessee service all male persons of color.[8] In Memphis in September a procession of several hundred free blacks marched through the streets under the command of Confederate officers. "They were brimful of patriotism, shouting for Jeff Davis and singing war songs."[9] One black company was sent to Augusta, Georgia to serve with the 3rd and 4th

Georgia Regiments.[10] In Montgomery blacks were seen being drilled and armed for military duty.[11] Two companies of black Confederates were formed in Ft. Smith, Arkansas. They had no weapons, but prepared themselves by drilling and declared themselves determined "to fight for their masters and their homes."[12]

Similar occurrences took place in Virginia. In Lynchburg 70 men enlisted to fight for the defense of Virginia soon after it seceded; a local newspaper raised "three cheers for the patriotic Negroes of Lynchburg."[13] A week later a group in Richmond volunteered "the work of defense, or any other capacity required" and were ordered to report "to the Captain of the Woodis Riflemen."[14] In late April, 60 black southerners carrying a Confederate flag asked to be enlisted. In Hampton 300 blacks volunteered to serve in artillery batteries.[15] In Petersburg a group of blacks who had volunteered to work on defenses held a mass rally at the courthouse square. The former Mayor, John Dodson, presented them with a Confederate flag and promised them "a rich reward of praise, and merit, from a thankful people." Charles Tinsley, a bricklayer and spokesman for the group, accepted the flag and said "we are willing to aid Virginia's cause to the utmost of our ability. We do not feel that it is right for us to remain here idle, when white gentlemen are engaged in the performance of work at Norfolk that is more suitable for our hands and of which it is our duty to relieve them. We promise unhesitating obedience to all orders that may be given us."[16] Off they went, probably dressed in red shirts and black pants, bearing the flag of the Confederacy "of their own free will."[17]

The largest demonstration of all came in New Orleans. A mass meeting attended by black residents was held just after the news had arrived from Ft. Sumter. They declared themselves resolved and "ready to take up arms at a moment's notice and fight shoulder to shoulder with other citizens."[18] Later one black man said to a commanding General of the State Militia, "our fathers were brought here as slaves because they were captured in war, and in hand to hand fights, too. Pardon me, General, but the only cowardly blood we have got in our veins is the white blood."[19] They proceeded to organize a regiment of black Confederate troops with black officers, a unit that will be discussed in more detail later in this essay. Thus all over the South there were black men who responded to the news of war by making public demonstrations of their support for the Confederacy.

Free blacks and slaves provided much of the infrastructure of the Southern war effort. In the course of four years of war hundreds of thousands worked on fortifications. Breastworks, trenches, forts, and other defensive works were built in nearly every city and town in the South, largely by black laborers. Indeed, one of the persistent themes in Confederate politics was the labor question. How should black labor be used? What compensation should be given owners of slaves used on national projects? Blacks staffed Southern hospitals and ran the weapons manufacturing plants in Virginia and Georgia. One historian estimates that at least 20% of the workers in the Confederate Ordnance Department were black. Another states that half of the workers at Richmond's Tredegar Iron Works, the largest and most important in the South, were black.[20] Blacks built the enormous Chimborazo Hospital in Richmond; drove wagons for Southern armies; planted and harvested the crops on Southern plantations while whites were in the army, and dug coal and saltpeter out of Southern mines. As James Brewer has shown, blacks played a central and essential role in Virginia's Quartermaster and Commissary Departments, in Confederate Naval and Ordnance works, the Quartermaster Department, hospitals, railroads, and as transportation workers.[21] By February of 1865, 310 out of 400 workers at the Naval works in Selma were black, and by September of 1864 there were 4,301 black and 2,518 white workers in Confederate iron mines.[22]

Southern blacks also supported the rebellion in individual ways. In New Orleans, black lithographer Louis Pessou produced and sold beautiful full-color pictures of Confederate camp scenes and a copy of the Ordinance of Secession in his shop.[23] In Fort Smith, Arkansas, a black-sponsored ball raised money for soldiers.[24] Richard Kinnard of Petersburg gave $100, and Jordan Chase of Vicksburg, a veteran of the War of 1812, gave a horse for Confederate cavalry and pledged an additional $500 to the cause. A New Orleans real estate broker also gave $500 to the war effort. Not all could give money, but even some of the poorest slaves supported the war: an Alabama slave gave a state regiment a bushel of sweet potatoes, possibly all he had to give. The black residents of Helena, S.C., rounded up $90 for soldier relief and in Charleston a little black girl sent "a free offering of 25 cents."[25] The free black women of Savannah made uniforms for Southern soldiers and among the subscribers of a Confederate loan in Columbus, Ga., was a free man who contributed $300.[26] The "Ladies Gunboat Fund" in Savannah, which eventually produced the *C.S.S. Georgia*, had significant black support.[27] Free blacks in Vicksburg held a ball to raise money for soldiers in Virginia. "The colored folks in every town in the South had given balls, parties, and fairs, for our benefit, and sent thousands of dollars, clothes and blankets, etc..." wrote one Southerner. Blacks even echoed the white tendency to brag about their fighting prowess. "In truth, our servants feel as much pride in this holy war as we do, and are ever ready, as we have frequently seen to prove in battle 'dat de Soufren colored man can whip a norfern nigger and de Yankee to back him.' "[28]

In the town cemetery of Canton, Mississippi, just outside of Jackson, stands a 20' obelisk in memory of the black Mississipians who served in a partisan unit attached to Nathan Bedford Forrest's cavalry in 1864 led by a young Mississippian, Addison Harvey, and known as "Harvey's Scouts." It was built sometime between 1894 and 1900 by William Hill Howcott, a private in the unit. It is dedicated to "the good and loyal servants who followed the fortunes of Harvey's Scouts during the Civil War." It carries a tribute to the "faithful servant and friend Willis Hoscott, a colored boy of rare loyalty and faithfulness whose memory I will cherish with deep gratitude."[29]

The feelings of black Southerners about the war have received scant attention from historians. Perhaps the concept of freedom is so overwhelming in our culture that we assume that all black Southerners believed that victory by the North would bring freedom, whatever might be their interpretation of that idea, and that they naturally sympathized with the North. Certainly this is the framework of perception that Northern soldiers carried south with them.[30] Just as surely we have been misled by the Southern writers before, during and after the war who propagated and endorsed the "myth of the happy slave" to support their view of slavery as a benign institution. We have apparently just begun to comprehend the minds and hearts of black Southerners during the war, and to study and understand how they truly felt about it, and how the war actually affected their lives.

Recent research suggests a very different sensibility. Some sided with the South, some with the North, but the majority were loyal to themselves and their families, and tried to do what was the best for themselves, without regard to abstract political causes.[31] One recalled that he had fought for both North and South, "but I neber fought for the Yankees till dey captured me and put me in a corral and said, 'Nigger, you fought for de South; now you can fight for de North.' "[32] Black Southerners gave support to both sides, and that support was conditional, based on individual assessments of the situation at hand. For the majority, the war brought not elation and joy but anxiety, wariness, and difficult choices. As Clarence Mohr, a historian of slavery, has written recently, there is much to suggest that throughout the war black Southerners "maintained a strong sense of local identity and a bittersweet affinity for the land of their birth." He went on to conclude that during the war "an almost bewildering array of emotions and private considerations" shaped the behavior of individual bondsmen:"

> Concern for friends or relatives in slavery, uncertainty over the war's outcome, personal esteem for white owners, disillusioning contacts with racially prejudiced Northerners, awareness of religiously inspired efforts at ameliorative reform, and the actual expansion of slavery's customary prerogatives all served to bind particular Afro-Americans to the Southern cause.[33]

The primary fact was that the South was home. Some of the 4,000,000 who lived there had roots going back over 200 years. The African "griot" tradition of a village "historian" passing family and tribal history down the generations orally often kept family traditions alive.[34] Despite the oppression of slavery and racism, and sometimes because of it, they had developed intricate networks of relationships to families, friends, (both black and white) in local towns and on plantations. Many felt a strong sense of attachment to their home states, towns and rural areas. In New Orleans, Mobile, Richmond and Charleston, black Southerners had long served in local militia units and had played a significant role in the Revolution and War of 1812. Their strongest loyalty and bittersweet affinities lay with their local area and state, not the Federal government, or some far-off ideal world. Like whites, they thought of themselves as Virginians, Carolinians and Louisianians, or members of a local community, *not Americans*. As Bell Wiley has pointed out, even some of those who followed the Union armies away from their homes returned after short periods of time. Homesickness and a growing awareness that the army could not care for them drove them back to where they started.[35] As Benjamin Quarles, one of the leading black historians of this century has said, "like thousands of white Southerners who personally hated slavery and felt that it was doomed with the coming of the war but who nevertheless defended the Confederacy, these free Negroes had a sense of community responsibility which impelled them to throw their lot with their neighbors."[36]

Many hoped that a victorious South would show its appreciation of its black citizens and loosen the bonds that held them. As one body servant said when he was captured with his master and was questioned about his loyalty by a Northern officer, "I had as much right to fight for my native state as you had to fight for your'n, and a blame sight more right than your furriners, what's got no homes." He was paroled as a member of the Seventh Virginia Cavalry.[37] On the march to Gettysburg one servant talked to a wife of a Pennsylvania farmer who suggested that he slip away from the army and remain in Pennsylvania, a free man. He refused and she asked him "are you treated well?" "I live as I wish," he boldly replied, "and if I did not, I think I couldn't better myself by stopping here. This is a beautiful country, but it doesn't come up to home in my eyes."[38] Another black Confederate underscored the wish to improve life in the South by defending it when he stated they hoped to raise esteem for blacks amongst both blacks and whites by fighting for the South: "no matter where I fight," he said, "I only wish to spend what I have, and fight as long as I can, if only my boy may stand alone in the street equal to a white boy when the war is over."[39]

Many reasons existed for black Southerners not to perceive the North as a land of freedom and opportunity. Stories circulated throughout the South that the Yankee soldiers were monsters who would treat them badly, as indeed they often did.[40] Sherman's troops in Georgia were especially rough on black Southerners.[41] Several Northern states had laws prohibiting black immigration and even residency, and all had discriminatory laws. Lincoln himself, "Father Abraham" to some, repeatedly declared that he was no abolitionist, and did little to make

Southern blacks feel they were welcome in the North. Combined with the difficulty of the escape process, these factors probably caused some to seek ways to work within the context of the Civil War South.

In addition to psychological and emotional ties, many free black Southerners had economic and material reasons for siding with the South. Significant divisions existed between free blacks and slaves, and some free blacks aligned themselves with whites against slaves. In their eyes, the degradation of slavery elevated their own status just as the degradation of all blacks elevated the status of all whites.[42] John Chavin, a free Negro preacher and schoolteacher, opposed emancipation and urged his friends to oppose abolitionism.[43] Ethnic and religious differences also caused divisions because slaves, noted a writer in the *New Orleans Picayune*, felt that free blacks "put on too many airs, and he scoffs at him and hates him accordingly."[44]

The number of affluent free blacks in the South grew dramatically in the 1850s, a decade of unprecedented prosperity and continuous economic expansion in the South. In Charleston, 75 whites rented homes from blacks. By 1860, there were 26 free black residents of Nashville who, with no property in 1850, had managed to accumulate net assets of $1,000. Labor shortages caused increases in wages for skilled craftsmen, and free blacks prospered as bricklayers, barbers, machinists, carpenters, and in many other professions.[45]

Many prosperous free blacks were mulattos who had been given or inherited property from their white parent. While marriage between blacks and whites was outlawed, racially mixed couples were numerous, so much so that in Louisiana a special term, "placage,"was coined to designate it. They became successful as plantation owners as well as farmers, artisans and skilled craftsmen. By 1860 in Charleston alone they owned $500,000 in property. They formed small clans of related families and friends and aligned themselves with the planter aristocracy. For example, the two wealthiest black farmers in Virginia were Priscilla Ivey and Frankey Miles, both of whom had been mistresses of white slaveowners. A successful North Carolina barber-planter was the son of a prominent merchant-shipper and an Ibo woman. Former slave Robert Rentfro owned a famous hotel in Nashville. St. Louis had a long Spanish and French Creole tradition and there the four most prosperous free families were all descendants of white settlers and black women. Louis Rutgers, who eventually amassed an estate of $50,000, was the slave son of a Dutch immigrant.[46]

Perhaps the group that had the strongest vested interest in seeing the South victorious were the black slaveowners. In 1830 approximately 1,556 black slaveowners in the deep South owned 7,188 slaves. About 25% of all free blacks owned slaves.[47] A few of these were men who purchased their family members to protect or free them, but most were people who saw slavery as the best way to economic wealth and independence for themselves. The American dream in the antebellum South was just as powerful for free blacks as whites and it included the use of slaves for self-improvement. They bought and sold slaves for profit and exploited their labor just like their white counterparts. In South Carolina, John Stanley owned 163 and William Ellison owned 97. The Metoyer clan of Louisiana owned nearly 400. By 1860, so many black women in Charleston had inherited or been given slaves and other property by white men, and used their property to start successful businesses as caterers, dressmakers, and other small businesses, that they owned 70% of the black-owned slaves in the city.[48] Horace King of Russell County, Alabama, was born a slave but was freed and became a highly skilled and successful bridge-builder, employing slave labor in his business. During the war he was a frequent contributor to the Southern cause and furnished uniforms and money to the sons of his former master.[49] These black slaveowners undoubtably understood that a Northern invasion and victory would bring economic and social ruin to them. And it did.[50]

Even some slaves might believe they had a vested interest in a Southern victory. Skilled labor was in great demand before and during the war, and slaves with training benefited from the economic pressure. They were often rented out by their masters for goodly sums and because of their value were given incentives to do good work and stay with their masters. Some were allowed to live on their own away from their owners and to live nearly as freely as whites. They earned wages that made many whites envious and the war stimulated this trend. One slave blacksmith bragged that his income exceeded that of "any white man in the shop with him." In addition, skilled slaves could keep any money they earned in their spare time. For example, in 1864 one black Southerner made $7.50 per day in basic wages, plus an additional $6.00 for each breech-band he made for Southern cannon. He made $127.50 in one month in overtime wages alone.[51]

Finally, like their white counterparts, some young black Southerners went off to war because it was an exciting thing to do, the great adventure of their generation. A servant from South Carolina wrote a letter to his sister which summed up his feelings in battle as well as his self-identity, as many other black Southerners must have felt, as a soldier:

> I've bin havin' a good time ginerally--see a heap of fine country and a plenty of purty gals. . . I have also bin on the battle fields and hear the bullets whiz. When the Yankees run I . . . got more clothes, blankets, overcoats, and razors than I could tote. I've got an injin rubber cloke with two brass eyes keeps the rain off like a meetin' house. Im a made man since the battle and cockt and primed to try it again. If I kin kill a Yankee and git a gold watch, and a pair of boots, my trip will be

> made. How other niggers do to stay at home, while we soldiers are havin' such a good time is more than I can tell.[52]

Black Southerners found their way into combat in Confederate armies in three ways, but perhaps the largest numbers were the ubiquitous "body servants." At Fort Mill, South Carolina, there is an unusual monument, with the following inscription:

> Dedicated to
> the faithful slaves
> who, loyal to a sacred trust
> toiled for the support
> of the Army with matchless
> devotion . . . guarded
> "Our Confederate States of America."[53]

These were not the laborers in work-gangs, nor were they the soldiers who volunteered on their own. Body servants were those slaves who before the war had been cooks, butlers, carriage-drivers and other skilled workers who had not worked in the fields but in the "big house" on plantations and on small farms with whites. As Eugene Genovese has pointed out, they often grew up with the children of their masters and had close, though often ambivalent, relationships with them.[54] Sam Newsom of Tennessee remembered the relationship he had with a white boy and linked it to his Confederate service:

> We was sort of brought up together, master Will and I was, and maybe that's why everybody seemed to sort of trust him to me. I used to rock him to sleep. He got to be a fine and reckless sort of gentleman. Then the war came. I went with master Will. Nothing could stop him and I knew he would need me. He got to be a first lieutenant in the cavalry. I slept in the same tent. When he was fighting I stayed with the ambulances. . . I got wounded once at the battle of Sullivan's Creek. Master Will was killed at Chickamauga. I brought his body home. I smuggled him by the pickets, hired a wagon and got him to Chattanooga. From there I brought him on home.[55]

When an English observer estimated that there were 30,000 body servants in the Army of Northern Virginia in 1862 he meant the cooks, valets, and personal attendants.

Blacks seemed to be everywhere in Southern armies, especially early in the War. A Union surgeon, caught behind Confederate lines in

1862, observed the Army of Northern Virginia moving toward Sharpsburg and remarked in his diary on the presence of black Confederates:

> Wednesday, September 10
> At 4 o'clock this morning the Rebel army began to move from our town, Jackson's force taking the advance. The movement continued until 8 o'clock P.M., occupying 16 hours. The most liberal calculation could not give them more than 64,000 men. Over 3,000 Negroes must be included in the number. . . They had arms, rifles, muskets, sabers, bowie-knives, dirks, etc. They were supplied, in many instances, with knapsacks, haversacks, canteens, etc., and they were manifestly an integral portion of the Southern Confederacy army. They were seen riding on horses and mules, driving wagons, riding on caissons, in ambulances, with the staff of generals and promiscuously mixed up with all the Rebel horde.[56]

Black Southerners, and especially body servants, became an integral, important part of Southern armies. One soldier sent his servant home to get supplies and wrote a note to his wife about him:

> He is a great darky-worth his weight in gold even in these hard times. . . He can tell you what things I principally need & more fully than I can write-he knows more about it anyway than I do, knows more about what I have and what I need-he attends to it all.[57]

In 1861 the 3rd Alabama Infantry marched to war with 1,000 white soldiers in the ranks, and almost as many blacks. This was not unusual. Of the 3,000 free blacks in Alabama, nearly all served the Confederacy in one capacity or another.[58] One brigade had a "washing corps" of 150 blacks.[59] Some became superb foragers and made important contributions to food supplies.[60] For their masters, and often for many others, they set up and struck tents, cleaned clothes, cared for the sick and wounded; in the Navy they stoked the fires in steamships and tended the sails on older ships. In short, they performed virtually every act of labor of a personal sort one can imagine.

There were so many black musicians in Southern armies that in April of 1862, the Confederate Congress passed a law authorizing their use and setting their wages as the same as white musicians.[61]

The Confederate government acknowledged their presence in various ways. For example, Samuel Cooper, Adjutant and Inspector General, issued an 1862 order that "the adjutants of the regiments throughout the Army will inquire into and report all cases of slaves serving with their respective regiments without written authority from their masters."[62] In other words, the Confederate government recognized that black Southerners had gone off to join the army: the *Southern* army.

Not all were slaves, owned by whites; many were free blacks with attachments--economic and otherwise-to the people they served. Robert Greene, in *Black Defenders*, lists several who were hired, not owned, and who served for three or four years.[63] Stonewall Jackson's servant, Jim Lewis, was "inconsolable" at Jackson's death. He led Jackson's horse in the funeral procession, then returned to the army and served Colonel "Sandie" Pendleton until Pendleton died at Fisher's Hill in 1864. Lewis was eventually buried in Lexington, not far from where Jackson and Pendleton rest.[64] Peter Vertrees, a Kentucky mulatto, served his white uncle as Assistant Surgeon for three years.[65] Silas Young of Alabama served for three years.[66]

It was not unusual for a servant to work for more than one person over a period of time. Several of the men in Greene's study not only served the entire war, but also with several individuals.[67] Benjamin Singleton of Beaufort, South Carolina entered the army as a servant of Capt. John H. Thompson and stuck with him until he was killed at Second Manassas in 1862. He then worked for Sergeant William Thompson and later Corporal David Thompson until late in the War, when he was with Robert and James Thompson of the Citadel Cadets.[68] It is not recorded whether these were all members of the same family.

Others revealed their dedication to the South's war effort in different ways. One servant who was captured by a Yankee was made to serve a Northern officer, but when sent to a spring to get water, kept on going through the Confederate lines and returned to his former master, taking two Yankee horses with him.[69] Another, Leroy Jones of the 4th Tennessee, joined up with his master and was captured with him. When his master died of typhoid fever, Jones slipped through the lines and went to his master's home, where he remained until given his freedom. Fifty-nine years later he applied for a pension and had several whites support his application.[70] Some of the servants indicated their military feelings by wearing uniforms. The Cahaba Rifles had servants who "with gray blankets, haversacks, and cedar canteens strapped on their shoulders and wearing the Confederate gray uniform, marched behind the company."[71] One slave was even more loyal to the cause than his master. Both were captured and sent to Point Lookout, then exchanged, whereupon they were asked to sign an oath of loyalty to the Union. The master signed, the slave did not. When asked why he refused to sign as his master had, the slave replied: "Massa has no principles."[72]

Servants occasionally captured white or black Northerners. Colonel Arthur Fremantle, a British officer of the Coldstream Guards, visiting the Army of Northern Virginia in 1863 spotted a black

Confederate, "dressed in full Yankee uniform, with rifle at full cock, leading along a barefooted white man, with whom he had evidently changed clothes. General Longstreet stopped the pair, and asked the black man what it meant." The black Confederate said that two white Confederates had captured the Yank, then had a bit too much Brandy, whereupon they turned the prisoner over to him. Fremantle was impressed with the slave's earnestness and seriousness, as well as the "supreme contempt with which he spoke to his prisoner."[73] At another point about 20 servants, on their own initiative, made a night raid on a Northern camp and captured a number of black laborers.[74]

One Confederate reported that when his regiment went into battle their servants went in too, picking off Federal officers. During one charge they found that a half-dozen blacks had actually preceded them, and each brought back a black Federal prisoner. The Southerners kicked and abused the Federals, saying:

> you black rascal you!-does you mean to fight agin white folks, you ugly niggers, you? Suppose you tinks yourselves no 'small taters' wid dat blue jacket on and dem striped pants. You'll oblige dis Missippi darkey by pulling dem off right smart, if yer doesn't want dat head o' yourn broke" said one of our cooks to his captive; "comin' down Souf to whip de whites! You couldn't stay 't home and let us fight de Yanks, but you must come along too, eh! You took putty good care o' yourself, you did, behind dat ole oak! I was a lookin' at yer; and if you hadn't dodged so much, you was a gone chicken long ago, you ugley ole Abe Lincolnite, you![75]

And of course they were occasionally captured in battle by Union troops. Hiram Conaway, a cook, was captured early in the war near Winchester, Va., and held until the end of the war.[76] Eli Dempsey of the 1st North Carolina Artillery was captured in 1862 and held as a regular soldier until 1864.[77] Another servant said "I am proud of my war record." He had been taken prisoner on two occasions, escaped, and returned to his regiment with valuables that had been given to him for safekeeping.[78] Robin, captured with his master during Morgan's raid into Ohio, was imprisoned apart from him. Robin was offered his liberty several times in exchange for taking an Oath of Loyalty. He refused, saying "I will never disgrace my family by such an oath."[79] A number of servants captured at Vicksburg were offered their freedom with Federal protection, but rejected the offers and chose instead to be sent to Northern prisons with those they served.[80]

Since they were a part of the army, they were often drawn into battle. Pompey Tucker was helping a doctor at Second Manassas when "a shell blew off the head of the horse we were driving. Shrapnel from the same shell wounded the doctor." They got separated, and Tucker searched for the doctor while continuing to work with the wounded. A day and a half later he found him as well as another white man from his home area, both severely wounded. He found two horses, loaded them both in a wagon and drove 15 miles to a railroad where he put them on a train bound for Chimborazo Hospital in Richmond. Tucker went with the men, cared for them in the hospital and eventually helped the Confederate effort at home in Virginia, where "I helped the South by capturing six Yank guerrillas-three colored, three white near Mortar Branch, hardly five miles from where I live now," he recalled.[81]

Occasionally the North's mistaken image of the black Southerner --that he could not possibly be expected to fight for the South--was used against them. A servant of Captain George Baylor of the 12th Virginia Cavalry lured an unsuspecting detachment of Yankees into a Confederate ambush.[82] Sam Collier had a similar experience. He had worked for his owner's nephew, and when Colonel Edwards was shot at Belmont in 1861 Collier took care of him. Decades later he remembered:

> When the Yankees came into Madison County, I hid Colonel Edwards' uniforms up in the attic. Then they came to our house that night, and Colonel Edwards told me to burn it up, so I slipped it out early the next morning before daylight and burned it up, so the Yankees could not see it, and find out that he had been in the Confederate Army.[83]

William Bibb had been a carriage driver and waiter for Algernon Bibb in Alabama. When Algernon organized a company in 1861, William went with him. In 1921 Algernon's widow testified that William "had screened his master from being captured by the Federals by joining with them and riding his master's horse for several hours and then made his escape back to Captain Bibb, riding a horse which had been presented his master by General Walker."[84] One black Southern woman was permitted, because Northerners could not imagine a slave spying for the South, to frequently cross into Yankee territory. Called "Confederate Mary" by Northern troops, she secretly delivered messages for Confederate forces and smuggled medicine back into Southern lines.[85] Indeed, black spies were so common that U.S. Rear Admiral David Ammen noted that many of the slaves that had been driven away by Federal troops had returned to Confederate lines with accurate accounts of numbers and dispositions of National troops.[86]

Stories of servants caring for wounded masters abound. Anthony Watts of South Carolina stayed with his wounded master until he died, and then took the body home. Zack Brown was a servant of Robert Coleman, who was shot and taken to the hospital. Brown stayed with him as a nurse until they were captured. Jim Hampton summed up his experience and that of many black Confederates when he remembered that "Samuel Wilkes was killed in July(1862) and I came home with his body." When Captain Cothran of Orr's Rifles was wounded at Second Manassas, servant Wade Childs carried him on his back to the rear of the lines.[87] At Missionary Ridge a wounded 13th Tennessee private was carried by his body servant, Alf, four miles behind the lines. Alf took care of him for months, then returned to the war to work for his master's brother. Alf disappeared at the end of the war, but the three were reunited forty years later at a veteran's convention.[88] George Mills was at Big Bethel, Manassas, Seven Pines, Fair Oaks, Malvern Hill and Antietam with with Captain William Bryson of Hendersonville, N.C. in Ransom's Brigade. Bryson was killed at Antietam. Mills put the body in a rough pine coffin and started off to North Carolina. In Fredericksburg, Va., he used some of the money Bryson had given him for safe keeping to ship the remains by rail to Greenville, Tennessee, where he hired a wagon and a white driver and and finally reached home.[89] Henry Nelson told a similar story and added "that shows you I was a friend to the Southern army. I hid the meat from the yankees to keep them from taking everything we had."[90]

Alex Wharton served two brothers from Tennessee through the Atlanta campaign where both were wounded. Wharton took care of them and others at Chickamauga, Missionary Ridge, and Atlanta.[91]

Others actually took up arms and fought. When one white Confederate refused to go forward with his company at Mechanicsville, a servant named Westley came forward and asked permission to put on the deserted accouterments and took up the gun. He then went into action with the company "and though minie balls of the enemy were falling thick and fast about him, Westley never wavered, but brought down a Yankee at every fire," one of the men remembered.[92] A servant named Edward shot a Yankee soldier who had "made himself especially obnoxious" according to one Confederate Major.[93] Teen Blackburn, servant of Capt. Augustus Blackburn was at Manassas when the Captain got into trouble. Teen picked up a sword, fought off an oncoming Yankee, and thus saved his master's life.[94] One servant encountered a Federal soldier leading two horses; he shot the man, then led the horses into Confederate lines.[95] Another old vet remembered that his regiment's cooks "would not remain in camp, but marched out with the rest, and fought behind their masters." He remembered one man named Archie in particular, for he braved enemy fire to get water and ammunition on more than one occasion. The black Confederates, he recalled, "usually behaved like trumps."[96] It is recorded that at Seven Pines a cook and minister with an Alabama regiment got excited and in the midst of everything took up a rifle and went into battle. He was heard to yell at the regiment "De Lor' hab mercy on us all, boys, here dey comes agin! Dar it is," he exclaimed, as the Yankees fired over their heads, "just as I taught! Can't shoot worth a bad five-cent piece. Now's de time, boys!" and as the Alabamians returned a withering fire and mounted a furious charge, he was heard to shout "Pitch in, White folks-Uncle Pomp's behind yer. Send all de Yankees to de 'ternal flames, whar dere's weeping and gnashing of-sail in Alabama; stick 'em wid de bayonet, and send all de blue ornery cusses to de state of eternal fire and brimstone!"[97]

Stories of servants actually fighting are numerous. One Confederate officer recalled that his servant William, a strong 23 year-old and part Indian, was six feet in height, and "when with me as bold as a lion, having fought by my side in more than one affair."[98] Another officer remembered that at Brandy Station "my negro servant Edmund, formed the officers' servants and colored cooks in line immediately in the rear of the regiment and flourishing an old saber over his head, took command of them. As the troops moved into battle their servants went too, but when the artillery shells started landing, they scattered in every direction."[99] At the same engagement, Tom and Overton, two servants in the 12th Virginia Cavalry, picked up rifles discarded by Northerners and joined the 12th in a charge. They captured the black servant of a Union officer and marched him back to camp at gunpoint, where they proceeded to hold him prisoner. For two months the Yankee servant waited upon the Southerners.[100] Servant Levin Graham refused to stay behind in camp when the time for battle came, instead grabbing a musket, he "fought manfully" and "killed four of the Yankees."[101]

Even the cooks got into the action. Perhaps some of their enthusiasm comes through in the story related in terms common to the Civil War era if not to ours. One veteran remembered that the cooks of his company often joined in the fight:

> You might as well endeavor to keep ducks from water as to attempt to hold in the cooks of our company, when firing or fighting is on hand. In fact, an order has been frequently issued to keep darkies in the rear in time of battle, but although I lectured my boy about it, I was surprised to find him behind me at Manassas, rifle in hand, shouting out: "Go in, Massa! give it to 'em, boys! Now you've got em, and give em H-ll!"[102]

And of course, many black Confederate servants were killed or wounded. One recalled that servants started looking for their masters as soon as they heard they were wounded, whether the fighting had ended or not. Alfred Brown, a Surgeon's Assistant from Georgia, was often close to the lines of battle, and was "wounded twice in one day" at Chickamauga. "A ball was shot through his left thigh and he was wounded in the right leg by a piece of a . . . shell."[103] Hutson Longstreet, a servant for four years, caught a bullet in the neck at Granada, Mississippi,[104] while Wade Watkins of Tennessee was shot in the right leg yet continued to serve the 48th Tennessee Cavalry throughout the rest of the war.[105] J. K. Knight of South Carolina was wounded at Petersburg, and Spencer Copeland had a foot amputated after injuring it while digging barefoot on the breastworks at Charleston.[106] Monroe Jones of the First Mississippi Light Artillery lost both legs at Snyder's Bluff near Vicksburg when a shell exploded.[107]

While body servants, cooks and others found their way into combat as circumstances dictated, other black Southerners enlisted, some officially and some sureptitiously, in regular units as individuals. Any estimate of the numbers involved will be merely a guess, though one reliable historian believes there were 3,000 from Louisiana alone.[108]

Perhaps the most numerous were the nameless individuals who took up the Southern cause. The first Northern officer killed in battle was Major Theodore Winthrop, member of an old, distinguished New England abolitionist family, shot by an unnamed black sniper at Big Bethel. He was a member of the Wythe Rifles of Hampton, Virginia, whose Captain had told him that the "Yankees would take you to Cuba and sell you. If you wish to stay with your wife and children, drive them out of Virginia."[109] General George H. Gordon, the man who ordered the charge at Battery Wagner, noted that "there was sharp picket firing from Wagner, in which many men from my command were killed, and strange stories were bruited about of the fatal precision and fire of a Negro marksman, a Rebel."[110] The Sheriff of Henderson County, North Carolina wrote a letter to a militia commander of his state asking him the bring all free blacks in his company in to check their papers.[111] A black artilleryman fired the last cannon shot at Federal forces as the Confederates abandoned the breastworks (built by slaves) at Yorktown in 1862.[112] William H. Dove and at least two others in the 5th North Carolina Cavalry was officially listed on the muster-rolls as "a free Negro-has no home."[113]

Numerous black Confederates enlisted and served as musicians. Henry Brown of Camden, South Carolina is probably a representative example. While his status at birth in 1830 is unclear, by 1861 he was a highly respected free Negro brickmason who joined a local defense unit, the Darlington Guards, as a drummer. He went with them to Charleston in 1861. After that unit disbanded he went to Virginia with Capt. W. H. Evans' company of the 8th South Carolina Infantry and later transferred to Capt. S. H. Wilds' company of the 21st South Carolina infantry.[114] General John B. Gordon had Josepheus Black and two other musicians in his entourage,[115] and Charles McCuller served as a drummer in the 7th North Carolina Cavalry ("Claiborne's Partisan Rangers") in 1864.[116] Another, "Old Dick" Slate was a veteran of the Mexican War who enlisted as a drummer with the 18th Virginia Infantry in 1861. Along with fellow drummer George Price and fifer Austin Dix, all were listed as "free men of color." One Northerner who managed to observe Confederate troops on the march noted that "the only real music in their column today was from a bugle blown by a Negro. Drummers and fifers of the same color abound in their ranks."[117] James Clark, a free Negro born in Georgia enlisted at the age of 57 in Co. K, 28th Georgia Infantry and served as a fifer until 1865. Several members of his company testified that Clark had not been actually mustered in service but had joined on his own account and was paid by the members of the company for his services.[118] Charles Binger, a veteran of the Seminole War, signed on as a Fifer with the 2nd Georgia Infantry Battalion in May 1861 and served through the Seven Days and at Malvern Hill before being discharged in July 1862 at the age of 68![119] Indeed black musicians were so common that the Confederate Congress passed an act in 1862 providing that "whenever colored persons are employed as musicians in any regiment or company, they shall be entitled to the same pay now allowed by law to musicians regularly enlisted."[120]

Perhaps typical of the many who found their way into the army as individuals was Primus Kelly of Texas. Born a slave in North Carolina, Kelly moved to Texas before the War with the John W. S. West family. They settled in Grimes County, and became successful cotton planters. Kelly grew up with West's three sons, Robert, Richard, and John, Jr. When the war came the three sons joined the 8th Texas Cavalry, part of Terry's Texas Rangers. On the day the regiment boarded a train in Houston to head East, Kelly showed up on his own and went with them. Being black, Kelly was prohibited from officially joining, and no official records carry his name. Yet he donned a gray uniform and carried a gun. Richard was wounded twice in battle, and each time Kelly carried him home to Texas. And each time when Richard returned to the war, Kelly went with him. At Woodsonville, Shiloh, Bardstown, Perryville, Murfreesboro, Chickamauga and Knoxville, all four members of the West family fought, black alongside white. After the war Primus Kelly returned to Texas, bought a small farm near his "brothers," and lived quietly until his death in 1890.[121]

In Sumter County, South Carolina, John Wilson Buckner grew up a free Negro, the son of a mulatto mother and black father. He was also the grandson of William Ellison, one of the most successful free blacks in Antebellum America.[122] Ellison had been born a slave in 1791, probably the son of a black mother and white plantation owner. Ellison was trained as an artisan, making and repairing cotton gins. He was emancipated in 1816, and quickly went into business for himself. Between then and 1860 he developed a very successful cotton gin manufacturing and repair business and diversified into cotton planting. He eventually owned around 100 slaves and his family became a central part of a larger group of black slaveowners in and around Charleston. His two sons tried to join the Confederate service but were rejected, apparently on account of race. They did not, however, shrink from serving the South in other ways. Their chroniclers note that

> few planter families compiled a better war record than the Ellisons. They more than fulfilled every obligation the government imposed. As soon as the call went out, they quit growing cotton and began producing food crops. They supplied their neighbors and the rebel armies with provisions. They hired out their skilled slaves, apparently for war-related work. They paid all their taxes on time and invested their profits in government notes. Rather than slackers, the Ellisons were model Confederates.[123]

Despite being black, John Wilson Buckner joined the 1st South Carolina Artillery in March of 1863. He was wounded in action on July 12, 1863, at Battery Wagner, in the campaign that involved the 54th Massachusetts. His obituary noted that "he was always a freeman and at the breaking out of the war enlisted as a regular soldier in Capt. P. O. Gaillard's company. He served subsequently in Capt. Boykin's company and later as a scout. He was a faithful soldier. . ."[124]

There were many black Confederates in Louisiana, including one who fought at Gettysburg. For the story of Charles F. Lutz and the other black Confederates in Louisiana, see Arthur Bergeron's essay.

Blacks took part in every area of fighting. Hattie Carter was a female free Negro who served as an ammunition runner in Richmond throughout the war.[125] In Mississippi in 1861 or 1862, Elias, a slave belonging to Mr. Baber killed another named Jim. Elias was condemned to be hung. Instead he was given the option to go into the army and fight for the Confederacy. He was released and went into the army.[126] James Young enlisted in Company K, 29th Alabama as a Private in 1862 and stayed in the army until May of 1865, throughout the Atlanta campaign and at Bentonville, despite suffering from frostbitten feet. He was given a pension in 1902, but it was challenged in 1912 by the State Board of Pension Examiners because he was a Negro. In Young's favor a Judge wrote that Young had served in the 29th Alabama and that "he not only deserves the pension for actual fighting service rendered, but as he is now almost eighty years old, he deserves to be advanced into a higher class."[127] Numerous other blacks in Alabama also received pensions for their service.[128] Similarly Tom Bing served as a private in Colcock's Regiment of South Carolina troops under Capt. Bill Peeples for the entire war.[129] Phil Reese and George Dance served in the 8th Tennessee and "remained with the Army until the surrender."[130]

Some black Confederates seemed to have a felicity for use of the rifle. Several accounts of black Confederate sharpshooters exist. The appearance of one during the Peninsula Campaign in 1862, firing at members of Hiram Berdan's First U.S. Sharpshooters caught the imagination of the unit's historian. His account deserves extensive quotation:

> For a considerable time during the siege the enemy had a Negro rifle shooter in their front who kept up a close fire on our men, and, although the distance was great, yet he caused more or less annoyance by his persistent shooting. On one occasion while at the advanced posts with a detail, the writer with his squad had an opportunity to note the skill of this determined darky with his well aimed rifle. Being stationed at a pit on the edge of a wood fronting the treeless stretch of ground around the opposing works, with sand bags piled up for cover, during the forenoon this rebellious black made his appearance by the side of an officer and under his direction commenced firing at us. For a long time this chance shooting was kept up, the black standing out in plain view and cool drawing bead, but failed to elicit any response, our orders being to lie quiet and not be seen. So the Negro had the shooting all to himself, his pop, pop, against the sand bags on the edge of the pit often occurring, while other close shots among the trees showed plainly that he was a good shot at long range. He became pretty well known among the scouts and pickets, and had established quite a reputation for marksmanship, before he came to grief. Emboldened by his having pretty much all this promiscuous shooting unopposed, the pickets rarely firing at him, he began to work at shorter distance, taking advantage of the ground and scattering trees. This was what our men wanted, to get him within more reasonable range, not caring to waste ammunition trying to cripple him at the long distance he had at first been showing himself. They wanted to make sure of him. In the meantime our boys would when opportunity offered, without being seen, post a man forward to await in concealment for the adventurous darky. The scheme succeeded and his fate was sealed. A scouting party was sent out, cornered the black sharpshooter in a chimney top a quarter of a mile in front of their lines, and shot him.[131] A similar account around the same time claims that another black sharpshooter "had done more injury to our men than any dozen of his white peers. . ." He perched in a big tree, behind its trunk and shot at Yankees in front of Yorktown. At one point he was nearly surrounded, and a Federal supposedly shouted at him: "I say, big nigger, you better come down from there." When told that he had been captured he replied "not as this chile knows of"

> and resumed firing, whereupon he was quickly shot through the head.[118]

Finally, black Confederates served in the Navy as well as the Army. When the *C.S.S. Shenandoah* arrived in Liverpool in November of 1865, one black seaman, Edward Weeks, was on board, and thus became one of the last Confederates of any color to cease fighting. At least two seamen were carried on the rolls as "Private(col'd).[132] In one of the three photographs of the *C.S.S. Alabama* a black crewman can be seen peering out at the camera from behind and between two officers.[133] At least three free blacks served as sailors aboard the *C.S.S. Chicora* under Commander Ingraham in the defense of Charleston.[134] The Savannah squadron apparently had several black seamen, the most famous of which was Moses Dallas. He joined the Federal army for a short period but soon deserted and joined the Savannah squadron where he became "the best inland pilot on the coast,"and drew praise and and pay increases because of his effectiveness. On the night of June 2-3, 1864, he led a party of 132 Confederates on an attack that succeeded in sinking a Federal gunboat in Ossabaw Sound at the mouth of the Ogeechee River. He guided the raiders up to the *U.S.S. Water Witch*, and in the ensuing battle apparently was killed, or so it was officially reported. Three months later he quietly reappeared in a blue uniform. He ended up as a Corporal in the 128th U.S. Colored Infantry.[135]

Black Southerners supported the Confederate war effort not only as servants, as individuals in regularly enlisted white units, but also in units that were composed entirely, or almost entirely, of blacks, both free and bonded. These fall naturally into three categories. The first category are units for which our knowledge is exclusively anecdotal. The second category are units of regularly-enlisted black Southerners who were usually free. The all-black units of slaves raised by the Confederate government in March and April 1865 make up a third category.

At least three units of black Confederates were seen during the war, far enough apart in space and time that they cannot be confused with one another. In August of 1861 a Federal officer observed a group he called the "Richmond Howitzer Battery" near Newport News, Virginia that was manned by blacks.[136] A correspondent from the *New York Times* riding with Ulysses S. Grant reported in 1863 on a black artillery crew in Tennessee. "The guns of the rebel battery were manned almost wholly by Negroes," he noted, with "a single white man, or perhaps two, directing operations."[13] An Indiana soldier wrote a letter to his hometown newspaper about an exchange of fire with a group of black Confederates in the Fall of 1861. The story which was then reprinted all over the North:

> . . . a body of seven hundred Negro infantry opened fire

> on our men, wounding two lieutenants and two privates. The wounded men testify positively that they were shot by Negroes, and that not less than seven hundred were present, armed with muskets. This is, indeed, a new feature in the war. We have heard of a regiment of Negroes at Manassas, and another at Memphis, and still another at New Orleans, but did not believe it till it came so near home and attacked our men . . . One of the lieutenants was shot in the back of the neck and is not expected to live.[138]

These units could have been free or bonded men, like those described by John Parker, a slave who was pressed into service as an artilleryman at First Manassas. He had been a fieldhand on a large plantation. The master went off to war in 1861, followed soon by the overseer. He had been sent to work on earthworks around Fredericksburg, Winchester, and Richmond. He records the black population's excitement grew as the battle neared, when "all the colored people" were sent off to the front lines to fight. "I arrived at the Junction two days before the action commenced," he recalled.

> They immediately placed me in one of the batteries. There were four colored men in our battery, I don't know how many there were in the others. We opened fire about ten o'clock in the morning of Sunday the 21st; couldn't see the Yankees at all and only fired at random. Sometimes they were concealed in the woods and then we guessed our aim. . . My work was to hand the balls and swab out the cannon; in this we took turns. The officers aimed this gun; we fired grape shot. The balls from the Yankee guns fell thick all around. In one battery a shell burst and killed twenty, the rest ran. I felt bad all the time, and thought every minute my time would come; I felt so excited that I hardly knew what I was about, and felt worse than dead.[139]

Perhaps more noteworthy, and certainly more well-known to historians, were the units of free blacks who enlisted together. As we have already seen, black Confederate musicians abounded throughout the Southern armies, and at least one Confederate brigade had an all-black or predominately-black band. McCreary's 1st South Carolina Infantry had such a group, for we are able even now to name 14 of its members. All were listed as "free persons of color" except one, William Rose, a slave who apparently ran away from his master to join the Confederate army.[140] They were listed on the muster-rolls of each company, apparently serving the company as drummers and fifers, then switching to other instruments as appropriate for regimental and brigade-level occasions. Two of the men who enlisted in this group were blind, and one served six months before he dropped out.[141] The band served as the regimental band for McGowan's brigade, a unit that fought through the entire war with the Army of Northern Virginia, including Gettysburg.[142]

The Sixth Louisiana Cavalry had at least nine blacks in its ranks, and probably many more. Most of what we know comes from pension records filled out decades after the war ended. The men were all from the area around Campti, in Bossier Parish, and apparently joined Capt. Thomas W. Fuller's Bossier Cavalry company in April, 1862, soon becoming Company H, Sixth Louisiana. There were mulattos who "lived white, in almost all respects," recalled one descendant. There was "hardly any aspects of Compti life or society. . ." in which they "were not freely accepted. Almost all of the old [white] Compti families were their relatives and freely acknowledged it."[143]

The free black residents of New Orleans had a large, vibrant subculture, one with a long history of military service to their colony and state. Blacks had been a part of the Louisiana militia since the 1720s. They had fought against pirates in 1727, and later both slaves and free blacks had helped the French against the Choctaw Indians and in other wars. When the Spanish took over the area in the 1760s they continued to depend upon black militia. Don Bernando de Galvez marched them against the English forts at Natchez and Baton Rouge in 1779 and even more slaves and free blacks joined Galvez's army when it captured Pensacola in 1780. After the U.S. purchase in 1803 blacks still served in Louisiana, it being the only state where black participation was permitted in the early part of the century. They helped suppress a slave revolt in 1811 and at least two companies were with Andrew Jackson in the Battle of New Orleans.[144] Another source lists several units of "free men of color" in the Louisiana militia in the War of 1812.[145]

The Louisiana Native Guards were a direct result of the "monster rally" of free people of color in April of 1861. On May 12 Governor Thomas O. Moore issued a proclamation providing for the enrollment of free blacks in an all-black regiment with some black officers. Their mission was the defense of New Orleans and by early 1862 approximately 3,000 men had joined this regiment and assorted other units in and around New Orleans. Their officers were skilled tradesmen, craftsmen, and even a few slaveowners. While the exact racial heritage of all officers is not known, the majority were apparently mulattos with substantial influence in the community. Capt. Noel Bachus, 40, was a carpenter and landowner; Capt. Michael Duphart was a 62 year-old wealthy shoemaker, and Lt. Andre Cailloux was a cigarmaker, a boxer, and had the reputation of being "the blackest man in New Orleans." (He joined the Union forces after the surrender of New Orleans and was killed leading a charge at Milliken's Bend). There were several sets of fathers and sons and also sets of brothers in the regiment, and all the males in the large Duphart family were members. Like most Southern militia regiments early in the war they provided all their own uniforms and equipment.[146]

However, they apparently weren't well provided for. One of the few existing documents, a morning report for January 10,1862, records many absences due to lack of uniforms.[147] On the other hand, there are several accounts of them on parade in New Orleans fully armed and in complete, gray uniforms. "We must pay a deserved compliment to the companies of free colored men, all very well drilled, and comfortably uniformed," said the *New Orleans Picayune*. "Most of these companies, quite unaided by the administration, have supplied themselves with arms without regard to cost or trouble. One of these companies, commanded by the well-known veteran, Capt. Jordan, was presented, a little before the parade, with a fine war flag of the new style."[148]

The rolls in the National Archives list 1,307 men, including officers.[149] While their service was mostly relegated to guard duty in New Orleans, including serving as Provost Guards,[150] there is some indication that at least part of the regiment saw action at Fort Jackson during the New Orleans campaign.[151] As Federal troops approached and captured New Orleans in 1862, the Native Guards refused to abandon the city and surrendered. No parole or surrender documentation is available.

A community of free blacks was founded in the early 18th century in the area southeast of Natchitoches, Louisiana, between the Cane and Red Rivers.[152] The area is known as the Isle Brevelle, and has some of the richest farm land in the South. The forbearer was a mulatto woman who had been a lover of a white plantation owner and was given her freedom in the mid-18th Century. By the Civil War her descendants had grown to several hundred people in several families, with the Metoyer family as more or less the pole around which the rest clustered. These hard-working, industrious people had built several fine mansions along the rivers and had developed large cotton plantations totaling some 15,000 acres. Owners of nearly four hundred slaves, they hired private tutors for their children and built a Catholic Church which served the community. On a Sunday one could attend the church and witness black people sitting in the front pews with whites in the rear. They were a quiet, soft-spoken people and visitors often commented on their "gentlemanly manners," describing them as "honest and industrious, and . . . good citizens in all respects." By 1860 they felt themselves separated from their slaves by class, economics, education, religion and even race. They regarded themselves as a "third race," neither white nor black. When the war came they concluded that a northern victory would be a disaster for them, and would probably bring the end of their status and destroy their property and prosperity. They felt no special kinship nor feelings for their slaves, and indeed actively opposed abolitionism.

When the news of Ft. Sumter came they were elated and loudly proclaimed their Confederate patriotism. Throughout the war they provided Southern troops with tons of forage and sent many of their slaves off to build earthworks for defense of the Red River. They quickly organized their own local defense force, including two companies of all black men. The Augustin Guards, named for a patriarch, Augustin Metoyer, had one white officer. Like the Native Guards, they too supplied their own horses, uniforms, and arms. The Monet Guards, a company of infantry, were named after another family in the Isle. Unfortunately no official documentation of these groups has survived, so we know neither the names of all the men nor their exact number. However, if the best estimate of the historian most knowledgeable about them is correct, the two companies enrolled about 150 men, which was virtually the entire adult male population of the community.[153]

They took their work seriously, and apparently became good cavalrymen. An observer from a local newspaper noted:

> The squadron of cavalry, so skillfully trained by Dr. Bordin, their uniformity and precision were admirable. The firm commands and good cadence of the captain[sic], also that of the officers, the intelligent enthusiasm produced by all the soldiers; the excellent horsemanship by the squadron; all contributed to amaze the public who had come to attend these maneuvers. For us who have often attended cavalry drills in Europe, we wonder how, in so little time, these men have been able to attain this degree of perfection. The company of infantry, newly formed, has need of practice, but we are convinced that having a little, their drills will be executed with as much precision as in the cavalry.[154]

The writer also reported that the cavalry drilled by setting up a dummy with the name "Abe Lincoln" on its chest and attacking it with sabers.

The Augustin Guards volunteered their services to the Confederacy but were rejected because of their race. They continued to drill and in May 1862 were making plans to help defend New Orleans when it was captured. They kept together until early 1864 but apparently saw no combat. Their white officer died just before the Union began its Red River campaign, and the Guards never reorganized. When Banks moved up the river the Guards came together one night, but, due to squabbles amongst themselves, were not able to offer any resistance. The Union troops noticed the existence of a people they thought were peculiar--quiet and reserved--and burned their plantations and crops anyway.[155]

In May of 1861 the free Negro planters of the area around Point Coupee, Louisiana, organized a volunteer home guard quite similar to those of Natchitoches, and elected Colonel F.L. Claiborne as their commanding officer. Their company numbered 80 men, "the flower of that description in the state." Claiborne spoke highly of them, calling them my "dragoon company of brave quadroons."[156]

Black Southerners in Mobile, Alabama, also took part in the defense of that city. As early as 1862 a citizen had written to the Government that he felt he could organize a regiment of "creoles"--the term for people of mixed-blood. He noted that:

> all of them are free under the treaty with France by which Louisiana was acquired. They are mostly property-holders, owning slaves, and a peaceable, orderly class, and capable of doing good service. They are as true to the South as the pure white race. As yet none of them have gone to war, but have been anxious to do so. If such a battalion or regiment can be received, I can raise it in a few days.[157]

In fact, by 1862 black Confederates were already organized and working actively on the defenses. In April of that year the *Mobile Evening News* carried the following notice:

> Creole Guards-Attention:
> Attend a drill of your Company this evening at 7 1/2 O'clock.
>
> -By Order
>
> Jerome Barnard, O.S. (PA)[158]

In November 1862 the state legislature of Alabama passed an act authorizing the raising of troops of "mixed blood . . . commonly known as creoles" for the defense of the city and county of Mobile.[159] They were to have white officers.[160] Major General Dabney H. Maury had written to Adjutant General and Inspector General Samuel Cooper, the Confederacy's senior officer, asking to enlist creoles in Confederate service as artillerymen in defense of Mobile. He noted that "they were very anxious to enter Confederate service" and that he believed they were "admirably qualified" to be artillerymen. Cooper sent the letter on the Secretary of War James A. Seddon. Seddon, in a sort of written wink, indicated the problems involved and how to get around them. "Our position with the North and before the world will not allow the employment as armed soldiers of Negroes," he wrote. However, "If these creoles can be naturally and properly discriminated from Negroes, the authority may be considered as conferred; otherwise not, unless you can enlist them as 'navvies'(to uses the English term) or for subordinate working purposes."[161] In other words, if Cooper could call them something other than blacks, he could go ahead. Apparently, he did, because in August of 1864 the Confederate commander of Mobile formed a special unit of cavalry with some blacks in it, and in October he ordered the city to enlist creoles and free blacks. An artillery unit was formed in 1864 and another in the Spring of 1865. At least one company of Native Guards was formed in the spring of 1865. The commander was the Assistant Chief of Police and the other officers were Creoles.[162] Thus it appears that at least five different units of black troops were active in Mobile.

In March of 1865, after several months of official debate, the Confederate government finally began actively recruiting and enlisting black soldiers. The Confederacy had steadfastly opposed enrolling blacks in the armed services except as servants and laborers. In addition to the race question, early in the war it was felt that there were more than enough white southerners to whip the Yankees. By the middle of the war, as the clamor grew, Jefferson Davis and others believed, as Seddon had said, that the foundation of the Southern theory of the racial superiority of whites would crumble if blacks were allowed to enlist. As Howell Cobb, a powerful Georgia planter and politician, and perhaps the richest man in his state, said, "If slaves will make good soldiers our whole theory of slavery is wrong . . ."[163]

But as the bloodbath of 1864 dragged on and Southern troops melted away from desertion as well as the fighting, more white voices were heard in favor of black Confederates.[164] In early 1865 Robert E. Lee himself publicly advocated the enlistment of black troops, and in March the Confederate Congress authorized the Administration to raise 300,000 new troops "irrespective of color." General Ordinance No. 14 went on the say that "no slave will be accepted as a recruit unless with his own consent and with the approbation of his master by a written instrument conferring, as far as he may, the rights of freedmen . . ."[165] In the end, even Howell Cobb changed his mind and came out in favor of black Confederates. His son offered to raise a company from the family's plantations and even send a white overseer along as an officer.[166]

Several messages were sent out authorizing individuals to begin raising black troops,[167] and soon drilling was taking place. Indeed, on the day that the act was passed, "two companies [of black Confederates] were seen parading with a battalion . . ." Another witness recorded that "the streets of Richmond were filled with 10,000 Negroes who had been gathered at Camp Lee on the outskirts of Richmond. Negroes were armed and placed in trenches near Richmond."[168] A Camp of Instruction was established near the Alabama River,[169] and two blacks in Confederate uniform were arrested in Richmond and held until a white officer secured their release.[170]

As pointed out previously, some black Southerners had spent the entire war supporting the Confederacy in numerous laboring roles in the infrastructure, and now they began to make the transition from support to combat. Thomas Morris Chester, a black newspaper correspondent from Philadelphia, was near Richmond at this time and interviewed several blacks soon after the fall of the city. He recorded that they were abuzz with a discussion of how they should react to the call to arms, and that "after a cordial exchange of opinions it was decided with great unanimity, and finally ratified by all the auxiliary associations everywhere, that black men should promptly respond to the call of the rebel chiefs, whenever it should be made, for them to take up arms."[171] Richmond's vast hospitals were a prime source of recruits. One writer observed that "the Battalion from Camps Winder and Jackson, under the command of Dr. Chambliss, will parade on the square on Wednesday evening at 4 1/2 O'clock. This is the first company of Negro Troops raised in Virginia" he noted. "It was organized about a month since, by Dr. Chambliss, from the employees of the hospitals and served on the lines during the recent Sheridan raid."[172] Another company raised by Major J. W. Turner was drilled daily in Richmond by Lt. Virginius Bossieux. On March 27 the *Richmond Examiner* reported that the company numbered 35 men, with new members coming in every day. The men were busily recruiting their friends, and it seemed that "the knowledge of the military art they already exhibit was something remarkable. They moved with evident pride and satisfaction to themselves. Their quarters in the rendezvous are neat, clean, warm and comfortable. Their rations are cooked in Libby Prison."[173]

Thus a few black Southerners finally saw combat in authorized Confederate units in 1865. Not only did Chambliss' regiment fight against Sheridan, but other units were noted at various points in the retreat to Appomattox. A Lieutenant in this regiment noted that "my men acted with the utmost promptness and good will. . . Allow me to state, Sir, that they behaved in an extraordinary suitable manner."[174] A Virginia private watched as one unit guarded a wagon train during the retreat. They were attacked by Yankee cavalry, but fired their rifles rapidly and successfully fought them off. The blue horsemen retreated and reformed on a nearby hillside, then proceeded to charge down on the wagon train, overrun, and capture the black Confederates.[175] A courier reported that on April 4 he saw black Confederates working on breastworks. "All wore good gray uniforms and I was informed that they belonged to the only company of colored troops in the Confederate service, having been enlisted by Major Turner in Richmond. Their muskets were stacked, and it was evident that they regarded their present employment in no very favorable light."[176]

In an action on April 7 the 108th New York Infantry captured an armed black Confederate. His name was Tom Brophy, and the Northern soldiers, rather than sending him to prison, made him their servant. He stayed with them until the regiment was disbanded, and then went North with them. He became a well-known resident of a small town in New York, where he died in 1888.[177]

The Southern armies that marched into Pennsylvania in 1863 and retreated to Atlanta in 1864 contained a good many black Southerners, marching as servants, as individual soldiers, and in black units. As C. Vann Woodward said, it is impossible to imagine any aspect of Southern society without them, and quite futile to try. Others have understood this, including British Colonel Arthur Fremantle. He travelled with the Army of Northern Virginia in 1863, and a comment he made might provide a fitting conclusion to this story. One does not have to agree with his reading of the motivations of black Southerners or the nature of their relationships with whites to appreciate his observations about their combat potential and the resistance of those in power in the Confederate government. From what he had seen of black Southerners,

> I am of the opinion that the Confederates could, if they chose, convert a great number into soldiers; and from the affection which undoubtably exists as a general rule between the slaves and their masters, I think that they would prove more efficient than black troops under any other circumstances. But I do not imagine such an experiment will be tried, except as a very last resort.[178]

Fremantle had correctly foreseen the future. As Lee retreated to Appomattox, and Johnston to North Carolina, their wagons were driven by blacks, and in them black Southerners rode as servants, caring for wounded white, and black, Confederate soldiers.

Notes

1. C. Vann Woodward, *American Counterpoint*, quoted in Eugene Genovese, *Roll, Jordan, Roll: The World The Slaves Made* (New York: Pantheon Books, 1974), preface.

2. Quoted in Michael P. Johnson and James L. Roark, *Black Masters: A Free Family of Color in the Old South* (New York: W.W. Norton, 1986), 293-295.

3. Charles Wesley, *The Collapse of the Confederacy* (New York: Russell and Russell, 1937), 153.

4. Quoted in Clarence Mohr, *On The Threshold: Masters and Slaves in Civil War Georgia, 1861-1865* (Baton Rouge: Louisiana State University Press, 1986), 66.

5. Wesley, *Collapse*, 244.

6. J.K. Obatala, "The Unlikely Story of Negroes Who Were Loyal To Dixie," *Smithsonian* 9(1979), 94.

7. Wesley, *Collapse*, 153.

8. *Ibid.*

9. *Memphis Avalanche* 3 September 1861.

10. H.C. Blackerby, *Blacks in Blue and Gray: Afro-American Service in the Civil War* (Tuscaloosa, Ala.: Portals Press, 1973), 18.

11. Charles H. Wesley, "The Employment of Negroes as Soldiers in the Confederate Army," *Journal of Negro History* 4(1919, 242.

12. *Rebellion Record*, 46.

13. *Ibid.*, 245.

14. Benjamin Quarles, *The Negro in the Civil War* (Boston: Little, Brown, 1955), 36.

15. *Ibid.*, 37.

16. Obatala, "Unlikely," 94, and Quarles, *Negro*, 35.

17. *Charleston Evening News*, May 1, 1861.

18. *New Orleans Picayune*, 28 April 1861.

19. Quarles, *Negro*, 38.

20. E. Smith, "Negroes in the Confederacy," 13.

21. James H. Brewer, *The Confederate Negro: Virginia's Craftsmen and Military Laborers, 1861-1865* (Durham, N.C.: Duke University Press, 1969).

22. Wiley, *Southern Negro*, 112.

23. Patricia Brady, "Black Artists in Antebellum New Orleans," *Louisiana History* XXXII(Winter, 1991), 5-28.

24. *Arkansas Historical Quarterly*, 3(1944), 77.

25. Quarles, *Negro*, 37.

26. T. Conn Ryan, *Confederate Georgia* (Athens: University of Georgia Press, 1943), 133-134.

27. Mohr, *Threshold*, 286.

28. *Battlefields of the South* (New York: John Bradburn, 1865), 282.

29. *Clarion* (Mississippi) *Ledger*, 3 May 1984.

30. See the chapter on "The Landscape of the South: The Union Soldier Views The South" in Reid Mitchell, *Civil War Soldiers: Their Expectations and Their Experiences* (New York: Simon and Schuster, 1988).

31. See Mohr, *Threshold*, for this viewpoint.

32. Quoted in George P. Rawick, Ed., *The American Slave: A Composite Autobiography* Vol. I. From Sundown to Sunup: The Making of the Black Community (Westport, Ct.: Greenwood Press, 1972), 136.

33. *Ibid.*

34. See for example Gary B. Mills' account of the free Negro community in North Louisiana in *The Forgotten People: Cane River's Creoles of Color* (Baton Rouge: Louisiana State University Press, 1977). It is the intention here to simply suggest motivational factors, not to discuss them in depth.

35. Wiley, *Southern Negro*, 12.

36. Quarles, *Negro*, 39.

37. Quoted in Blackerby, *Blue and Gray*, 34.

38. Washington Wills, quoted in Manly Wade Wellman, *Rebel Boast: First at Bethel-Last at Appomattox* (New York: Henry Holt and Company, 1956), 117.

39. Quoted in Blackerby, *Blue and Gray*, p. 34.

40. See the slave narratives in James Mellon, Ed., *Bullwhip Days: The Slaves Remember* (New York: Weidenfeld and Nicholson, 1988), and John Blassingame, *Slave Testimony: Two Centuries of Letters, Speeches, Interviews and Autobiographies* (Baton Rouge: Louisiana State University Press, 1977). These stories appeared from Virginia to Mississippi.

41. Mohr, *Threshold*, 94.

42. Ira Berlin, *Slaves Without Masters*. See especially the chapter on "Sources of Free Negro Identity."

43. *Ibid.*, 272.

44. *New Orleans Picayune*, 30 June 1860.

45. Berlin, *Slaves Without Masters*, 343-346.

46. Loren Schweninger, "Prosperous Blacks in the South, 1790-1880," *American Historical Review*, February, 1990, 31-56. See also his longer work, *Black Property Owners in the South, 1790-1915* (Urbana: University of Illinois Press, 1986).

47. Schweninger, "Prosperous," 36

48. Larry Koger, *Black Slaveowners: Free Black Slave Masters in South Carolina, 1790-1860* (Jefferson, N.C.: 1985). For other studies of black slaveowners, see Mills, *Forgotten People*; David O. Whitten, *Andrew Durnford: A Black Sugar Planter in Antebellum Louisiana*

(Natchitoches, La:, 1981); Michael P. Johnson and James L. Roark, *Black Masters: A Free Family of Color in the Old South* (New York:, 1984).

49. Walter Fleming, *Civil War and Reconstruction in Alabama* (New York: Columbia University Press, 1905), 208.

50. David Rankin, "The Impact of the Civil War on the Free Colored Community of New Orleans," *Perspectives in American History*, 11(1977-1978), 379-418.

51. Wayne R. Austerman, "Virginia's Black Confederates," *Civil War Quarterly* VIII(1987), 52. See also Berlin, *Slaves Without Masters.*

52. Quoted in Wiley, *Southern Negro*, 141-142.

53. Blackerby, *Blue and Gray*, ii.

54. Genovese, *Roll, Jordan, Roll;* see the chapter on "Life in the Big House."

55. Quoted in Greene, *Black Defenders_*, 85. See also Jay S. Hoar, "Black Glory: Our Afro-American Civil War Old Soldiery," *Gettysburg Magazine* January, 1990, 212.

56. Quoted in Isaac W. Heysinger, *Antietam and the Maryland and Virginia Campaigns of 1862,* (New York: Neale Publishing Company, 1912), 122-123.

57. Quoted in Genovese, *Roll, Jordan, Roll*, p. 347.

58. Fleming, *Civil War and Reconstruction in Alabama.*

59. *Battlefields of the South*, II, 59.

60. Wiley, *Southern Negroes.*

61. *OR*, IV, I, 1059.

62. *OR*, IV, 2, 86.

63. Robert Greene, Ed., *Black Defenders of America.*

64. Austerman, "Black Confederates," 51.

65. Scott E. Sallee, "Black Soldier of the Confederacy," *Blue and Gray,* 1990

66. Pension record of Silas Young, Alabama State Archives, Montgomery.

67. *Ibid.*

68. Alexia J. Helsley, "Black Confederates," *South Carolina Historical Magazine* 74(July, 1973), 186.

69. Austerman, "Black Soldiers," 47.

70. Leroy Jones, Pension Application, Tennessee State Archives, Nashville.

71. *Confederate Veteran*, May 1916, 216.

72. Blackerby, *Blue and Gray*, 1.

73. Walter Lord, Ed., *The Fremantle Diary, Being the Journal of Lieutenant Colonel James Arthur Lyon Fremantle, Coldstream Guards, on His Three Months in the Southern States* (Boston: Little, Brown, 1954), 225..

74. Bell Irvin Wiley, *The Life and Times of Johnny Reb* (Baton Rouge: Louisiana State University Press, 1978), 328.

75. *Battlefields of the South*, I, 157-158.

76. Hiram Conaway, Pension Application, Virginia State Archives, Richmond.

77. Greene, *Black Defenders*, 64.

78. *Confederate Veteran*, Sept., 1912, 410

79. *Richmond Whig*, January 27, 1864.

80. *OR*, 2, VI, 397-398.

81. Jay S. Hoar, *The South's Last Boys in Gray: An Epic Poem Elegy* (Bowling Green, Ohio: The Bowling Green State University Popular Press, 1986), 212-213.

82. Austerman, "Black Soldiers," 47.

83. *Ibid*, 62. Similar stories appear on p. 84.

84. William Bibb, Pension Application, Tennessee State Archives, Nashville.

85. Blackerby, *Blacks in Gray*, 36.

86. Daniel Ammen, *The Navy in the Civil War* (New York: Charles Scribner's Sons, 1883-1885), V.2, 43.

87. Helsley, "Black Confederates," 186.

88. *Confederate Veteran*, April 1927, 152-3

89. Sam Collier, Pension Application, Tennessee State Archives, Nashville.

90. Henry Nelson, Pension Application, Tennessee State Archives, Nashville.

91. Alex Wharton, Pension Application, Tennessee State Archives, Nashville.

92. *Battlefields of the South*, 284.

93. Henry B. McClelland, *I Rode With Jeb Stuart* Ed. Burke Davis (Bloomington: Indiana University Press, 1958), 109.

94. Hoar, *South's Boys*, 462.

95. Wiley, *Southern Negro*, 139.

96. *Battlefields of the South*, II, 22-23.

97. *Ibid*, 253.

98. Capt. Thomas Nelson, *The Confederate Scout* (Washington, D.C.: The Neale Publishing Company, 1957), 122.

99. Blackerby, *Blue and Gray*, 13.

100. Austerman, "Black Soldiers," 47.

101. *New Orleans Crescent*, November 15, 1861.

102. *Battlefields*, 282.

103. Alfred Brown, Pension Application, Tennessee State Archives, Nashville.

104. Hutson Longstreet, Pension Application, Mississippi State Archives, Jackson.

105. Wade Watkins, Pension Application, Tennessee State Archives, Nashville.

106. Helsley, "Black Confederates," 186.

107. Monroe Jones, Pension Application, Tennessee State

Archives, Nashville.

108. John D. Winters, *The Civil War in Louisiana* (Baton Rouge: Louisiana State University Press, 1963), 21.

109. Moore, *Civil War in Song and Story*, 481.

110. George H. Gordon, *A War Diary* (Boston: Little, Brown, 1882), 194.

111. Blackerby, *Blacks in Gray*, 29.

112. George Alfred Townsend, *Rustics in Rebellion: A Yankee Reporter on the Road to Richmond, 1861-1865* (Chapel Hill: The University of North Carolina Press, 1950), 52.

113. Greene, *Black Defenders*, pp. 65, 79, 89.

114. Greg Tyler, "Rebel Drummer Henry Brown," *Civil War Times Illustrated*, February, 1989, 22-23. See also Greg Tyler, "Article Brings Notice to a Unique Rebel," *Civil War Times Illustrated* May/June 1990, 57.

115. Obatala, "Unlikely," 98.

116 . Blackerby, *Blacks in Gray*, 21.

117. *Ibid.*, 16.

118. James Clark, Pension Application, Department of Archives and History, Atlanta, Georgia.

119. Mohr, *Threshold*, 286.

120. *OR*, IV, I, 1059.

121. Carroll, "Dignity, Courage and Fidelity," 26-27.

122. Johnson and Roark, *Black Masters*.

123. *Ibid*, 306.

124. *Sumter Watchman and Southron*, August 28, 1895.

125. Jay Hoar, "Black Glory," 126.

126. William T. Lewis, *The Centennial History of Winston County, Mississippi* (Pasadena, Texas: The Globe Publishers, 1876), 77.

127. James Young, Pension Application, Alabama State Archives, Montgomery, Alabama. The Board rejected the claim, saying that "The board takes judicial knowledge of the fact that Negroes are not by law authorized to be enlisted in the Confederate State's Army or Navy and that as a matter of fact no Negroes were so enlisted in said army or navy. Therefore, the State Auditor is hereby directed to strike the name of the said James Young from the pension roll."

128. Letter from State of Alabama Department of Archives and History, February 6, 1991, in Young's application file.

129. Helsley, "Black Confederates," 187.

130. Major Henry B. Morgan, "The Birth of a County," *Moore County* [Tennessee] *News*, no date, p. 26.

131. Capt. C. A. Stevens, *Berdan's United States Sharpshooters in the Army of the Potomac, 1861-1865* (St. Paul, Minnesota: Price-McGill, 1892), 55-56.

132. Greene, *Black Defenders*, 79.

133. William C. Davis, *Images of the War* , IV, 193.

134. William N. Still, Jr, *Iron Afloat: The Story of the Confederate Armor Clads* (Columbia: The University of South Carolina Press, 1985), 114.

135. Mohr, *Threshold*, 289-290.

136. Austerman, "Virginia's Black Confederates," 50.

137. Obatala, "Unlikely," 99.

138. Quoted in Blackerby, *Blacks in Gray*, 5.

139. Quoted in James M. McPherson, *The Negro's Civil War: How American Negroes Felt and Acted During the War For The Union* (Chicago: University of Illinois Press, 1982), 22-23.

140. *South Carolina Troops In Confederate Service*, A.S. Salley, Jr., Comp. (Columbia: The R.L. Bryan Co., 1913), I, 218, n. 17. 219. It is nearly impossible to tell the length of these men's service. Most of the records are missing, and those available list many of them as deserters. On the other hand, several of them list their service in their pension records as with "McCreary's Regiment." McCreary did not command the Regiment until early in 1864, therefore it is logical to assume that those who described their Regiment as McCreary's served as late as 1864.

141. See *Black Defenders*. Also Blackerby, *Blacks In Gray*, 18, and *South Carolina Troops*.

142. J.F.J. Caldwell, *The History of A Brigade of South Carolinians, known first as "Gregg's" and subsequently as "McGowan's Brigade (Dayton: Morningside, 1974).*

143. Bergeron. "Free Men of Color," 251.

144. Mary Berry, "Negro Troops in Blue and Gray: The Louisiana Native Guards, 1861-1863," *Louisiana History* 8(1967), 165-190.

145. Powell A. Casey, *Louisiana In The War of 1812* (Privately Printed, 1963).

146. Berry, "Negro Troops in Blue and Gray."

147. National Archives Microcopy 320-94.

148. *New Orleans Picayune*, 10 January 1862.

149. Microcopy 320-94, National Archives.

150. *OR*, I, 6, 858.

151. *Ibid*, 852-858.

152. All of the information on this community is drawn from Gary B. Mills, *Forgotten People*, and Gary B. Mills, "Patriotism Frustrated: The Native Guards of Confederate Natchitoches," *Louisiana History* (Winter, 1977), 437-451.

153. *Ibid.*, 441.

154. *Ibid.*, 441-442.

155. *Ibid.*

156. Quoted in H.E. Strekx, *The Free Negro in Antebellum Louisiana* (Rutherford, N.J.: Fairleigh Dickinson University Press, 1972), 212.

157. *OR*, IV, I, 1088.

158. *Mobile Evening News*, 14 April 1862.

159. "Creole" is frequently used to describe people of Spanish-English or French-English blood. Since these two groups were considered legally white, no governmental action would be needed for them to serve. Therefore, I conclude that the references cited here are to people of black and white mixed blood, but it remains possible that this is a reference to the other groups.

160. *OR*, IV, 2, 197.

161. *OR*, IV, 2, 941.

162. Arthur Bergeron, *Confederate Mobile, 1861-1865* (Oxford: The University of Mississippi Press, 1992).

163. *OR*, IV, 3, 1009.

164. Robert F. Durden, *The Gray and the Black* (Baton Rouge: Louisiana State University Press, 1972).

165. *OR*, IV, 3, 1161.

166. Mohr, *Threshold*, 285.

167. To Majors J.W.Pegram and Thomas P. Turner, *OR*, IV, 3, 1144. Several more can be found in the *OR*.

168. Quoted in Blackerby, *Blue and Gray*, 27.

169. *OR*, I, 54 Part I, 818.

170. Richmond *Whig*, March 31, 1865.

171. Quoted in R.J.M. Blackett, Ed., *Thomas Morris Chester, Black Civil War Correspondent* (Baton Rouge: Louisiana State University Press, 1989), 248.

172. *Richmond Sentinel*, March 21, 1865.

173. *Richmond Examiner*, March 27, 1865.

174. Austerman, "Virginia's Black Confederates," 53.

175. *Confederate Veteran*, 1915, 404, 411.

176. Lt. Moses Purnell Handy, "The Fall of Richmond in 1865," *The American Magazine and Historical Chronicle* (Ann Arbor: Clements Library) Vol. I, No. 2, 1985-86, n.p.

177. George Washburn, *History and Record of the 108th Regiment of New York Volunteers* (Rochester: E.R. Andrews, 1894).

178. Walter Lord, Ed., *The Fremantle Diary, Being the Journal of Lieutenant Colonel James Arthur Lyon Fremantle, Coldstream Guards, on His Three Months in the Southern States* (Boston:Little, Brown, 1954), 225.

Louisiana's Free Men Of Color In Gray

Arthur W. Bergeron, Jr.

A number of writers have studied the use of blacks as soldiers by the Union and Confederate governments during the American Civil War. Most of these works have focused on the Union army since it employed large numbers of black soldiers during the conflict. When the authors do cover the Confederate side, they usually limit their coverage to the free blacks of New Orleans who formed a regiment of "Native Guards" for the Louisiana militia and to efforts late in the war to employ slaves as soldiers.[1] Various Southern states enacted legislation accepting free blacks as laborers or in other noncombat roles, but until early 1865, the official policy of the Confederate government prohibited blacks from serving as armed soldiers.[2]

Scholars who have investigated the role of blacks in the Confederate armies usually have described only the body servants who occasionally picked up a weapon during a battle, though several writers have discussed the largely unsubstantiated cases of slaves serving in other combat situations.[3] Two studies which look closely at blacks who aided the Confederate war effort fail to document satisfactorily the enlistment of free blacks as combat soldiers. One of these books exhibits a strong Confederate bias but cannot substantiate its assertion that "many of these [free blacks] were in active war participation."[4] In dealing with "the question as to whether or not any Negroes ever fought in the Confederate ranks," Professor Bell I. Wiley found no firm evidence to say that they did. He concluded, "If persons with Negro blood served in Confederate ranks as full-fledged soldiers, the per cent of Negro blood was sufficiently low for them to pass as whites."[5] Contrary to Professor Wiley's contention, a number of Louisiana free blacks did serve as soldiers, and their white comrades in arms did know them to be "free men of color."

Before discussing the men who enlisted in white units, it is important to look at those who formed militia units in the state. Like their white neighbors, the Pelican State's free men of color became caught up in the martial fever that swept through the South following the election of Abraham Lincoln and the secession of South Carolina. New Orleans was the home of "the most sophisticated and exclusive free colored community in antebellum America,"[6] and there they first began to organize to defend their state, their homes and their families.

News of South Carolina's secession from the Union reached the Crescent City on December 21, 1860, and it resulted in several raucous celebrations over the next several days.[7] In this atmosphere, a number of free blacks sent a letter to the editor of the *Daily Delta* expressing their support for their native state. The letter stated:

> . . . the free colored population (native) . . . love their home, their property, their own slaves, and they are dearly attached to their native land, and they recognize no other country than Louisiana, and care for no other than Louisiana, and they are ready to shed their blood for her defense. They have no sympathy for Abolitionism; no love for the North, but they have plenty for Louisiana; and let the hour come, and they will be worthy sons of Louisiana. They will fight for her in 1861 as they fought in 1814-15 . . . .

These free blacks said that they had not yet made any demonstrations "because they have no right to meddle with politics." They asked only that they be given a chance to prove themselves as "worthy sons of Louisiana." In reponse, the editor wrote, "The native free colored people of Louisiana have never given grounds for any suspicion, or distrust, and they have frequently manifested their fidelity in a manner quite as striking and earnest as the white citizens."[8]

On January 7, 1861, Louisiana elected delegates to a secession convention that was to begin meeting on January 23. Three days after the election, Governor Thomas O. Moore ordered state militia troops to seize the Baton Rouge Arsenal and Forts Jackson and St. Philip on the Mississippi River below New Orleans. Military companies began forming all over the state throughout the month of January.[9] "A. L. M.," who signed himself a "Creole of Louisiana," wrote to Moore on January 20. He complained about the mistrust of free blacks he had seen coming from some whites and expressed sentiments of loyalty similar to those sent to the editor of the *Daily Delta*. Much of the letter outlined the unique position of free blacks in the Crescent City, pointing out that they were well-educated and had amongst their number artists, physicians, craftsmen, mechanics and other businessmen.[10]

"A. L. M." assured the governor that the native free blacks of Louisiana "own property, slaves, have all their interest here, and are able to appreciate the benefit of slavery, very few of them have ever been slaves, they never associate with negroes, their education and good breeding preventing it, they have no sympathy for Abolitionists, knowing that the Abolitionists are the greatest enemies they have." He decried the lack of loyalty to Louisiana of the foreigners and Northerners in the city, saying "the French, Germans, Dutch, and Spaniards will not help us." This "Creole" then stated that "the old colored veterans of 1814-15" had begun talking to prominent white citizens about organizing "companies for the defense of Louisiana." All they hoped for when these units were formed was that all of the company officers come from their own ranks.[11] In this letter and that to the *Daily Delta* are early indications that the New Orleans free blacks were not only able but anxious to support the actions of their state, though the government did not yet take advantage of the offers made.

This attitude changed quickly after the rapid developments of mid-April. Fort Sumter fell, and on April 15 Lincoln called for volunteers to put down the "insurrection." The next day, the new Confederate government made its own call for troops. Governor Moore issued pleas on April 17 and 21 for a total of 8,000 troops to defend against an invasion of the South.[12] On April 21, a committee of ten prominent free blacks of New Orleans called a meeting for the following night at the Catholic Institute. These men expressed themselves ready "as soon as a call is made to them by the Governor of this State... to take arms and form themselves into companies for the defence of their homes."[13] Approximately two thousand people attended the meeting, listened to exhortations by several men and unanimously adopted the resolutions offering their services to the governor. Lists were opened, and fifteen hundred men signed up.[14]

Several New Orleans newspapers applauded this action by the free blacks. The *Daily Picayune* referred to the gathering as "representing the flower of the free colored population of New Orleans" and asked, "What will the Northerners have to say to this?"[15] The *Daily Crescent* reported that the governor had accepted the services of these men as part of the state militia. Jordan B. Noble, known as the "Drummer Boy of Chalmette" for his service under Andrew Jackson in the Battle of New Orleans, was raising a company, and another was in the process of organizing in Jefferson City, a suburb of the Crescent City. "Should their services be needed, they will be among our hardest and best fighters," the *Daily Crescent*'s story read. "When the down town free colored men form their regiment (and it will be a rousing one,) they will make a show as pleasing to all, as it will be surprising to many of our population."[16]

Jordan was one of the first to succeed in forming a company. It took the nickname Plauche Guards for Major Jean Baptiste Plauche, who had commanded the Orleans Battalion at the Battle of New Orleans. They were organized by May 22 and held company drill on Wednesday and Friday afternoons at their headquarters at the corner of Baronne and Perdido streets. On May 29, Governor Moore appointed Felix Labatut and Henry D. Ogden as colonel and lieutenant colonel, respectively, of the Regiment of Free Men of Color. The next day, Moore appointed S. St. Cyr as the regiment's major. Commissions were issued to the officers of five companies, including Noble's, on May 31. In keeping with the request made in January, all of these company officers were free blacks. Another company had been organized by June 4. The free blacks of the Barthelemy Settlement in nearby Plaquemines Parish were reported as forming a company with white officers, but it is unclear whether or not these men joined the regiment.[17]

Over the next several months, these companies drilled and tried to obtain uniforms and equipment. A parade scheduled for late

September had to be cancelled because some of the men did not yet have these items, although the Plauche Guards apparently did turn out for the commander of the state militia, Major General John L. Lewis. Some of the Union soldiers captured in the battle of First Manassas were sent to New Orleans for imprisonment. The first group was expected to arrive on September 25, and three companies of free blacks were ordered out as part of the escort. Unexpected events delayed the arrival of the Federals. Major General David E. Twiggs, Confederate commander in New Orleans, then decided not to use the free blacks in the escort when the prisoners finally did reach the city. He asked Lewis to convey this news to the men and said, "He [Twiggs] thanks them for the promptness with which they answered the call, and is assured that they will be equally ready upon a more important occasion."[18]

Other companies continued to form, and on October 1 commissions were issued to officers of three new units. Another company joined the regiment on November 14. Nine days later, the regiment, or portions of it, participated in a grand parade through the streets of New Orleans. A newspaper report placed the regiment's strength at 750 men. The account described Captain St. Albin Sauvinet's company as "a fine corps of 82 men, very well uniformed, and which may be relied upon in case of danger."[19] An undated muster roll for this company which was probably prepared at the time of this parade, states that the men had only ten muskets among them, "no other arms whatever."[20] Since the Native Guards, as they called themselves, had been organized only for defense of New Orleans, they had little chance of obtaining any of the limited number of weapons being distributed by state authorities. There were white militia companies that were having the same problems.

On the night of December 7, the Beauregard Native Guards, which had probably just been organized, was presented with "a fine silk flag" by a young lady of the free black section of the city. Unfortunately, no description of the flag has survived, so it is impossible to state whether it was a Louisiana or Confederate flag. The next day, one of the older companies turned out and was accompanied by a brass band. A newspaper account of both ceremonies stated that these men "are of opinion, just as companies of white men, they can as well have a lively time until the enemy invade our soil." The reporter went on to say, "In both cases, a pleasant collation [light meal] followed the military manifestation."[21]

The Regiment of Native Guards again participated in a grand parade and review on January 8, 1862, this one in celebration of Jackson's victory over the British on that date in 1815. They received compliments in a description of the event in the *Daily Picayune*. The paper stated that the men were well drilled and uniformed. Most of them had used their own resources to obtain weapons, "without regard to cost and trouble." Just prior to the parade, Noble's Plauche Guards had received "a fine war flag, of the new style," in a ceremony at Mr. Cushing's store on Camp Street. Noble reportedly gave "one of his most felicitous speeches" after receiving the banner.[22] From this brief description, the flag was undoubtedly one of the Confederate battle flags, which had been designed in part by Louisiana native General Pierre Gustave Toutant Beauregard.

A regimental morning report dated January 10 indicates that three companies, some 200 men, of the regiment had not participated in the parade or in the muster that day because they still did not have all of their uniforms. This report placed the regiment's strength at 1,022 rank and file. As a result of the unit's obvious deficiencies in equipment, General Lewis on January 17 ordered his quartermaster general to issue knapsacks, haversacks and canteens to each of the company commanders. Several days later, Lewis made the same provisions for Noble's company, which seems to have severed its formal relationship to the regiment and acted as an independent unit.[23]

Based upon these latter orders and surviving muster rolls and reports, the composition of the 1st Louisiana Regiment of Native Guards at this time was as follows: Native Guards, Captain St. Albin Sauvinet, 85 men; Savary Native Guards, Captain Joseph Joly, 85 men; Beauregard Native Guards, Captain Louis Golis, 52 men; Young Creole Native Guards, Captain Ludger B. Boquille, 76 men; Labatut Native Guards, Captain Edgar C. Davis, 110 men; Mississippi Native Guards, Captain Marcelle Dupart, 64 men; Economy Native Guards, Captain Henry Louis Rey, 100 men; Meschacebe Native Guards, Captain Armand Lanusse, 90 men; Order Native Guards, Captain Charles Sentmanat, 90 men; Crescent [City?] Native Guards, Captain Virgil Bonseigneur, 63 men; Perseverance Native Guards, Captain Noel J. Bacchus, 60 men; Louisiana Native Guards, Captain Louis Lainez, 75 men; and Ogden [or Turcos] Native Guards, Captain Alcide Lewis, 85 men. Captain Jordan Noble's Plauche Guards numbered 100 men.[24]

Under an act of the state legislature reorganizing the militia, Governor Moore renewed the commissions of the Native Guards' regimental field and staff officers as well as those of the officers of the Plauche Guards on February 15. The fall of Forts Henry and Donelson resulted in a call for reenforcements for the Confederate army in Tennessee. Major General Mansfield Lovell at New Orleans responded by ordering away all of his volunteer regiments and several 90-day units. In early March, he asked Moore to provide 10,000 volunteers to defend the various entrenchments around the city. The Native Guards Regiment was one of the units that offered its services in this capacity. These men were never called out, however. Flag Officer David G. Farragut's Union naval squadron steamed past Forts Jackson and St. Philip and appeared at the city on April 25. Lovell attempted to get the militiamen to report at Camp Moore near Tangipahoa, but the majority of them, including the Native Guards, chose to remain in New Orleans.

The regiment ceased to exist, but in the Fall many of its members reorganized as the 1st Louisiana Native Guards for service in the Union army.[25]

Though not as well documented as the New Orleanians, there were companies of free blacks in several other areas of Louisiana. The *Baton Rouge Weekly Gazette & Comet* reported on April 27, 1861, that Captain Henry B. Favrot, a prominent white, had begun to enroll a company of free blacks from the town's populace. At that time, he had already enlisted thirty men. The paper's editor praised Favrot's efforts, wished him success, and stated that he would count on the company "as a host in any emergency . . . in this perilous hour." By early October, the company was complete and had been armed. There is no record of how many men Favrot was able to enlist in his unit, which became known as the Baton Rouge Guards. The men drilled throughout the fall and winter, and they had become very proficient by early April of 1862. In that month, the men turned their Mississippi rifles over to a white militia company that had no weapons or substandard weapons and rearmed themselves with shotguns.[26]

This company of free blacks apparently disbanded the next month when Union forces occupied the town. An unidentified member of the company may have fought with Major General John C. Breckinridge's Confederate army when it attacked the Union garrison at Baton Rouge on August 5. After that battle, a reporter noted that one of "the most conspicuous of the rebels" involved in the attack on the position of the 14th Maine Infantry Regiment was "a huge negro." This man was "armed and equipped with knapsack, musket and uniform" and helped lead the attack. Eventually he was killed by the Federals. The Confederates in this area of the battlefield were Kentuckians, and it seems likely that Breckinridge and his subordinates would have welcomed the assistance of a former militiaman in guiding their units through unfamiliar terrain toward the enemy positions. In his report of the battle, Breckinridge stated that armed citizens of the area had joined his army in its attack on Baton Rouge.[27]

Free blacks in Pointe Coupee Parish, northwest of Baton Rouge, also offered their assistance to the state. In early May, a number of them assembled at the courthouse and obtained from the police jury permission to organize a military company. Initial reports stated that they had chosen two white men, Ferdinand L. Claiborne and Ovide Lejeune, as their captain and first lieutenant, respectively. A newspaper article in early June said that the company had completed its organization and had 92 members. They elected Louis H. Trudeau as captain and three other whites as the other company officers. The editor of a Baton Rouge paper roundly criticized the free blacks for "displacing" the highly esteemed Claiborne, calling their action "insulting and impudent." Nothing else is known of this company except that it was still drilling with the white militia of the parish as late as November of 1861.

Appointments for the officers of the Pointe Coupee Light Infantry were made on February 15, 1862, and commissions issued on March 13 (both effective June 15, 1861), so it appears the company was still in service in the spring of 1862.[28]

As early as May of 1861, free blacks in the area near Natchitoches known as Isle Brevelle had begun forming two militia companies. The first to organize was a cavalry company nicknamed the Augustin Guards, and an infantry company called the Monet's Guards quickly followed. Although supervised by white planters, the officers of the units appear to have come from the free black population. The cavalrymen furnished their own uniforms, weapons, equipment and horses. One historian has estimated that approximately 150 men served in the two companies. Dr. Jean N. Burdin, who was born in France, drilled both units. The men offered their services for the defense of New Orleans to Governor Moore. Though they and local officials expected them to go to the Crescent City in early 1862, Union forces captured New Orleans before the companies could leave the parish. Both companies occasionally continued to drill, but their only official duty was to participate as part of the honor guard at the funeral of a white soldier who had died of disease in Arkansas. Union soldiers passed through the area during the Red River Campaign of 1864. The companies had become largely disorganized by that time and ceased to exist afterwards.[29]

Some fairly tenuous evidence exists that free blacks in the Opelousas area attempted to offer their services to either state or Confederate authorities. In a suit filed thirty years after the war against the federal government for damages sustained at the hands of Union troops, there was testimony that one of the aggrieved parties had offered to form a company. William C. Johnson, formerly a lieutenant and enrolling officer, stated that Auguste Donato, Jr., told Confederate officers in 1864 that he had proposed raising a company but was turned down. This claim was made when Donato was about to be conscripted as a laborer and thus may have been an attempt to escape that duty. Another person testified in the same case that he did not know if Donato had made such an offer. The fact that several free blacks from this area did enlist in regular Confederate units may lend some support to the idea that their friends and relatives attempted to organize a militia unit.[30]

Professor John D. Winters has estimated that nearly three thousand free blacks had volunteered for militia duty by early 1862, but that figure is too high. There were probably no more than 2,000 men who joined the companies discussed above.[31] Whatever the total might have been, however, with so many men in militia service, it seems reasonable that a few individuals could have seen combat duty. I have been able to document fifteen free blacks who volunteered for and served in regular Confederate units as privates, although I have information that leads me to believe several others also saw service. Twelve of these men enlisted in Louisiana volunteer regiments, two in a reserve or home guard unit and one in a Texas cavalry unit. Three of the first twelve fought in several battles, and two of the three received wounds.

The three most prominent examples of free blacks who volunteered for Confederate military service all came from St. Landry Parish.[32] The three were Charles F. Lutz, Jean Baptiste Pierre-Auguste, and Lufroy Pierre-Auguste. Charles F. Lutz, born in June of 1842, was the son of Frederick Guillaume Lutz and Caroline Marx (or Manse), a mulatto woman. Charles Lutz joined Captain James C. Pratt's Opelousas Guards company, which became Company F, 8th Louisiana Infantry Regiment, on June 23, 1861. This regiment went to Virginia and formed part of a brigade commanded by Brigadier General Richard Taylor. The 8th Louisiana fought in the battles of Winchester, Cross Keys, Port Republic, the Seven Days, Second Manassas, Sharpsburg and Fredericksburg. In the battle of Second Fredericksburg, or Marye's Heights, on May 3, 1863, Lutz fell into enemy hands with more than one hundred of his comrades. He remained in Federal prisons for about two weeks before being exchanged to rejoin his unit. At the battle of Gettysburg, on July 2, 1863, Lutz received a severe wound in his left forearm and again became a prisoner.

After holding him in a prison hospital in New York, Federal authorities exchanged Lutz on September 16, 1863, at City Point, Virginia. He went home on furlough after his release. About June 30, 1864, while at Opelousas, Lutz became involved in some kind of difficulty. As a result of this mysterious event, Lutz lost his right arm. He claimed in land and pension applications filed after the war that he was shot in the arm, resulting in its amputation, but did not elaborate on the nature of the affair. Lutz went to Texas to live with his brother in Polk County. On May 9, 1865, he received a discharge at the general hospital in Houston on the basis of a surgeon's certificate of disability. Lutz married after the war and later moved to Westlake in Calcasieu Parish. After two attempts, Lutz finally received a Confederate pension from the state of Louisiana in 1900. He died in Westlake on April 9, 1910, after a long illness. Of the men discussed here, Lutz was probably the only one who passed for and enlisted as white. His discharge papers describe him as 5 feet 8 inches tall, with fair complexion and hazel eyes. The Federal censuses of 1880 and 1900 list him as white.[33]

Jean Baptiste Pierre-Auguste was born in St. Landry Parish in May 1842. He was possibly the son of Ursin and Caroline Pierre-Auguste, both free persons of color. Jean Baptiste joined Captain James W. Bryan's company at Lake Charles in early 1862. He may have been living in Calcasieu Parish when the war began. Bryan's unit became Company I, 29th Louisiana Infantry Regiment, on April 15, 1862. The regiment went to Vicksburg, Mississippi. There it participated in various campaigns in defense of the city, particularly the battle of Chickasaw Bluffs, December 28-29, 1862. The 29th Louisiana was part of the Confederate garrison besieged at Vicksburg between May 19 and July 4, 1863. The men repulsed two major Union assaults on their trenches. Jean Baptiste received a slight wound to his thigh during one of these actions. Following the surrender of the Confederate garrison, he went home on parole.

The men of the 29th Louisiana returned to duty in the summer of 1864 near Alexandria. From that time until the end of the war, the regiment did little except routine garrison duty. In February and March of 1865, Jean Baptiste was detailed as a cook for his company's officers, possibly a duty he received because he was a free black. A clothing-issue book kept by Captain Bryan shows Jean Baptiste in service as late as May 12, 1865. The 29th Louisiana disbanded near Mansfield about May 19, and the men went to their homes without official paroles. Jean Baptiste was married at least twice. The 1900 census for Calcasieu Parish lists him as a single parent, but he stated that he had a wife and four children when he applied for a Confederate pension in 1912. The State Board of Pension Commissioners originally rejected his application because he had no official parole. Several of his former comrades sent in affidavits attesting to his service until the end of the war, and he received his pension in 1915.[34]

Lufroy Pierre-Auguste was born in St. Landry Parish about 1830. He was the son of Pierre Pierre-Auguste and Gabriele Tessier, free persons of color. The 1860 census shows that Lufroy worked as a stock herder for Francois P. Pitre, Jr. Lufroy left his farm and joined Captain Daniel Gober's Big Cane Rifles, which became Company K, 16th Louisiana Infantry Regiment. The first two muster rolls of this company list him as a free man of color—the only such instance I found in researching these men. None of the men discussed in this paper, except for Lutz and possibly one other, pretended that they were white. The other men in their companies undoubtedly knew them as free blacks.

The 16th Louisiana fought in the battles of Shiloh, Farmington and Perryville. On December 8, 1862, while in camp at Murfreesboro, Tennessee, Lufroy received a discharge from Confederate service. All men not subject to the conscript act passed the previous April were being released. As "a colored man," Lufroy was excluded from the provisions of the draft law. He went home, but he did become involved in one other incident before the war's end. On May 13, 1865, near Opelousas, he surprised two Jayhawkers. These men made up part of a band of outlaws, deserters and draft dodgers who resisted Confederate authority. The two Jayhawkers fired at him, and he returned fire, hitting one of the men. Lufroy married in 1869, but no further information on his life after the war has come to light so far.[35]

Two free men of color—Evariste Guillory, Sr., and Evariste

Guillory, Jr.—saw some service as home guards. Both father and son were free mulattoes living on Bayou Mallet west of Opelousas when the war began. They joined Captain M. McDavitt's Company I, 2nd Louisiana Reserve Corps. No information exists on when they enlisted in this unit, but the regiment did not form until July of 1864. The Reserve Corps consisted primarily of men who were over or under draft age or who were in some manner ineligible for regular service, such as discharged or disabled former soldiers. The men of the Reserve Corps saw practically no fighting with the enemy, but Confederate authorities called them out to chase Jayhawkers and deserters when needed for such service. They sometimes acted as drovers gathering cattle for the army in the field. Both of the Guillorys surrendered to Federal authorities and received their paroles at Washington, Louisiana, on June 17, 1865.[36]

Jacques Esclavon, a forty-year old free mulatto farmer of Calcasieu Parish, saw service in a Texas military unit late in the war. Jean Esclavon and Adelaide de la Fosse, free mulattoes, possibly were his parents. On September 11, 1864, he enlisted in Company A, Ragsdale's Battalion of Texas Cavalry. This unit had moved into southwestern Louisiana to perform guard and picket duty around the Calcasieu and Mermentau rivers and had enlisted several dozen Louisianans. It is possible that the Texans did not know that Esclavon was black, but existing battalion records showing his assignment to menial duties such as teamster and company cook may indicate they knew his status. Official records show Esclavon in service until at least March 1865. He may have remained on duty until his command broke up and dispersed to their homes at the end of the war.[37]

The remaining free men of color who wore the gray all came from the area of Campti, and did not, with one exception, join a military unit until relatively late in the war. There appear to have been more men enlisted than the nine mentioned here, but other names have not yet been discovered. An authority on this area of northwestern Louisiana has observed that these free blacks "lived as white, in almost all respects. There was hardly an aspect of Campti life or society (male, that is)" in which they "were not freely accepted. Almost all of the old Campti families (white) were their relatives and freely acknowledged it."[38] Thus, it is not hard to understand why they easily entered easily a predominantly white military company.

Gabriel Grappe became the first of these north Louisiana free blacks to enlist. On April 6, 1862, at Monroe, Grappe joined Captain Thomas W. Fuller's Bossier Cavalry company. Gabriel, born in 1825, was the son of Jacques Grappe and Marie Rose de la Cerda. Jacques Grappe was "half negro, one-eighth Chitimachas Indian and three-eighths French." Rose de la Cerda was of Spanish ancestry and probably had no black ancestors. The 1860 census shows Gabriel Grappe was a wagoner, but when he enlisted, he gave his occupation as farmer. From Monroe, Fuller's company went to Tennessee and fought in skirmishes both there and in Northern Mississippi. Grappe appears on a muster roll for January and February of 1863 as being absent sick at Okalona, Mississippi, and makes no further appearance in official records until October 1, 1864. On that date, a Confederate officer in Natchitoches wrote that Grappe had joined Captain Robert B. Love's Company H, 6th Louisiana Cavalry Regiment. It is possible that Grappe received a discharge from Fuller's company and later enlisted in Love's. He may have transferred from one company to the other shortly after the formation of the 6th Louisiana Cavalry (the Bossier Cavalry now serving as Company C of the regiment). The regiment saw no combat duty in late 1864 or early 1865 but served on courier and guard duty. Grappe surrendered and received his parole at Natchitoches on June 15, 1865.[39]

The eight remaining free men of color from the Campti area served in Company H, 6th Louisiana Cavalry, with Gabriel Grappe. One man was Gabriel's brother McGhee (or Margil), born in 1835 and by occupation a carpenter.[40] Two of the men were father and son—Jesse (or Jessy) and William Gardner. William was the son of Jesse and Jane Laury and was born February 24, 1840.[41] Two others—Joseph G. and Alphonse Perot—were brothers born in 1843 and 1838, respectively. They were sons of Valery Perot and Marie Felonize Condet, and both men operated farms.[42] Sylvester Perez was, as his name indicates, of partial Spanish ancestry. He married his first cousin, also a free person of color, Trinidad Armandine Simon, whose ancestors came to Campti from the Opelousas area.[43] Ambroise Lebrun was a descendant of Paul Etienne Le Brun dit Dagobert, a Frenchman who with Suzette Grappe, a sister of Jacques, fathered a number of mulatto children.[44] Little information has come to light on John Adams, the last of the Campti group. Born in 1842, he made his living as a shoemaker. A descriptive list gives his complexion as "quadroon."[45]

The service of these men first came to my attention through a letter written by Lieutenant J. Alphonse Prudhomme, the Confederate enrolling, or conscript, officer in Natchitoches. On October 1, 1864, Prudhomme wrote to his superiors in Shreveport that he had discovered the Perot brothers and McGhee Grappe in possession of passes from one of their lieutenants. The three privates told Prudhomme that the other five men had joined Captain Love's company also. Prudhomme reported that he had enrolled the Perots and Grappe under provisions of an order calling for conscription as laborers of free men of color. He also said he intended to send the men to Alexandria to work on fortifications there. Prudhomme then asked for instructions.[46]

While awaiting a reply, Prudhomme allowed Grappe to go home for clothes. Under this pretext, Grappe sought assistance from a family friend. On October 7, P. A. Morse, an influential citizen of Bossier Parish, wrote to the commander of the Louisiana conscript district and had Grappe take the letter to Shreveport. Morse stated that he knew well the Grappe family and recounted some of their family background. He asked for orders permitting the Grappe brothers to stay in Captain Love's company because they wished to remain in it and because Prudhomme had enrolled them illegally. Morse pointed out that although their father was a free man of color, the Grappe's mother "was a Mexican white woman." Colonel Edmund G. Randolph responded quickly to Morse's letter. The next day, he ordered McGhee Grappe back to Natchitoches and advised Prudhomme to send him back to his regiment. Grappe continued to serve with his unit until he surrendered and received his parole.[47]

The Perot brothers did not fare as well as McGhee Grappe. Prudhomme sent Alphonse on October 7 to Alexandria to serve as a laborer. Joseph received orders to appear before a medical examining board no later than October 16 to determine if his health would permit him to do heavy labor. No further information on him has come to light, and his ultimate fate is unknown. Prudhomme finally caught John Adams, enrolled him on December 30, and sent him on the same day to work on the Alexandria fortifications.[48] No other official records exist to show what happened to Jesse and William Gardner, Sylvester Perez or Ambroise Lebrun. If any of them remained in Captain Love's company after the controversy of October of 1864, none received a parole at the end of the war. Prudhomme's record book showing enrollments of free blacks contains no entries after December of 1864. He may have eventually enrolled these last four men as laborers or at least forced them out of active service in Love's company.

Unfortunately, none of the men discussed here left any letters, diaries or memoirs yet discovered either to elaborate on their wartime activities or to explain why they chose to enlist as volunteers in Confederate units. This leaves us to speculate on their motivation in risking their lives for a cause many people would not expect them to espouse. They undoubtedly followed a stronger urging of the same impulse which led thousands of their fellow free blacks to form militia units. In assessing the actions of New Orleans free blacks, David C. Rankin and Mary F. Berry emphasize the historical state-patriotism these men felt as well as their long tradition of service in the militia.[49] General studies of the roles played by free blacks elsewhere in the South, whether in labor or militia units, center on their state loyalty. As Benjamin Quarles noted, "These Negro volunteers placed the cause of their respective commonwealth above every other public duty."[50]

Gary Mills's study of the free blacks in the Natchitoches area also speaks of state loyalty but adds, "Most . . . realized that a Union victory would mean the complete destruction of their economy, the basis of their livelihood, and their special status as gens de couleur libre." Claude Oubre has written that St. Landry Parish's free blacks "knew where their loyalties lay" when the war started because they stood to lose "the status they enjoyed as a free people." These writings fall in line with the statewide study done by H. E. Sterkx, who observed that "many well-to-do colored freemen prized their distinctive economic positions so strongly that they deplored any prospect that would endanger it. . . Equally feared by this group of colored planters was the prospect of a general emancipation, which would submerge them in the great black mass of Negroes."[51]

Another factor, which is related to this view of their place in society, comes into play when considering the Campti free blacks (except Gabriel Grappe) and the Guillorys of St. Landry Parish. These men found themselves faced with a choice in the late summer or early fall of 1864—they could enlist in combat units or wait for conscription as laborers. A Natchitoches free black wrote from one labor camp, "We are in a way slaves." He described the squalor of the camp and told his wife, "The negroes [slaves] are treated better than we are. We are obliged to do the hardest kind of work and the negro looks on."[52] To avoid the degrading conditions and work of the labor camps, where they would find the same treatment given the slaves around them, these men chose an action that would emphasize their distinctiveness from other blacks.

Several historians have questioned the sincerity of the free men of color who formed Confederate militia units. They say that those men did so out of fear or under pressure from whites. They also point accurately to the facts that the Native Guards Regiment disbanded when New Orleans fell into Union hands and that most of the men later joined the Union army.[53] These historians may indeed be correct in appraising a few of the free blacks who served in the state militia. Yet fear or coercion does not seem to have motivated the majority of the men discussed in this paper, especially those who joined regular Confederate units. As I have stated, Confederate law prohibited any blacks from serving in combat units. If coercion forced these men to enlist, why didn't many more free blacks face the same pressure? We should not doubt the sincerity of these fifteen men, especially the ones from St. Landry Parish. A study of that area states, "the Opelousas Patriot was the mostvirulently anti-Free Negro journal in the whole of Louisiana." Many residents of the parish advocated the expulsion of mulattoes from the state, and in fact, some eighty-one free persons of color left St. Landry for Haiti in 1860.[54]

The actions of these free blacks seem to argue for what may be to some an unpopular conclusion. By volunteering for combat duty in regular Confederate service, these men took what can be seen as the final step of their acceptance or acculturation into the local white societies where they lived. Their decision reinforces what Gary Mills and others have written about the social and economic interactions of certain segments of Louisiana's antebellum population. In areas of Natchitoches, St. Landry, Calcasieu, Bossier and possibly other parishes, many whites and free blacks must have enjoyed a freedom of association that has received relatively little attention by social scientists. The actions of these free men of color in volunteering for—and of their white comrades in accepting them into—military units should lead us to take a closer look at race relations in Louisiana's pre-war period.

In summary, state or local patriotism and the desire to protect their standing which kept them above blacks in slavery would seem to have motivated all of the men discussed here to join the Confederate army. There is no evidence that anyone forced them to take that step. Rather, it seems that they followed the dictates of their consciences and made a bold move many whites shunned.

NOTES

1. George W. Williams, *A History of the Negro Troops in the War of the Rebellion, 1861-1865* (New York: Harper & Bros., 1888); Joseph T. Wilson, The Black Phalanx: *A History of the Negro Soldiers of the United States* (Hartford, Conn.: American Publishing Co., 1890); Benjamin Quarles, *The Negro in the Civil War* (Boston: Little, Brown & Co., 1955); Dudley Taylor Cornish, *The Sable Arm: Negro Troops in the Union Army, 1861-1865* (New York: Longmans, Green & Co., 1956); James M. McPherson, *The Negro's Civil War* (New York: Pantheon Books, 1965).

2. Williams, *History of the Negro Troops*, 82; Mary Frances Berry, *Military Necessity and Civil Rights Policy: Black Citizenship and the Constitution, 1861-1868* (Port Washington, N. Y.: Kennikat Press, 1977), 116 n. 12; *War of the Rebellion: A Compilation of the Official Records of the Union and Confederate Armies* (Washington, D. C.: Government Printing Office, 1880-1901), Series 4, Vol. I, 1095, 1111, and Vol. II, 941 hereafter cited as *OR*, all references to SEries i unless otherwise noted; General Samuel Cooper to Major General Dabney H. Maury, Sept. 28, 1863, Letters and Telegrams Sent by the Confederate Adjutant and Inspector General, 1861-1865, Chap. 1, Vol. 38, 458, Record Group 109, War Department Collection of Confederate Records, National Archives.

3. Charles H. Wesley, "The Employment of Negroes as Soldiers in the Confederate Army," *Journal of Negro History*, IV (1919), 243; J. K. Obatala, "The Unlikely Story of Blacks Who Were Loyal to Dixie," *Smithsonian*, IX (1979), 94-101.

4. H. C. Blackerby, *Blacks in Blue and Gray: Afro-American Service in the Civil War* (Tuscaloosa, Ala.: Portals Press, 1979), 6; Robert E. Greene, *Black Defenders of America, 1775-1973* (Chicago: Johnson Publishing Co., Inc., 1974), 53-102. Greene discusses sixty-six blacks who had applied for Confederate pensions after the war, but none of the men served as infantrymen.

5. Bell I. Wiley, *Southern Negroes, 1861-1865* (1938; reprint Baton Rouge: Louisiana State University Press, 1974), 160-61.

6. David C. Rankin, "The Politics of Caste: Free Colored Leadership in New Orleans During the Civil War," in *Louisiana's Black Heritage*, ed. by Robert R. MacDonald, John R. Kemp, and Edward F. Haas (New Orleans: Louisiana State Museum, 1979), 125.

7. Jefferson Davis Bragg, *Louisiana in the Confederacy* (Baton Rouge: Louisiana State University Press, 1941), 24.

8. *New Orleans Daily Delta*, Dec. 28, 1860.

9. Bragg, *Louisiana in the Confederacy*, 226-27, 49, 51.

10. "A. L. M." to Thomas O. Moore, Jan. 20, 1861, Letters Received by the Executive, 1860-1865, Louisiana State Archives.

11. *Ibid.*

12. Bragg, *Louisiana in the Confederacy*, 56

13. *New Orleans Daily Picayune*, Apr. 21, 1861.

14. *Ibid.*, Apr. 23, 1861.

15. *Ibid.*

16. *New Orleans Daily Crescent*, Apr. 27, 1861.

17. *New Orleans Daily Picayune*, May 22, 1861; Miscellaneous Register of Officers, Louisiana Militia, 1856-1862, pp. 103, 138, 171, Louisiana State Archives; Order Book, Adjutant General's Office, Louisiana State Troops, 1862-1864, 164, 165, Louisiana State Archives; Daily Crescent, May 29, 1861.

18. *Daily Picayune*, Sept. 25, 1861; Maj. Gen. John L. Lewis to ——, Sept. 24, 1861, Letters Sent Book, Louisiana State Troops, 1861-1862, 21, Louisiana State Archives; *OR*, Series 1, Vol. LIII, 746.

19. *Daily Picayune*, Nov. 24, 1861; Order Book, Adjutant General's Office, Louisiana State Troops, 1862-1864, 185, 213, Louisiana State Archives; Compiled Service Records, M320, Rolls 94 and 412.

20. Compiled Service Records of Confederate Soldiers Who Served in Volunteer Organizations from Louisiana, Microcopy No. 320, Roll 94, National Archives.

21. *Daily Picayune*, Dec. 9, 1861.

22. *Ibid.*, Jan. 10, 1862.

23. Compiled Service Records, M320, Roll 94; Orders No. 30, Headquarters Louisiana Militia, Adjutant General's Office, Jan. 17, 1862, Order Book, Adjutant General's Office, Louisiana State Troops, 1862, 101-102, Louisiana State Archives; Orders No. 61, Headquarters Louisiana Militia, Adjutant General's Office, Jan. 31, 1862, *ibid.*, 113.

24. Compiled Service Records, M320, Rolls 94-95, 412; Orders No. 30, Headquarters Louisiana Militia, Adjutant General's Office, Jan. 17, 1862, Order Book, Adjutant General's Office, Louisiana State Troops, 1862, 101-102, Louisiana State Archives; Orders No. 61, Headquarters Louisiana Militia, Adjutant General's Office, Jan. 31, 1862, *ibid.*, 113.

25. Miscellaneous Register of Officers, Louisiana State Troops, 1861-1862, pp. 13, 79, 98, 120, 130, 139, 146, 160, 161, 175, Louisiana State Archives; *OR*, XV, 557; Napier Bartlett, *Military Record of Louisiana* (Baton Rouge: Louisiana State University Press, 1964), 255-6.

26. *Baton Rouge Weekly Gazette & Comet*, Apr. 27, Oct. 5, 1861, Apr. 5, 1862.

27. *Daily Delta*, Aug. 7, 1862; Grenada Appeal, Aug. 7, 1862; *OR*, XV, 79.

28. *Baton Rouge Weekly Gazette & Comet*, May 11, 1861; *Pointe Coupee Democrat*, June 8, Nov. 2, 1861; *Baton Rouge Daily Advocate*, June 12, 1861; Miscellaneous Register of Officers, Louisiana Militia, 1856-1862, 139, 161, Louisiana State Archives.

29. *Daily Picayune*, May 22, 1861; Gary B. Mills, "Patriotism

Frustrated: The Native Guards of Confederate Natchitoches," *Louisiana History*, XVIII (1977), 440-49; Gary B. Mills, *The Forgotten People: Cane River's Creoles of Color* (Baton Rouge: Louisiana State University Press, 1977), 233-36.

30. Cornelius Donato, Administrator, for August Donato, deceased, vs. the United States, #9570, U. S. Court of Claims, Congressional Jurisdiction, Record Group 125, National Archives.

31. John D. Winters, *The Civil War in Louisiana* (Baton Rouge: Louisiana State University Press, 1963), 21.

32. I owe a special debt of gratitude to Mrs. Jan Tate, who assisted me in locating historical and genealogical information which identified these three men and two others who I will discuss later.

33. Population Schedules, Eighth Census of the United States, St. Landry Parish, Louisiana, 1860, National Archives; Compiled Service Records, M320, Roll 194; Application File of Charles F. Lutz, Confederate Pension Files, Louisiana State Archives; Population Schedules, Tenth and Twelfth Censuses, Calcasieu Parish, 1880 and 1900.

34. Population Schedules, Seventh Census, 1850, St. Landry Parish; Compiled Service Records, M320, Roll 355; Notebook, J. W. Bryan Papers, Louisiana Adjutant General's Library, Jackson Barracks, New Orleans; Return of Company I, 29th Louisiana Infantry, March 1865, Bryan Papers; Clothing Issue Book, Company I, 29th Louisiana Infantry, 1864-1865, Bryan Papers; Population Schedules, Twelfth Census, 1900, Calcasieu Parish; Application File of Jean Baptiste Pierre-Auguste, Louisiana Confederate Pension Files.

35. Population Schedules, Eighth Census, 1860, St. Landry Parish; Rev. Donald J. Hebert, Southwest Louisiana Records, 31 vols. (Cecilia, La., privately published, 1974-1983), IX, 14; ibid., III, 691; Compiled Service Records, M320, Roll 273; Captain E. John Ellis to Pa, Nov. 29, 1862, E. John and Thomas C. W. Ellis Family Papers, Louisiana and Lower Mississippi Valley Collection, Special Collections, Louisiana State University Library; Opelousas Courier, May 20, 1865; Population Schedules, Tenth Census, 1880, St. Landry Parish.

36. Population Schedules, Eighth Census, 1860, St. Landry Parish; Opelousas Courier, July 9, 1864; Compiled Service Records, M320, Roll 114.

37. Population Schedules, Eighth Census, 1860, Calcasieu Parish; Compiled Service Records of Confederate Soldiers Who Served in Volunteer Organizations from Texas, Microcopy No. 323, Roll 210; Hebert, Southwest Louisiana Records, III, 686.

38. Elizabeth Shown Mills to author, Nov. 8, 1981. Mrs. Mills provided historical and genealogical information helping to establish the identities of these nine men.

39. Ibid.; Compiled Service Records, M320, Roll 22; Succession Book 25, Office of the Clerk of Court, Natchitoches Parish; Population

Schedules, Eighth Census, 1860, Natchitoches Parish; Lieutenant J. Alphonse Prudhomme to Lieutenant [?] Goodwill, Oct. 1, 1864, Letter Book, July 12, 1864-May 15, 1865, p. 51, J. A. Prudhomme Papers, Louisiana Adjutant General's Library.

40. Population Schedules, Eighth Census, 1860, Natchitoches Parish; Mills to author, Nov. 8, 1981.

41. Records of Baptisms, 1851-1873, Church of the Nativity, Campti, La., no. 1862-4 and no. 1863-15; Mills to author, Nov. 8, 1981.

42. Records of Baptisms, 1851-1873, Church of the Nativity, no. 1864-1; Joseph Galion Perot to Marie Terencine Lamather, Records of Burials and Marriages, 1851-1905, ibid., unnumbered page; Succession Book 21, Clerk of Court, Natchitoches, Succession of Marie Felonize Condet; Enrollment Book, Natchitoches Parish, La., 1864-1865, Louisiana Historical Association Collection, Manuscripts Department, Special Collections Division, Howard-Tilton Memorial Library, Tulane Univeristy.

43. Records of Burials and Marriages, 1851-1905, Church of the Nativity, 268; Mills to author, Nov. 8, 1981.

44. Mills to author, Nov. 8, 1981.

45. Enrollment Book, LHA Collection.

46. Prudhomme to Goodwill, Oct. 1, 1864, Prudhomme Letter Book, 51.

47. Enrollment Book, LHA Collection; P. A. Morse to Col. Edmund G. Randolph, Oct. 7, 1864, with endorsement by Randolph, Oct. 8, Prudhomme Papers; unnumbered order, Conscript District of Louisiana, Oct. 8, 1864, ibid.; Compiled Service Records, M320, Roll 22.

48. Enrollment Book, LHA Collection.

49. David C. Rankin, "The Forgotten People: Free People of Color in New Orleans, 1850-1870" (unpublished doctoral dissertation, Johns Hopkins University, 1976), 166-67; Mary F. Berry, "Negro Troops in Blue and Gray: The Louisiana Native Guards, 1861-1863," *Louisiana History*, VIII (1967), 172. See also Obatala, "The Unlikely Story," passim, and Roland C. McConnell, *Negro Troops in Antebellum Louisiana: A History of the Battalion of Free Men of Color* (Baton Rouge: Louisiana State University Press, 1968), *passim*.

50. Quarles, *The Negro in the Civil War*, 38; see also McPherson, The Negro's Civil War, 24.

51. Gary B. Mills, *The Forgotten People*, 230, 244; Claude Oubre, "St. Landry's Gens de Couleur Libre: The Impact of War and Reconstruction," in Vaughan B. Baker and Jean T. Kreamer, *Louisiana Tapestry: The Ethnic Weave of St. Landry Parish* (Lafayette: Center for Louisiana Studies, 1982), 82; H. E. Sterkx, *The Free Negro in Ante-Bellum Louisiana* (Rutherford, N. J.: Fairleigh Dickinson University Press, 1972), 213.

52. Alexander S. Dupre to wife, Sept. 29, Oct. 2, 1864, Melrose Collection, Archives Division, Northwestern State University Library, Natchitoches.

53. Rankin, "The Forgotten People," 168; Wilson, *The Black Phalanx*, 483-84; Quarles, *The Negro in the Civil War*, 38-39; McPherson, *The Negro's Civil War*, 24.

54. Geraldine Mary McTigue, "Forms of Radical Interaction in Louisiana, 1860-1880" (unpublished doctoral dissertation, Yale University, 1975), 173, 174.

Different Drummers: Black Virginians As Confederate Loyalists

Ervin L. Jordan, Jr.

On December 2, 1859, the day John Brown was executed for attempting to ignite a slave insurrection at Harpers Ferry, a group of Scottsville, Virginia, blacks led by a slave named Ben hanged him in effigy as an "old murderer, horse thief and traitor" and proclaimed their willingness to use his pikes to defend their owners against abolitionists. In May of 1861 a black Culpepper County resident declared: "If old Lincoln does put his foot on old Farginny I can raise a regiment of [negroes] . . . the negroes here understand all about it, the people have informed them as to the true state of things, they know that the South are their real friends." One hundred thirty-three years later, an African-American scholar observed: "When you eliminate the black Confederate soldier, you've eliminated the history of the South. . . . [We] share a common heritage with white Southerners who recall that era. We shared in the plantation scheme of things as well as the forces that fought to keep them."[1]

This essay evaluates Afro-Virginian loyalty to the Commonwealth of Virginia and, by extension, the Confederacy. Several thousand, and not just "faithful" body servants caught up by the thrill of battle, took up arms or otherwise volunteered for the South and staunchly worked in its behalf. One in six of the Confederacy's 3,653,000 blacks were Virginians. Half a million resided in the state (490,000 slaves, 59,000 free blacks), more than in any other place in North America.

Reminiscences, newspapers and similar sources indicate that approximately 15 percent of Virginia's slaves and 25 percent of her free blacks supported the Confederacy. Although the majority of the South's blacks lived in the Old Dominion, this is not to imply Afro-Virginians were more likely to be Confederate loyalists as compared to blacks in other seceded states or as representational of African-American sentiment as a whole. However, as products of a racial caste in a particular Confederate state, they are representative of this phenomenon.[2]

"It is worthy to assemble facts to put truth in the face of legend," Stephen Vincent Benet once said, "to investigate impartially, to throw new light on an old problem."[3] While the names of thousands of prominent and little known white Confederate civilians, soldiers and politicians are writ large on the pages of history, ignored are the black men and women without whom the nascent Confederacy could not have mobilized.

Black historians have rejected the authenticity of Confederate blacks. Joseph Thomas Wilson designated Southern efforts to enlist black soldiers as "unrealized dreams" and censured blacks who boasted the loudest of their desire to fight Northerners as doing so only for white approbation and in hopes of obtaining extraordinary liberties. Benjamin Brawley and William E. B. Du Bois denied the existence of black Confederate soldiers; white Southerners who believed in black volunteers were "equally misguided" according to Charles Harris Wesley. These scholars acknowledged the value of slaves as agricultural and military laborers and that if the Confederacy had actually fielded black troops during 1861-1863, large numbers could have been obtained. John Hope Franklin believed black Confederate soldiers would have been truly loyal to the South; Benjamin Quarles agreed but added "without their hearts being in it." Regardless, a Union soldier shot by a black Southerner was just as dead as if killed by a white Southerner.[4]

The notion is not so farfetched, and history offers many instances where racial or cultural minorities allied themselves with their ancestral oppressors: sepoys and Gurkhas in British India; tejanos (Mexicans) who fought and died with Texan-Americans during the Texas Revolution; Native American scouts and the U. S. Army during the subjugation of western Indian tribes; and the nisei, Japanese-Americans who served with American armed forces in World War II despite their families' being ordered from their homes and businesses and sent to internment centers in Arizona, Arkansas, California, Idaho, Utah and Wyoming.[5]

Black Confederate patriotism took many forms: slaves devoted to their owners, free blacks who donated money and labor, blacks who joined the Confederate army and slaves who loyally supervised plantations of absentee-owners. An unidentified black Winchester resident became a local hero after being jailed and allowed only bread and water because of his support of the South and refusal to work for the Union. The old man was forced to chop wood with an iron ball and chains attached to his arms and legs, but stubbornly vowed to support the Confederacy to his last breath. A Charlottesville newspaper reprinted an interview with James Ward, a slave who fled "Yankeedom" but returned with warnings to his fellow slaves of abuse and racism in Union army camps. He declared he would rather be the slave of "the meanest masters in the South" than to be a free black man in the North: "If this is freedom, give me slavery forever."[6]

Horace Holmes, a black Richmond resident, purchased a new Confederate army lieutenant's uniform and proudly wore it as he attended to his business. City policemen, annoyed at the sight of a black man wearing the hallowed gray, arrested and dragged him before the provost marshal. Holmes protested that he was unaware that it was illegal to make such a purchase. After a brief consultation, the gold lace and insignia were removed and a relieved Holmes was permitted to go his way with the remainder of his uniform.[7]

Holmes and other Virginia free blacks were as enthusiastic to publicly demonstrate their bravery and patriotism as white Southern males. Heedful of their perilous situation, free blacks too, supported the Confederacy at public rallies. They tended to be loyal to their county or town and sought to demonstrate their allegiance in order to preserve their freedom and nullify suspicion of them as dissidents or Northern collaborators. They shared the universal opinion of their white neighbors that the South was going to win the war.

Spotsylvania County free blacks placed themselves and their property at Virginia's disposal in August of 1861, and a black Fairfax County farmer sold twenty-eight acres of his 150-acre farm and donated the money to the state's defense. Robert Butt of Portsmouth declined to become a candidate to represent his district in the Federal Congress as long as the city was under Union occupation: "No, gentlemen, I will leave this position to some one who is more anxious to act the traitor, and have his name written high upon the page of infamy." James T. Ayer, a black farmer in Suffolk, sold so much food to Southern quartermasters that Union officers accused him of being an employee of the Confederate commissary department. Numerous Union officers reluctantly acknowledged the presence of "black rebels" throughout the Old Dominion.[8]

There are numerous but forgotten examples of Afro-Virginian civilians who were Confederate patriots. "Uncle Billy," owned by Bedford County customs collector Micajah Davis, buried Davis's official records during a Union raid in 1864 and proudly returned them to a surprised Davis after the war. Lewis, a Mecklenburg County slave who served with the Boydton Cavalry as its bugler during antebellum times, was denied permission by the Confederate War Department to enlist when it became the 3rd Virginia Cavalry. He donated his forty-dollar bugle plus an additional twenty dollars to the regiment.[9]

A Winchester newspaper gleefully reported the outcome when Union raiders carried off nine slaves belonging to a local slaveowner. In Maryland, the slaves were offered a choice of freedom or return to their owners; they unanimously stated a preference for the Old Dominion, their wives and children and claimed devotion to their masters. Flabbergasted, Unionists "set them on the Virginia shore again and the negroes are now at home contented and happy, fearing nothing." After two weeks of freedom in Pennsylvania, four Clarke County slaves, disgusted with the North, demanded to be returned to Virginia but were instead sold. Two slaves captured in King George County escaped from their "rescuers," complaining Northerners worked and whipped them twice as hard as Southerners. An ex-slave from Gloucester County named Fanny escaped from her owners yet sent back money in equal amounts of silver, gold and greenbacks for the benefit of her grateful owner's children.[10]

Pro-Southern blacks provided financial support to the Confederacy. Pompey Scott of Amelia County donated twenty dollars and William, property of Dr. W. H. Rives, patriotically invested $150 in Confederate States loan bonds "as a . . . rebuke to the hypocrites of the North. Intelligent slaves know that they have no friends in the world but the Southern white people."[11]

Seventy "patriotic free negroes of Lynchburg" proffered their services to Governor John Letcher "to act in whatever capacity may be assigned them" in defense of Virginia. One newspaper article gleefully noted both free and enslaved Afro-Virginians seemed equally dedicated to the state and the South. Even blacks from Vicksburg, Mississippi, held a fundraiser for "de boys in Varginny" which netted one thousand dollars. Norfolk blacks voluntarily erected breastworks while Charles Tinsley, spokesman for a group of black volunteers from Petersburg, vowed they would gladly serve their native state in her hour of trial and stood ready to obey any and all orders. An October of 1861 illustration in *Harper's Weekly* of a Confederate recruitment parade in Woodstock was led by a public-spirited black man bearing a Virginia state flag.[12]

After their capture, a group of white Virginia slaveowners and their slaves were asked if they would take the oath of allegiance to the United States in exchange for their freedom. A free black among them indignantly-replied, "I can't take no such oath. I'm a secesh negro." A slave from this same group, upon learning that his master had refused, proudly exclaimed, "I can't take no oath dat Massa won't take." A second slave agreed: "I ain't going out here on no dishonorable terms." On another occasion a captured planter took the oath but his slave remained faithful to the Confederacy and refused. This slave, returned by a flag of truce boat, expressed disgust of his owner: "Massa had no principles."[13]

When two Union soldiers tried to entice a Shenandoah County slave named George with tales of the good life that awaited him and other blacks in the North after the publication of the Emancipation Proclamation, they were met with respectful but firm leeriness. He answered their stories with the curt remark that there were already more people up north than there ought to be. The soldiers tried a different approach by asking him if he was free. "No," George replied, "but I am comfortable; got a good house." He had no intention of forsaking the Old Dominion, and other such examples of black faithfulness were acclaimed by Confederates: "To the honor of the negroes it must be said, that they adhered in general with great fidelity to the cause. . . . This was a great surprise to the enemy, who had supposed that at the first signal the whole slave population would be in arms, and rush at every hazard to their standards."[14]

A small number of pro-Confederate free blacks and slaves spied for the South under the supervision of Confederates such as Belle Boyd or military officers like Colonel John Singleton Mosby, who appreciated the information they provided on Union troop movements across the

Old Dominion. So frequently did Afro-Virginians commit espionage that exasperated Union officers grumbled that military operations in the state were being thwarted by ubiquitous black spies and counterspies whom they characterized as sworn allies of the South. Unsung Afro-Virginian scouts, guides and safehouse caretakers acted as part-time Southern secret agents; only racial prejudice caused white Confederates to regard them as untrustworthy or lacking in patriotism, aptitude and nerve for the dangerous duty of wartime military espionage.[15]

But some black Confederates paid a high price for their fealty. A free black pastor in Hampton named Bailey, permitted to purchase his family's freedom and two houses, took the Confederate side to protect both. His fellow blacks considered it a sign of divine justice when his houses were destroyed by fire after Confederates burned the town in the summer of 1861. Another black Baptist minister, grateful to whites for allowing him to purchase his beautiful daughter and save her from the sexual advances of licentious slaveowners, was so appreciative that he publicly offered the services of himself and his sons to the Old Dominion. Enraged fellow Afro-Virginians rebuked him for this act and at first he tried to defend his actions with the excuse that he had done what he thought best for his race. As his congregation dwindled to almost nothing, he became alarmed and desperately attempted to restore himself in their good graces by way of apologies but was ostracized by the black community.[16]

Northerners miscalculated the quantity and sincerity of Southern blacks as agricultural, industrial and military allies: "It is just absurd to talk of a three year's War for the Union. An Army and a General competent to beat the Rebels will be competent to *pin* them so that they must fight or throw down their arms. A protracted Guerrilla war can not be maintained in such a region as the South, and amid such peasantry as the Slaves." Typical was an unidentified black man employed at Richmond's Howard's Grove Hospital who exhorted Afro-Virginians to stand by the South and join her armies to "help drive the ruthless invader from the sacred soil of Virginia." Other slaves even helped recapture runaways.[17]

The Confederate military became so dependent on Afro-Virginian laborers that by 1864, General Robert E. Lee and General Jeremy Gilmer, chief of the War Department's engineer bureau, made plans to organize them into Confederate Negro Labor Battalions as companies, regiments and battalions within their home counties. A hundred comprised a "gang" under a manager assisted by three white overseers. Eight gangs (800 blacks and 28 whites) formed a battalion commanded by a superintendent and were assigned an assistant purveyor, a clerk and a physician; three battalions (2,400 blacks and 84 whites) were a "force" under the command of a director assisted by two clerks. Afro-Virginians were forwarded to army conscript camps under and formally enrolled into the service by field grade officers with muster rolls, regular inspections, individual service records on file and other trappings of military order and discipline basically as unarmed militia. Such organizations could be rapidly converted into fully armed military regiments as necessary.[18]

Virginians became particularly sensitive about abuses of free black laborers and demanded they be treated fairly. When an extortion scheme to cheat them of their wages was uncovered in 1862, a newspaper editorial thundered angrily:

> In paying the negroes at work on the fortifications, we understand that most villainous abuses have been practised [sic]. The paymaster requires them to be identified by their overseers, and we are informed that it has been a common practice for some of the overseers to charge these poor creatures ten per cent of their pay as fees for their identification. Who are these overseers, and who is responsible for their conduct? Some of them hunt up free negroes in the city, giving them the alternative of paying black mail or of being carried to the jail and whipped. One of the most awful and revolting specimens of the barbarity of these creatures was related yesterday, where a free negro on the fortifications had his back actually cut into a mangle of bleeding flesh, the driver having given him, as we were told by a policeman, five hundred and sixty-one lashes with the whip... In the name of God, is there no justice to be found in the courts of human justice for iniquities like this?[19]

Nearly 180,000 Afro-Virginians served as noncombatant laborers. They generally suffered poor rations and health care, shoddy clothing and were frequently overworked. One suspects that many were not loyal to the Confederacy or the Union but to themselves and their families. However, indicative of black allegiance were those who volunteered or willingly sought employment. Free black carpenters and blacksmiths were hired while others were employed at mines, military hospitals, railroads and factories. Three hundred and fifty Norfolk black volunteers were welcomed by the chief engineer in charge of the city's defenses and efficiently constructed batteries and earthworks. Seven hundred free blacks worked to erect Richmond defensive works which stymied the advance of the Army of the Potomac in 1862. The ability to earn fair and regular wages (even slaves who worked overtime were usually allowed to keep their earnings) boosted the quality of life for free black families and gave Afro-Virginians an ego boost and incentive to remain true to the Old Dominion.[20]

Several Afro-Virginian body servants identified with the

Confederate cause. When Lt. John L. Cochran joined the 19th Virginia Infantry in 1861 shortly before First Manassas, accompanying him was a family servant, Tarleton. When Cochran apologized for not providing him a new suit of clothes, Tarleton bragged that his shabby clothing would very soon be replaced from the bodies of Northern soldiers he would slay during his first battle. Jack Foster, a body servant belonging to a member of the 36th Virginia Infantry, found the life of a body servant pleasant; apparently he had so much free time that he concluded his letters home with personal requests for more books. The 9th Virginia Cavalry's contribution of $262 for a monument to Stonewall Jackson was supplemented by the regiment's body servants' donation of ten dollars.[21]

Confederate body servants occasionally captured Union servants on the battlefields and treated them as personal prisoners. These captives, denounced as "Lincolnites," were abused, ridiculed and put to work under their supervision. Tom and Overton, body servants with the 12th Virginia Cavalry, captured a Union officer's servant at gunpoint at the battle of Brandy Station in 1863 and thereafter shared him as their own slave. But a slave boy who escaped and was recaptured during the battle of First Manassas by two Afro-Virginians suffered a grisly fate. The body servants in the camp condemned the boy as a traitor and executed him as an expression of their allegiance to the South.[22]

Body servants fought if given the chance, sometimes taking the place of timorous whites. At the battle of Port Republic on June 8, 1862, Edmund Drew, a barber assigned to the Charlottesville Light Artillery, bravely took over after an Irish substitute named Brown deserted his post as driver of the battery's lead caisson. During the Seven Days campaign, a Confederate soldier confessed his fright to his superior officer and Westley, a body servant, received permission to take the coward's rifle and place. Westley gave a good account of himself during the battle by killing a Union soldier with every shot. In the winter of 1864, officers of the 16th Virginia Infantry posted a young Afro-Virginian named Ben to guard the regiment's rations. While on duty, he mortally wounded a white private who tried to steal the supplies, and only the intervention of General William Mahone (later the "Hero of the Crater") prevented Ben from being lynched.[23]

A slave named Tom Hester joined a state regiment and served until wounded and captured. Levi Miller, a Rockbridge County slave, served gallantly with the 5th Texas Infantry Regiment in Virginia, Pennsylvania, Georgia and Tennessee during 1861-1864 as a body servant. He refused Northern enticements to desert during the Gettysburg campaign and saw combat at the Wilderness in May of 1864. In recognition of his bravery and patriotism, the 5th Texas enrolled him as a full-fledged soldier. Miller received a Confederate pension in 1908 and a hero's burial in Lexington in 1921.[24]

Afro-Virginians first became eligible for state pensions of $25 annually with the passage of a 1924 statute:

> Under the provisions of this act any person who actually accompanied a soldier in the service and remained faithful and loyal as the body servant of such soldier, or who served as a cook, hostler or teamster, or who worked on breastworks under any command of the army and thereby rendered service to the Confederacy, shall be entitled to receive an annual pension of twenty-five dollars, proof of service and right to be enrolled to be prescribed by the auditor of public accounts.

To prove his entitlement, a petitioner had to file an application with a local court, accompanied by affidavits from two white ex-Confederate soldiers; if none were available certificates from two local whites of good reputation were acceptable substitutes. This statute denied pensions to runaways, blacks who served as soldiers or laborers for the Union Army and black women. White women who were widows (even those who remarried) of Confederate sailors, soldiers, marines or who had been hospital matrons, were eligible not only for pensions but also funeral expenses paid for by the state. The 1928 General Assembly amended the 1924 act to include former slaves who had performed guard duty, buried Confederate dead or "who worked in railroad shops, blacksmith shops, or Confederate hospitals." About 270 black men met the requirements of the application process.[25]

Afro-Virginian enthusiasts for the Confederacy assumed that by identifying and actively supporting the Southern cause, white postwar gratitude would lead to expanded privileges and rights. Their fidelity did not result in racial equality nor granting of social and political rights. White Southerners considered them temporary indigenous allies but never formally recognized them no matter how loyal they seemed to be. Clearly, the motivations of black loyalists were either sincerely patriotic or represented alarmed individuals acting on behalf for their own selfpreservation and economic interests.

Several were slave and property owners who deemed their way of life threatened by the North and yearned to prove to their white neighbors that they, too, were Southern patriots. Approximately 169 free blacks owned 145,976 acres in the counties of Amelia, Amherst, Isle of Wight, Nanesmond, Prince William and Surry, averaging 870 acres each. Twenty-nine Petersburg blacks each owned property worth a thousand dollars and purchased more throughout the war.[26]

Free black residents of Hampton and Norfolk owned property of considerable value; 17 black Hamptonians possessed property worth a total of $15,000. Thirty-six black men paid taxes as heads of families in Elizabeth City County; they were employed as blacksmiths, bricklayers, fishermen and oystermen. One hundred sixty blacks in three Norfolk

County parishes (Elizabeth City, Portsmouth and St. Brides) owned a total of $41,158 in real estate and personal property. Black families surnamed Cuffe, Elliot, Civils, Smith and Wilkins were prominent on Norfolk tax rolls. One of the wealthiest, Samuel Smith, Sr., of St. Brides, was a fortune teller whose net worth was $3,000; Cullen Smith of Portsmouth Parish was worth $7,000. Several Petersburg blacks were substantial property owners and taxpayers. Two brothers, Thomas and James Bolling, together were worth $4,000.00; blacksmith Armistead Wilson's holdings totaled $1,600, twice the amount he paid for his freedom. Robert Clark, formerly a hotel slave, owned a carriage and horse hiring business valued at $9,000.[27]

Black Virginians also owned slaves. Gilbert Hunt, ex-slave blacksmith, owned two slaves, a house valued at $1,376, and $500 in other properties at his death in 1863. Betsey Fuller, a self-employed free black woman peddler in Princess Anne County, owned her husband. The mother of five children, Betsey prudently evaded mentioning ownership of her husband to census enumerators. But her husband sided with the Confederacy, and after the capture of Norfolk in 1862, he imprudently proclaimed his pro-Confederate sentiments. Union authorities put him to work on a city chain gang; Confederate propagandists praised him as a loyal Southerner.[28]

Patience and property ownership meant survivability. After the war, approximately fifty Afro-Virginians filed claims with the Federal government for wartime damages to their property caused by Union soldiers. These claims totaled $49,972.47, averaging $1,041.09 per claim. The two largest single claims were submitted by a Prince William County free black miller named James C. Muschett for $6,474.50 worth of livestock, food and household goods, and William Cook of Spotsylvania County, also free born, for $3,290.30 in losses of tools and livestock. These petitions are illustrative of the complexity, ingenuity and survival skills of members of the Afro-Virginian community. The amount of their estimated losses dispel assumptions of blacks as unable and unlikely to accumulate wealth.[29]

Slave-soldiers had been enthusiastically proposed in antebellum Southern periodicals: "A slave population, the most effective laborers for a warm climate under the best discipline and most skillful direction of any other people, in numbers sufficient to raise the means of army subsistence for any probable war, too well fed, clothed and taken care of, to be restless or unruly, and the least dangerous from insurrection." White Virginians found themselves experiencing the same debates and fears of their Revolutionary forefathers relating to the problem of arming black men to kill white males, even if those males happened to be the enemy. Nevertheless, one Campbell County planter advised his Confederate soldier-son: "[Do] not let Sam go into the fight with you. Keep him in the rear, for [he] is worth a thousand dollars." By November of 1861, the wife of a Confederate staff officer forthrightly predicted that the South would soon have no choice but to enroll black soldiers. Theoretically, 237,000 Afro-Virginian males (census returns enumerated 12,500 free blacks and 225,00 slaves) of military age were available. Approximately 680,000 Southern blacks (18 percent of the black population) were available for Confederate military duty by 1865.[30]

One nineteenth-century black historian, George Washington Williams, wrote: "From the earliest dawn of the war the rebel authorities did not frown upon the action of local authorities in placing arms into the hands of free Negroes." In 1862, state legislators candidly pondered a program to enlist Afro-Virginians as soldiers. A member of the House of Delegates proposed the enrollment of free blacks but admitted their families would lack means of support while their sole wage earners were away. The delegate hastened to explain that his proposal was not the result of any personal friendship toward free blacks since if it were in his power he would "convert them all to slaves."[31]

Confederate Secretary of War James Seddon agreed: "Our position with the North and before the world will not allow the employment as armed soldiers of negroes." But as the tide of white public opinion changed, *The Index*, a Confederate propaganda weekly published in London, suggested 500,000 black men could be spared for the front and replaced by black female slaves who were healthier, hardier and stronger than the peasant women of Europe. Southern blacks and whites understood and had "perfect confidence in each other's character," according to this publication. Blacks possessed obedience, intelligence and insensibility to danger: "They would . . . be more effective in the field with the more primitive weapons which the blacksmith's shop on every plantation could forge out of the implements of husbandry. A hundred thousand negro pikemen or scythemen could probably be a more formidable body for immediate service than the same number of raw recruits trusted with unwonted weapons."[32]

Throughout the fall of 1861, local Confederate commanders in Virginia were arming free blacks and slaves due to manpower shortages. In December, New York soldiers on patrol from Newport News were attacked near Newmarket Bridge by a Confederate force comprised of white cavalrymen and armed blacks. The New Yorkers killed six before retreating; their officers later complained: "If they fight us with Negroes, why should we not fight them with Negroes, too? . . . Let us fight the devil with fire." These Afro-Virginians, organized in response to immediate threats in the form of Union raids, were disbanded after the danger had passed. Extraordinary public attention surrounded the arrival of a wreath and letter in Richmond sent by Mrs. Judith C. Judah, an Afro-Virginian woman, as a contribution to the memory of "A Colored Southern Soldier," her husband. "I send you my willing contribution of flowers," Mrs. Judah wrote, "as an offering to the gallant dead of the Richmond Light Infantry Blues of which my husband . . . fell in the service. I hope they all sleep sweetly across the river under the shade of trees to rise again at another trumpet."[33]

Afro-Virginians fought for the Old Dominion before First Manassas. A black with the 1st Virginia Cavalry single handedly killed a Union soldier on July 2, 1861, during a skirmish at Falling Waters near Martinsburg. An entire company of the 15th Pennsylvania Volunteers was captured with the exception of three men killed while resisting capture or trying to escape. Sergeant Major Philip H. Powers of the Clarke Cavalry later wrote his wife: "One fellow was creeping away under the cover of a fence when he was shot dead by the only negro in our party."[34]

Several blacks (mulattoes) posed as whites and served in state regiments, some as officers. George and Stafford Grimes of Caroline County enlisted with the Fredericksburg Artillery in 1862, though both later deserted. George was recaptured and plans were made to court-martial him for desertion. However the court decided against this because as a "Negro" he could not be a soldier nor tried as one. According to census records, Stafford was a 23 year old mulatto laborer with a personal estate valued at $55.00.[35]

During the Yorktown siege several of the Confederacy's best sharpshooters were Afro-Virginians. After training, armed with a rifle and a handful of bullets, imaginatively camouflaged in natural or artificial positions, any illiterate black could be transformed into a lethal weapon. Any Union soldier killed or wounded reduced the number of foes, and if such blacks were slain or captured they were easily replaced. Alfred Bellard, 5th New Jersey Infantry, reported the shooting of two black snipers by Berdan's Sharpshooters during April of 1862. In June of 1863 George Hupman, a Union soldier stationed near Newport News with the 89th New York Infantry, and Herman Clarke of the 117th New York, wrote to homefolk about the shooting of black Confederate sharpshooters who refused to defect to the Union side.[36]

Flabbergasted Northern eyewitnesses reported the presence of armed blacks in the Army of Northern Virginia during the Sharpsburg campaign. Union Sanitary Commission employee Dr. Lewis H. Steiner recorded in his diary: "Most of the negroes . . . were manifestly an integral portion of the Southern Confederacy Army. . . . The fact was patent and rather interesting when considered in connection with the horror rebels express at the suggestion of black soldiers." Fifty black Confederate soldiers were sighted while on duty near the Rappahannock River during March of 1863, and a Union officer reported: "I could distinctly see negroes, [armed and uniformed], the same as white soldiers." Meanwhile, one of two Afro-Virginians aboard a steamship was accidentally killed while drilling each other in the manual of arms; a Richmond newspaper's comment on this incident merely denounced the arming of unsupervised blacks: "Guns in the hands of negroes are dangerous playthings, more apt to injure themselves than anybody else."[37]

Black zeal for military service was sincere. Shortly after the Confederate Congress authorized black enlistment in 1865, Afro-Virginians held several dances and parties, with the encouragement of local authorities, to recruit and raise funds on behalf of these regiments. "All colored men who will come forward and show their willingness to save their country" would receive a one hundred dollar bounty, according to the *Petersburg Daily Express* in April 1865; slaves were offered "freedom and undisturbed residence at their old homes in the Confederacy after the war." The *Richmond Examiner* reported the organization and first public appearance of a company of black Confederate soldiers, comprised of twelve free blacks and twenty-three slaves. Their barracks were described as "neat, clean, warm and comfortable"; their rations were prepared at Libby Prison.[38]

John Scott, a Goochland County free black, appeared at a recruiting station in March of 1865 out of a desire for revenge after his canal boat was stolen by Union soldiers who robbed him and destroyed his livelihood during a raid in his county: "Now I wants to join right away. I wants to fight them Yankees that have treated me so bad. I've got nothing in de world but just what I'm wearing, and I wants to fight them that robbed me. I knows a heap about a gun, just let me git a bead on 'em and I'll bring 'em [down] every pop."[39]

Civil War scholars presume Confederate blacks were recruited and drilled but never saw combat. However, one Confederate courier witnessed a skirmish on April 4, 1865, in Amelia County: "I saw a wagon train guarded by Confederate negro soldiers, a novel sight for me." The convoy, manned entirely by black infantry, came under attack by Federal cavalry. The blacks successfully fought off the first charge of their foes. A second assault proved to be too much, and the black soldiers were captured and led away as prisoners. Two days later, a squad of twelve Afro-Virginian soldiers, armed with rifles and commanded by white officers, were seen throwing up fortifications near Farmville.[40]

Twenty-eight blacks surrendered and insisted on being paroled at Appomattox with Lee's army rather than accepting freedom. Among the Confederates imprisoned at Point Lookout, Maryland, in May of 1865 was "a negro Confederate soldier" described as "the only [black] reb" in confinement. White Confederates took oaths of allegiance and were released but this lone black Confederate steadfastly refused to betray Dixie and remained loyal to the last, last of the loyal, "unreconstructed and unreconstructible."[41]

Pro-Confederate blacks were riddles; white Southerners did not trust them, Northerners regarded them as lunatics, and the majority of blacks feared and scorned them as fools or racial traitors. Afterwards some black Confederates wanted to forget their service. Civil rights activist and anti-lynching crusader Mary Church Terrell recalled that one of her uncles, James Wilson, a black man with blue eyes, was so light-skinned that he was forced to serve in the Confederate army as a soldier. Whenever his family mentioned this after the war he became embarrassed and angry.[42]

Confederate Virginia was a biracial society, a society intertwined with black and white influences. As a minority within a minority, pro-Confederate blacks have received little scholarly research. Numerous Afro-Virginians, free blacks and slaves, were genuine Southern loyalists, not as a consequence of white pressure but due to their own preferences. They are the Civil War's forgotten people, yet their existence was more widespread than American history has recorded. Their bones rest in unhonored glory in Southern soil, shrouded by falsehoods, indifference and historians' censorship.

Notes

1. *The Liberator*, December 30, 1859, "Mock Hanging of John Brown By Negroes," 206; R. L. Patteson to "Dear Uncle" May 14, 1861, Folder "15 May 1861—December 21, 1861," Item 89-89b, Box 4, Patteson Family Papers, Virginia State Library and Archives, Richmond; Dr. Leonard Haynes, Department of English, Southern University, Baton Rouge, Louisiana, as quoted in an United Press International wire story, ca. June 22, 1992, distributed by a computer electronic bulletin board "News of the World."

2. See Charles Harris Wesley, "The Employment Of Negroes As Soldiers In The Confederate Army," *Journal of Negro History* 4 (July 1919): 241, and Wesley's *The Collapse of The Confederacy* (Washington, D. C.: The Associated Publishers, Inc., 1937), 142; Catherine Cooper Hopley, *Life In The South*, vol. 1, 264-265, 318-319; J. K. Obatala, "The Unlikely Story of Blacks Who Were Loyal To Dixie," *Smithsonian* 9 (March 1979): 94-101.

3. As quoted in Michael Kammen, *Mystic Chords of Memory: The Transformation of Tradition In American Culture* (New York: Knopf, 1991), 499.

4. John Hope Franklin, *George Washington Williams: A Biography* (Chicago: The University of Chicago Press, 1985), 235; Joseph T. Wilson, *The Black Phalanx: A History Of The Negro Soldiers of The United States In The War of 1775-1812, 1861-'65* (Hartford, Connecticut: American Publishing Company, 1888), 483, 495, 499; Benjamin Brawley, *A Short History Of The American Negro*, revised edition (New York: The Macmillan Company, 1924), 113; W. E. Burghardt Du Bois, *Black Reconstruction* (New York: Russell & Russell, 1935), 119-120; Wesley, *The Collapse Of The Confederacy*, 42; John Hope Franklin, *From Slavery To Freedom: A History of Negro Americans*, Fifth edition (New York: Alfred A. Knopf, 1980), 221; Johnson Publishing Company, 1988), 464; Benjamin Quarles, *The Negro In The Civil War* (Boston: Little, Brown and Company, 1969), 281; Obatala, "Unlikely Story," 94-101.

5. See Daniel Pipes, *Slave Soldiers and Islam: The Genesis of a Military System* (New Haven: Yale University Press, 1981), 39-45, for a historical overview of slave soldiers.

6. Diary of Nancy Emerson, June 26, 1863, Emerson Family Papers (#9381), Manuscripts Division, Special Collections Department, University of Virginia Library, Charlottesville (hereafter UVA); *Charlottesville Daily Chronicle*, March 30, 1864.

7. *Richmond Daily Dispatch*, May 25, 1863.

8. Felix Gregory De Fontaine, *Marginalia: Gleanings From An Army Note-Book* (Columbia, South Carolina: Steam Power-Press of F.

G. De Fontaine & Co., 1864), 16, 72; Tinsley Lee Spraggins, "Mobilization Of Negro Labor For The Department Of Virginia And North Carolina, 1861-1865," *North Carolina Historical Review* 24 (April 1947):166.9. Francis Springer," Beyond the Call of Duty," *Southern Partisan* (Spring 1985): 26, 28; Thomas P. Nanzig, *3rd Virginia Cavalry* (Lynchburg, Virginia: H. E. Howard, Inc., 1990), 3-4. See also Edward Spencer, "Confederate Negro Enlistments," in *The Annals of The War Written By Leading Participants North and South* (Philadelphia: The Times Publishing Company, 1879), 536-542.

10. "Negro Subordination," *Winchester Republican*, January 3, 1862; Colin Clarke to Maxwell Clarke, August 3, 1863, Maxwell Troax Clarke Papers, Southern Historical Collection, University of North Carolina at Chapel Hill.

11. *Warrenton Flag of '98*, May 21, 1861.

12. *Petersburg Daily Express*, April 23 1861; article on black loyalty in *Lynchburg Tri-Weekly Republican*, April 17, 1861; *Harper's Weekly*, October 5, 1861, 632.

13. "I can't take no such oaf as dat" episode from "T. Rowland Book" (scrapbook 1, p. 21) in the Kate Mason Rowland Collection, Eleanor S. Brockenbrough Library, The Museum of The Confederacy, Richmond, Virginia; John B. Jones, *A Rebel War Clerk's Diary* (New York: A. S. Barnes & Company, Inc., 1961), p. 500 [February 16, 1865 entry]; *Central Presbyterian* (Richmond), October 15, 1862.

14. "George" incident described in Sigismund Stribling Kimball Journal, March 29, 1863 (#2534), WA; *DeBow's Review*, March 1867, 226-227.

15. John Bakeless, *Spies Of The Confederacy* (Philadelphia & New York: J. B. Lippincott Company, 1970), 116, 139, 143, 149-150, 317-318; *The Norfolk Union*, June 8, 1862.

16. *American Missionary*, October 1861, 245; "The Contrabands At Fort Monroe," *Atlantic Monthly* (November 1861): 638.

17. *New York Daily Tribune*, June 27, 1861; Joseph H. Mudd, "The Confederate Negro," *Confederate Veteran* 23 (September 1915): 411; Charles L. Perdue, Thomas E. Barden, and Robert Phillips, *Weevils In The Wheat: Interviews With Virginia Ex-Slaves* (Charlottesville: University Press of Virginia, 1976), 210-211.

18. James Seddon to General Robert E. Lee, September 22, 1864, Jeremy F. Gilmer to Lee, November 19, 1864, Lee to Gilmer, November 21, 1864, "The Negro In The Military Service of the United States 1636-1866" (Washington, D. C.: National Archives Microfilm Publications, 1963), Reel 3, frames 0703-0704, 0712-0717; Robinson, "The Confederate Engineers, " 416.

19. *Daily Richmond Examiner*, January 9, 1862.

20. James H. Brewer, *The Confederate Negro: Virginia's Craftsmen and Military Laborers. 1861-1865* (Durham, North Carolina: Duke University Press, 1969), 7, 19-20, 135, 138.

21. Ervin L. Jordan, Jr., and Herbert A. Thomas, Jr., *19th Virginia Infantry* (Lynchburg, Virginia: H. E. Howard, Inc., 1987), 3; Jack Foster to his master, June 24, 1862, Tompkins Family Papers [MsslT5996d), Virginia Historical Society, Richmond; "A Noble Contribution," *Richmond Sentinel*, July 31, 1863.

22. Wayne P. Austerman, "Virginia's Black Confederates," *Civil War Quarterly* 8 (March 1987): 47; An English Combatant, *Battle-Fields of The South. From Bull Run To Fredericksburqh; With Sketches Of Confederate Commanders, And Gossip Of The Camps* (New York: John Bradburn, 1864), 279.

23. Edmund Drew incident in "Memoirs of Leroy Wesley Cox," #940, Albemarle County Historical Society (stored at UVA as accession number 5049), 10; An English Combatant, *Battle-Fields Of The South*, 284; Benjamin Trask, *16th Virginia Infantry* (Lynchburg, Virginia: H. E. Howard, Inc., 1986), 28.

24. Perdue, Weevils In The Wheat, 137-138; *Winchester Evening Star*, February 26, 1921.

25. *Acts And Joint Resolutions (Amending the Constitution) Of The General Assembly of the State of Virginia, Session Which Commenced at the State Capitol on Wednesday, January 9, 1924* (Richmond: Davis Bottom, Superintendent of Public Printing, 1924), 295-297; *1925 Roster of Confederate Pensioners of Virginia* (Davis Bottom, Superintendent of Public Printing, 1925), 113; *Acts and Joint Resolutions (Amending the Constitution) Of The General Assembly of the State of Virginia, Session Which Commenced at the State Capitol on Wednesday, January 11, 1928* (Richmond: Davis Bottom, Superintendent of Public Printing, 1928), 555-556.

26. Luther Porter Jackson, *Free Negro Labor and Property Holding In Virginia, 1830-1860* (New York: D. Appleton-Century Company, Inc., 1942), 3-33, 247-251.

27. Robert Francis Engs, *Freedom's First Generation* (Philadelphia: University of Pennsylvania Press, 1979), 11-13; "Property Owners, Norfolk County, 1860," *Lower Norfolk County Antiquary* 2 (1899): 1-11; "Property Owners, Norfolk County, 1860," *Lower Norfolk County Antiquary* 3 (1899): 12-18; "Property Owners, Norfolk County, 1860," *Lower Norfolk County Antiquary* 3 (1900): 62-69; Luther P. Jackson, "Manumission In Certain Virginia Cities," *Journal of Negro History* 15 (July 1930): 301-302, 307-308, 309.

28. Marie Tyler-McGraw and Gregg D. Kimball, *In Bondage and Freedom: Antebellum Black Life In Richmond, Virginia* (Richmond, Virginia: Valentine Museum, 1988), 54-58 (Hunt data); Betsey Fuller in the 8th U. S. Census, 1860, Virginia, Princess Anne County, p. 682, in which she described herself as a 40 year old Virginia native. See also "Slave Owners, Princess Anne County, 1840," Lower Norfolk County Virginia *Antiquary* 4 (1903): 174-178, and Luther P. Jackson, "Manumission In Certain Virginia Cities," 296-297, 301-305.

29. U. S. Congress, House of Representatives, Committee on War Claims, *Summary Reports Of The Commissioners of Claims In All Cases Pertaining to Congress As Disallowed Under The Act of March 3, 1871* (Washington: Government Printing Office, 1871-1880), vol. 1, 381, 394, 401, 563, 573, 576; vol. 2, 107, 110, 111, 116, 118, 240, 247, 253; vol. 3, 143-146, 148, 151-152, 157-158, 160, 287, 289-290, 299; vol. 4, 208, 213-215, 224-225, 229-231, 236, 241, 303-304.

30. *DeBow's Review*, May 1853, 443-445; Virginia Writer's Project, *The Negro In Virginia* (New York: Hastings House, 1940), 193; C. Vann Woodward, ed., *Mary Chesnut's Civil War* (New Haven: Yale University Press, 1981), 241; *Message Of The Governor of Virginia . . ., Document 1. Biennial Report Of The Auditor of Public Records, 1860 & 1861* (Richmond: William F. Ritchie, 1861), 633 and 647; Joseph C. G. Kennedy, Superintendent of Census, *Population Of The United States In 1860: Compiled From The Original Returns of The Eighth Census, Under The Direction Of The Secretary Of The Interior* (Washington: Government Printing Office, 1864), 514; James M. Guthrie, *Camp-Fires Of The Afro-American* (Philadelphia: Afro-American Publishing Company, 1899), 605.

31. George Washington Williams, *History Of The Negro Race In America From 1619 To 1880* (New York: G. P. Putnam's Sons, 1882), 278; Edward McPherson, *The Political History Of The United States Of America . . .*, Second edition (Washington, D. C.: Philip & Solomons, 1865), 281-281.

32. James Seddon, November 24, 1863, U. S. War Department. *The War of the Rebellion: A Compilation of The Official Records of The Union and Confederate Armies* (Washington: Government Printing Office, 1880-1901), Series IV, vol. 2, 941 (hereafter cited as *OR*); *The Index: A Weekly Journal of Politics. Literature, And News: Devoted to the Exposition Of The Mutual Interests. Political And Commercial of Great Britain And The Confederate States of America* (London, Great Britain, 1861-1865), "Arming The Negroes," September 10, 1863.

33. *National Anti-Slavery Standard*, June 1, 1861; OR, Series IV, vol. 3, 1059; Benjamin H. Trask, *9th Virginia Infantry* (Lynchburg, Virginia: H. E. Howard, 1984), 76; "A Colored Southern Soldier," Lexington *Gazette and Banner*, May 23, 1866. The Richmond Light Infantry Blues was Company A of the Forty-sixth Virginia Infantry.

34. *0R*, Series I, vol. 2, 185-186, 484; Robert J. Trout, Myerstown, Pennsylvania, January 21, 1990 to Ervin Jordan.

35. William M. Robinson, Jr., "The Confederate Engineers," The Military Engineer 22 (September-October 1930): 412; Robert K. Krick, *The Fredericksburg Artillery* (Lynchburg: H. E. Howard, Inc., 1986), 71, 103; *8th U. S. Census, 1860*, Virginia, Caroline County, p. 723 (George Grimes not listed); *Code of Virginia, 2nd Ed.* (Richmond: Ritchie, Dunnavant & Co., 1860), 510; Wilson, *Black Phalanx*, 123, 179,

180.

36. Wilson, *Black Phalanx*, 498; *National Anti-Slavery Standard*, May 10, 1862; *Alfred Bellard, Gone For A Soldier: The Civil War Memoirs Of Private Alfred Bellard*, ed. David Herbert Donald (Boston: Little, Brown And Company, 1975), 56-57; George Hupman to parents, June 25, 1863, George Hupman Papers, Special Collections and Archives, Rutgers University Libraries, New Brunswick, New Jersey; Harry F. Jackson and Thomas F. O'Donnell, *Back Home In Oneida: Hermon Clarke and His Letters* (Syracuse, New York: Syracuse University Press, 1965), 87. Black "rebel sharpshooters" in South Carolina are mentioned in James Henry Gooding, *On The Altar of Freedom: A Black Soldier's Civil War Letters From the Front*, ed. Virginia Matzke Adams (Amherst: University of Massachusetts, 1991), 54.

37. Lewis H. Steiner, *Report of Lewis H. Steiner. M. D., Inspector of the Sanitary Commission . . . During The Campaign In Maryland, September 1862* (New York: Anson D. F. Randolph, 1862), 20-21; First Lieutenant Lewis Thompson, Camp of the 2nd U. S. Cavalry, Falmouth, Virginia, to First Lieutenant Henry E. Noyes, March 11, 1863, and Noyes to Capt. T. C. Bacon, March 11, 1863, "The Negro In The Military Service Of The United States, 1636-1886," Reel 2, frames 0067-0068 (hereafter Negro Military Service); *Richmond Sentinel,* March 30, 1863.

38. *Daily Lynchburg Republican*, March 29, 1865; *Petersburg Daily Express*, April 1, 1865; "The Company of Negroes," *Richmond Examiner*, March 27, 1865.

39. *Richmond Daily Examiner*, March 29, 1865.

40. R. M. Doswell, "Union Attack On Confederate Negroes," *Confederate Veteran* 23 (September 1915): 404; *The Watchman* (New York), ca. April 1866 (?), Robert K. Krick, chief historian, Fredericksburg and Spotsylvania National Military Park, Virginia, to Ervin Jordan, June 15, 1989.

41. R. A. Brock, ed., "Paroles of The Army of Northern Virginia. . .," *Southern Historical Society Papers* 15 (1915): 45, 63, 487; Royall W. Figg, "*Where Men Only Dare To Go!*" (Richmond: Whittet & Shepperson, 1885), 236.

42. Rev. Edward P. Smith, *Incidents Of The United States Christian Commission* (Philadelphia: J. B. Lippincott & Co., 1871), 367; "A Negro Preaching Secession Doctrine," *The New York Herald*, October 5, 1861; Mary Church Terrell, *A Colored Woman In A White World* (New York: Arno Press 1980; reprint of 1940 edition), 11-12.

Servants and Soldiers: Tennessee's Black Southerners In Gray

Richard Rollins

On a warm spring day in 1921, Charles S. Ivie, a 65-year old white lawyer in the Middle Tennessee town of Shelbyville, was sitting in his office when an unexpected visitor appeared in his doorway. In hobbled an elderly African-American gentleman, cane in hand, gray hair and beard giving him a distinguished visage. Ivie had never seen the man before. He was astonished when the stranger introduced himself as Wiley Sutton Ivie, the servant of Charles' father, Major Thompson Baker Ivie, a Quartermaster in the Army of Tennessee. Charles Ivie had been just eight years old when the war and slavery ended, and had no memory of the man. Wiley Ivie explained that he had come from West Tennessee in search of the major, or his wife or son, Charles' older brother. All three were now dead, and Wiley had come to him in hopes of finding someone who could help him verify his service in the Confederate army.

The two sat down to discuss the matter. Charles asked Wiley to tell him "all you know of my father's service in the army and your association with him there as nearly as you remember it." What followed was an incredible tale of war and family travail, including stories of family, friends, slavery and freedom, and the relationships and experiences of whites and blacks in the war. He spoke of the Major's horse and many other topics, most of which Charles had heard before and some of which he had long forgotten. Wiley went "much into detail" about "many other things of common family knowledge and history which he could not have given had he not been with my father in the war," said the lawyer. In the end, Charles Ivie was convinced that "this old, dear, decrepit and needy negro man is telling the truth . . . but I know of no living witness to the facts he states—all with whom this applicant associated having passed away."[1]

Wiley Ivie was a servant in the armed forces of the Confederate States of America, a group about whom very little has been written. Indeed, black Southerners who served the Confederacy have been out of favor among historians, social scientists and other scholars for 130 years. They have been thrown into the dustbin of history, where they have remained, hidden from our scholarly sight. Yet when the Army of Northern Virginia marched into Pennsylvania in 1863, or the Army of Tennessee retreated to Atlanta in 1864, they were not all-white armies, as we have come to imagine them. Instead, thousands of black Southerners marched with them, as servants, nurses, surgeon's assistants, laborers, drivers, and even a few in combat roles. Most had only first names, or were referred to as "the General's Ned," or "Tom Boykin's Bill." Thousands now lie beneath Southern soil in unmarked graves, with no marker for their final resting sites and no Confederate flags to fly above their headstones on Confederate Memorial Day.[2]

Black Southerners became an important, integral part of Southern armies. One soldier sent his servant home to get supplies and wrote a note to his wife about him. "He is a great darky—worth his weight in gold even in these hard times. . . . He can tell you what things I principally need & more fully than I can write—he knows more about it anyway than I do, knows more about what I have and what I need — he attends to it all."[3]

How many blacks were there in Confederate armies? Unfortunately, it will not be possible to form an accurate answer. An English observer estimated there were 30,000 black servants in the Army of Northern Virginia in 1862.[4] Dr. Lewis Steiner, a member of the U.S. Sanitary Commission who happened to be in Frederick, Maryland, in the days just before Sharpsburg, noted their presence in the Army of Northern Virginia in 1862. The description he recorded in his diary probably could have been written at any time during the war, and it could also have been a description of the western armies. According to Steiner, about 5% of the army he observed was black, but he was probably counting only those who appeared to be in combat roles:

> Wednesday, September 10
> At 4 o'clock this morning the Rebel army began to move from our town, Jackson's force taking the advance. The movement continued until 8 o'clock P.M., occupying 16 hours. The most liberal calculation could not give them more than 64,000 men. Over 3,000 Negroes must be included in the number . . . They had arms, rifles, muskets, sabers, bowie-knives, dirks, etc. They were supplied, in many instances, with knapsacks, haversacks, canteens, etc., and they were manifestly an integral portion of the Southern Confederacy army. They were seen riding on horses and mules, driving wagons, riding on caissons, in ambulances, with the staff of generals and promiscuously mixed up with all the Rebel horde.[5]

One author has estimated that 12% of the Confederates' laboring manpower was black, while the North's was just 10%.[6] Samuel Cooper, Adjutant and Inspector General, issued an 1862 order that "the adjutants of the regiments throughout the Army will inquire into and report all cases of slaves serving with their respective regiments without written authority from their masters."[7] In other words, the Confederate government recognized that black Southerners had gone off to join the army: the *Southern* army.

Since the 1950s our understanding of the experiences of African-Americans in the Civil War has been expanded greatly with works like Ira Berlin's *Freedom: A Documentary History of Emancipation*,[8] C. Peter Riley's study of blacks in Civil War Louisiana,[9] Dudley Cornish's *The Sable Arm: Negro Troops in the Union Army, 1861-1865*,[10] Joseph Glathaar work on black soldiers and white officers,[11] and of course, the recent hit movie *Glory*. and Ken Burns' *Civil War* series, telecast on PBS in September, 1990.

Notice, however, that all of the above works concentrate on African-Americans—Southern and Northern—who fought for the North. Black Southerners who sided with the Confederacy have been essentially overlooked. The most substantial works are Bell Wiley's short chapter in his 1938 work on Southern Negroes, and a few entries in Robert Greene's survey of *Black Defenders of America*.[12].

This scholarly blindness is easily understood. The number of armed black Confederates was always small, and they had little if any direct impact on the war in combat situations. Body servants were not regularly enlisted, but taken to war or hired by, supervised by, and wholly accountable to individuals or small groups of whites. Thus they rarely appeared on muster-rolls and other official government documents. Most could not write, so only a precious few letters home to family and sweethearts or other accounts of the war by black Southerners exist. As a result, their voices have rarely been heard. The primary written legacy of these men consists of anecdotes in letters, diaries, and memoirs, reminiscences and unit histories written by white Confederates. These men served, as they so often lived their lives, with little visibility to historians. White Southerners assumed black inferiority, and also black support, and saw few reasons to write down their activities, thoughts, and experiences. Speaking of this lack of written records, historian James Brewer, in his study of black Southern laborers during the war has remarked that "the omission of the Confederate Negro from the pages of history seems like a striking instance of the death of the unfit in the struggle for historical survival."[13]

Yet the events of the postwar period shaped the historical consciousness of historians, producing an almost total lack of concern for the servants. Those who did remember them wrote in terms that furthered their own causes, rather than an understanding of the lives of the servants. Southerners who chose to carry on the war or to defend the Old South through propaganda and racial politics extended part of the antebellum pro-slavery argument into their present by continuing the "myth of the happy slave." Whereas they had argued before the war that slavery was a positive good and that most slaves had actually been satisfied in bondage, they now used black participation in Confederate forces as further evidence of the value and rightness of slavery and often described those living ex-slaves as "white man's Negroes" or in other pejorative terms.[14] In the North, historians built upon the abolitionist's description of slavery as an immoral institution and, like white Northern troops during the war, assumed that no black Southerner could have supported the Confederacy without coercion.[15] White Northerners, both during the war and after, perceived themselves as the embodiment of morality and the liberators of black Southerners and thus found it virtually impossible to imagine them doing anything to support the Confederacy, and did not recognize it when it happened.

In our own era of Civil Rights, the emphasis naturally has been on the contributions of African-Americans to the Union armies of liberation. In the wave of books on abolitionism, emancipation, blacks in the military and even on slavery, those who worked for the Confederacy have been largely ignored.[16] John Boles, in his otherwise comprehensive synthesis, *Black Southerners*, says virtually nothing about the Confederates servants.[17]

This lack of interest in black Confederates has begun to change. Two scholarly articles have appeared, the best of which, Arthur W. Bergeron's "Free Men of Color in Gray" graced the pages of *Civil War History*,[18] and is included here. A few articles have also shown up in magazines aimed at the general reading public.[19] They are often written with an air of amazement at the fact that a black Southerner did what he did, and a statement of his supposed uniqueness. One book has already appeared and at least two others are in the works.[20]

None of these works have examined the pension applications filled out by Wiley Sutton Ivie and others, now housed in the Tennessee State Archives in Nashville. In the spring of 1921 the Tennessee legislature passed an act providing pensions for African-Americans who had worked as servants to white officers and men in Confederate armed forces. Like white pensioners, they had to prove that they were indigent or disabled, and that they had been in the service at the close of the war. In addition, a recipient had to have lived in Tennessee during the war or, if they moved to the state after the war, have lived there for at least 10 years. Between May, 1921, and September, 1936, applications were filed by 285 individuals. Of those, 16 are now missing, and 21 more have information insufficient to verify actual service. Thus the files contain 249 useful sets of information. While a few similar pension applications exist in the archives of other Southern states, this probably constitutes the largest cache of evidence about the service of black Confederates, their lives and experiences, and the relationships between servants and masters.

Who were the men who applied for a Confederate pension, between 56 and 71 years after the end of the war? All but two of those who described their antebellum life indicated that they were not field hands, engaged in picking cotton, farming and other hard-labor chores. They were house servants—cooks, drivers, skilled craftsmen and workers and body servants. Often they grew up in the masters' house and developed close relationships. Typically, Sam Collier explained that he and his master, Col. William Edwards, "both grew up together" in the house of William R. Collier, "and for this reason I was the house boy and body servant" of the Colonel and nursed him after he was wounded until he died.[21] Alex Porter, who was hired out to Capt. Killis Clark in Nathan Bedford Forrest's command, "stuck to Capt. Clark like a brother" and was held "in the highest esteem because of his faithfulness and devotion to the camp."[22] Free born James Reeves explained that "I went off with John Reeves, Tom New and John New—I had lived with them all my life and went off with them."[23] Lee Webber grew up with Thomas B. and William R. Webber and served them from June 1862 until June 1865. They were part of Jefferson Davis' escort to Georgia in 1865. When the President was captured, the three Webbers and 75 other "Confederate soldiers" headed for Texas to join Gen. Edmund Kirby Smith, only to receive the news that the final surrender had occurred. They simply went home and never bothered to surrender themselves.[24]

Perhaps the story of Sam Newsom provides insight into these relationships. He was a skilled slave, a blacksmith who was hired out and had saved $3,500 of his own money by the time the war ended. As historian James Brewer has pointed out, this was not an uncommon situation, especially in cities, and these slaves often lived an autonomous life, owning their own homes quite apart from those who owned them.[25] He went off to war with the man who nominally owned him, Lieutenant William Newsom of the 4th Tennessee Cavalry. He recalled that

> we was brought up together, Master Will and I was, and maybe that's why everybody seemed to sort of trust him to me. I use to rock him to sleep. He got to be a fine an reckless sort of gentleman. Then the war came. I went with Master Will. Nothing could stop him an I knew he would need me. He got to be a First Lieutenant in the Cavalry. I slept in the same tent. When he was fighting I stayed with the ambulance. . . I got wounded once at the Battle of Sullivan's Creek. Master Will was killed at Chickamauga. I brought his body home. I smuggled him by the pickets, hired a wagon and got him to Chattanooga. From there I brought him on home.[26]

As Bell Wiley has pointed out in the most scholarly essay on Confederate servants, they performed nearly every job imaginable in the army, from barbering to caring for horses, cooking, polishing brass and foraging.[27] Tennessee's pension was specifically designed for body servants, and the form was written with the assumption that those who would apply were body servants. Most did not comment on their specific duties, but of those who did, 37 cited cooking as their primary duty. Eleven were described as servants or body servants; one was a "hostler and general utility man," and five as a waiter or camp servant. Eleven were described as drivers or wagoners, two as hospital workers, five as surgeon's assistants, three as foragers, one as a shoemaker, one as a fifer, one as a blacksmith and two as an orderly or horseman.

As one would expect of men applying for pensions so long after the war, they were mostly young men when they entered the army. Of the 221 whose age can be reasonably ascertained, all were born between 1823 and 1853; therefore, they ranged between approximately eight and thirty-eight when the war began. A majority, 161, or 73%, were born from 1840 to and including 1850, making them between eleven and twenty-one when the war broke out.

No estimate of the life expectancy of a male slave born in the 1840s or 1850s is available. The closest figure is for a white male born in Massachusetts in 1850. He had a life expectancy of 38 years.[28] Logic would seem to dictate that a person born a slave, whose life would consist of a poor diet, hard labor, and no education, not to mention the more horrible aspects of slavery and army experience as well, would have a much shorter life expectancy. Our applicants range from their late seventies to over 100 in age, so they undoubtably far outlived whatever age they might have reasonably expected to attain.

All applicants had to testify they were either indigent or disabled, so it is not surprising that their files are replete with descriptions of physical problems. A physician's description of Charles Murray, who was 18 in 1861 and 84 when he applied, is typical of the files. The doctor noted "marked evidence of old age." Although he seemed to be fairly well nourished, his speech was slow and he walked with a "slow dragging gait." He had had a stroke in 1905 and had only partially recovered. He had little control over his bodily functions and had impaired vision, headaches, shortened breath and general weakness. Among other things, the doctor noted that Murray had an enlarged heart, general arteriosclerosis and an enlarged prostate gland.[29]

Black Southerners served in all branches of Confederate armies, but none of the Tennessee pensioners reported naval or marine service. One was President Jefferson Davis's body servant, while others reportedly belonged to two other headquarters' outfits and another group worked for quartermasters. They cited service in 40 different Tennessee infantry units; 15 Tennessee cavalry units; 15 non-Tennessee infantry units; five non-Tennessee cavalry units and three artillery units. Of these, only nine reported serving in the Virginia theater, the remainder serving in the western or trans-Mississippi areas. They reported taking part in 35 separate engagements or campaigns, almost entirely in the western theater.

The line between servant and soldier was a fine one, and occasionally crossed in critical situations. While the precise number of Tennessee applicants who actually saw combat in Confederate service is difficult to pin down, at least 13 reported actual battle experience in the applications. Two of those were wounded and an additional 14 claimed wounds as a result of hostile fire. Another 17 were captured and of these six escaped back to Southern forces.

Some reported their own experiences in battle situations and some of their white witnesses recalled seeing them in action. It should be noted that this was not required for a pension. In fact it was not expected by those who made up the application form, since they did not specifically ask for this information. Instead, these comments came out in conversations with the Board or in letters. Henry Neal recalled that "both of my young masters were killed in the Battle of Shiloh and I was shot in my left leg."[30] Also at Shiloh, William Easley was wounded,[31] and Taylor Kinnard's two masters were killed and he was shot in the arm.[32] A white man wrote of Henry Gore "I knew him before the war and have known him since the war. I know that he was with Col. Gore during the war. He was the servant of Col. Gore but when in battle, the applicant would engage in the battle."[33] Bob McClarson "was always found ready to do his duty in camps, on the march or along the firing line. . ."[34] Alexander Ransom "was there, often times in the thick of the fray."[35] When Wade Watkins' master, a surgeon, was killed, Watkins "was shot at the same time in the right leg."[36] Ned McCullough "was wounded in the Battle of Murfreesboro and at Chattanooga, and have holes in my body now."[37] Monroe Jones had both legs shot off at the knees at Snyder's Bluff in the Vicksburg campaign.[38] Lee Fuller's master was killed in 1862 and he was wounded when he was barely 15 years old.[39] Ike Anderson was "captured by the Federals soon after the battle of Ft. Donelson in 1862 and was shot in the leg and badly wounded by them." He said "I was carried to Nashville Tennessee by them where I was kept till close of the war and then released."[40] Alfred Brown was wounded twice at Chickamauga when a shell passed through his leg.[41]

In addition, certain terms were used to describe the experiences of several of the applicants, by themselves and by their witnesses, that could indicate a perceived experience beyond mere servitude. For example, "this old negro" Jacob Coleman was described as having "made a good soldier."[42] The term "soldier" may have had any number of definitions, and surely meant different things to different people. As Arthur Bergeron has shown in an essay published in *Civil War History* and included in this anthology, a few black Southerners did indeed enroll as privates in Confederate units.[43] It may also have meant that he had picked up a gun in the midst of battle, as others had done.[44] One can think of numerous other possibilities, including that it may have been an act of recognition of a long and close relationship between master and servant in a stressful period of their lives; and that it may have meant nothing at all. Henry Yourie was said to be "a true and loyal Confederate — stayed all the time — was always interested in the movements of our army and enjoyed victories as much as the soldiers themselves."[45] David Jarnigan was described by his ex-master as a "guard" who "was of as much benefit to the cause as if he had been a regular soldier,"[46] while George Matthewson was also described as "a soldier in the Confederate army."[47] The latter's witness went on to mention that Matthewson was a member in good standing in the United Confederate Veterans, recognized by "the camp and by all Confederate soldiers, as being one of their number," as well as listed in a local history book as having fought for the South. R. H. Bradley, who was wounded, was described as "a faithful soldier . . . never guilty of unbecoming conduct, in fact his record was excellent."[48] Ben Jones recalled that he "enlisted just after Vicksburg in the 3rd Tennessee regiment" and told the Board that "I am a veteran of the Civil War and a Confederate soldier."[49] Combat was not their only remarkable experience. Sam Kirk, a hospital worker in the Army of Tennessee, traveled a great deal more than a slave might expect, all in the the service of his country:

> Before the surrender, a few days after Christmas, 1865 [sic], Dr. Lagree and his hospital forces were ordered back to Richmond, and we were going from Corinth, Miss., to Richmond, and we got as far as West Point, Ala., the yankees run in on us, captured our supplies and burned up a part of our hospital appliances, and we went to Atlanta aiming for Richmond, reached Stone Mountain where we were ordered to put off of the train and get out of the way, and at Stone Mountain Mr. Dow Mercer got me, and took train to Atlanta, and I walked to Dalton, and I was placed in prison at Chattanooga, two days, and the yankees put me on a train, with a lot of soldiers, like they would a lot of stock, and I came to Murfreesboro.[50]

James Maney, 20 years old in 1863, told a similar story:

> I, James Maney, colored, was a slave of Dr. James Maney, the grandfather of Lieut. James Keeble, who was an aid on the staff of Gen'l George Maney. Dr. James Maney, at the breaking out of the war was the owner of a large plantation 2400 acres in Mississippi, and I was on that plantation at the time. When the Federals took possession of that part of the state in 1863, I, with other slaves, was carried to Georgia, and was put at work in the "Dixie Works" at Macon, Ga, from which place, in the latter part of 1863, I was sent to Dalton, as a body servant for my young master, James Keeble, who as stated was on the staff of Gen'l Maney. I went with him through all the Dalton campaign, up to the time Hood came into Tennessee. When

> Hood left for Tennessee, I was put in charge of a horse belonging to Col. Richard Keeble, at Aberdeen, Miss. When Hood returned from Tennessee, I rejoined my master, went with him through Alabama, Georgia, South Carolina, and up into North Carolina, and was with him when the army surrendered, at Greensboro, and then came home with him. We came by way of Chattanooga, where I was put in a "bull pen," and the next day was on the train for Murfreesboro, with my master, and reached home at 4 o'clock in the morning.[51]

George Washington Yancey was captured with the Georgia militia, escaped, went to Chickamauga and "got with the Southern troops again, but was captured again at Missionary Ridge." He escaped a second time and joined the Confederates at Atlanta. He was captured again at Macon and imprisoned. "I was loyal to the Confederate states," he asserted, and escaped again, spending the rest of the war foraging for the Confederate troops.[52] Dawson Pugh was captured by the Yankees in March, 1863, escaped, and returned to his owner and master, Lt. Frank Pugh.[53] Clay Hickerson was captured and when the Yankees tried to take him North with them he refused to go and returned to his owner, who told him he was free anyway.[54] In the spring of 1865, Dave Burns was captured along with "most of my company." He escaped and returned to his "old master."[55] A witness for Henry Church remembered that he had been at Ft. Donelson in early 1862:

> At the surrender he escaped with Burr Church and went with Capt. Perkins' Co. till Capt. Church was exchanged when he went to the [48th Tennessee Infantry] again at Vicksburg and stayed with Capt. Church till after the battle of Nashville where Capt. Church lost his leg.... Henry brought him back home and then went on South with floo[?] and was with the Regiment at the surrender.[56]

As for Henry Church, who returned to the army by himself after leaving his master at home, military service was a strong attraction for some black Southerners. Thus James Reeves, a free Negro, went off to war as a hired servant with John Reeves, Tom and John New. When John Reeves was killed, he remained in the army with the New brothers, but when John was killed he was called home. He was let out of his agreement but only with the proviso that he would not return to the army.[57] Harrison Mayes was a slave but "volunteered to serve" with another man. When that person was killed, he returned to his owner.[58] Rush McNeely recalled that he went to war with a young master who died of disease, whereupon he returned to his master's brother, who in turn prevented him from returning to the army, despite his plea to return.[59] Charles Wilkerson "stayed in the army until the last gun was fired."[60] When Charles Cannon's master was killed at Murfreesboro he "went back to the regiment and stayed with Mr. Bill Simmons of the same mess in co. B until the close of the war."[61]

Black Southerners used their skills in support of the Confederacy in ways other than labor. Historians of slavery in recent years have discussed the ways in which some slaves managed to gain some control over their own lives by deceiving their masters. They utilized and even fostered the stereotypes some whites had of them — shiftless, lazy, etc.— as a means of working less. "The only weapon of self defense I could use successfully, was that of deception," recalled one slave.[62] They often hid their intelligence and skills behind the facade of these stereotypes and used cunning to manipulate their world to their advantage. Thus a driver with the responsibility of getting work done and pleasing a master might learn to make a whip crack just off the skin of his charges. Songs sung in the fields might have double meaning, one on the surface for the whites to hear and a deeper sense that communicated something rather different to its black hearer.[63]

Many Northern whites not only shared these images but also had their own special stereotyped conception of what Southern blacks thought and felt about the war and about them. They believed all black Southerners were glad to see them, that they automatically sided with the North, perceived Union troops as liberators and would help them fight white Southerners. They could not believe that black Southerners would help the Confederacy, so Northerners assumed that any information given them was accurate. Like all stereotypes, this one had a nugget of truth to it, but was not completely true.

Thus black Southerners could, and did, use this false impression in the minds of Union troops to their advantage. Henry Nelson, just 15 when he rode off to war with Russell's Cavalry, hid his master from Federal troops. When they were at home on leave,

> the yankees came while he was at home, and ask me was it any soldiers anywhere a round there. I told them a lie. I told them that it wasn't any soldiers a round there. At the same time my mastery[sic] was there walking around with the yankees. I hid my mastery[sic]. I could have turn him up if I had been mean enough to turn him up. I was not a enemy of my mistress and mastery. I hid my mastery[sic] horses in the thicket to keep the yankies[sic] from getting them. That shows you I was a friend to the southern army. I hid the meat from the yankies to keep them from taking everything we had... I thought I would let you know part not telling you near all to let you know that I was in the army with

my mastery[sic].[64]

In the same vein, William Bibb "screened his master from being captured" by leading the Yankees in the wrong direction, away from where his master was hiding.[65] When Northern troops came to the house where Col. William Edwards was visiting during the war, his servant Sam Collier grabbed his Confederate uniform and took it outside and burned it to prevent him from being found out and taken prisoner, then kept his secret while Northern troops were present.[66] George Sewell was captured at Ft. Donelson and sent to Camp Chase in Columbus, Ohio as a prisoner. He went to work for a surgeon in an Ohio regiment, and when they got to Chattanooga "having accomplished the purpose for which I hired myself to him, namely, to get back south, I quit him."[67]

The range of the level of rank of their masters is surprising. Bell Wiley's assertion that few servants were left in the army after 1862 except those of higher officers seems reasonable, given the South's reputation for starving and inadequately clothing the fighting men. Indeed, when servants are mentioned in other works, that seems to be the accepted generalization.[68]

This would lead to the prediction that the vast majority served with colonels or generals. That is not the case. Of the 185 Tennessee applicants whose master's rank can be determined, the largest group, 65 in number (35%), served privates. They had to be in the army at the end to qualify, so most served two years or longer, with enlisted men. Twenty-four served lieutenants, 45 worked for captains; 13 for majors; 15 for colonels, just seven for generals. Thus 134 out of 185, or 72%, served at the level of captain or lower. In addition, 15 served with Surgeons and one served as the body servant of the President.[69]

The relative youth of the servants and their masters during the war may be a function of the date at which the pension applications were made. Nearly six decades had passed since the end of the war. It may well be that the older servants had already passed away, and that the higher ranking men had servants who were also older.

One might readily assume that all the Tennessee servants were owned by the men they served, but this too was not always the case. One line in the application form asked them to identify their owner, another to identify the person they served in the army. Five individuals indicated that they had been free-born men who were hired to go to war. One-hundred fifty-one (61%) indicated they were the slaves of their master (or their masters' father), while 54 (36%) indicated they had been given or hired out to individuals who were not their owners or their owners' family members.

A small amount of information about the masters is available. Between 1914 and 1922, the Tennessee State Archives and the Tennessee Historical Commission sent questionnaires to all known Tennessee

Civil War veterans. They returned 1,650. These questionnaires asked the veteran to give in-depth information about their life before and during the Civil War.[70] The forms were filled out by all classes, from very poor to wealthy, and vary in information from full to sparse. The questions range from date and place of birth to enlistment data and company rosters, war service and prison and hospital life. The compilers had originally conceived of them as a source of information for a study of the Old South, so they contain measures of social status, ownership of slaves, genealogical data, educational and religious data and much more. The objective of the questionnaire's authors was to show that the social relations before the war had been egalitarian in nature, so most questions were framed with that in mind. The compilers were not interested in black Southerners at all, and asked no questions about them or their lives.

Unfortunately, a search of the questionnaires revealed that only three of the owners or masters of the servants who filed pension applications had themselves filled out questionnaires. One even mentioned the name of the slave. Dick Tuggle had gone off to war as a servant with Capt. Needham F. Harrison of the 13th Tennessee in 1863, and stayed with him until the end of the war. Tuggle's application, filed in 1923, is thin, with no age given for him and little information. The only remarkable entry is a letter from a white veteran who said that whenever he went into battle, "I always give him my small things to carry home if I should get hurt as he was our cook & laundry man."[71] The 13th fought at Belmont, Shiloh, Richmond and Perryville early in the war, then with the Army of Tennessee from Chickamauga to Atlanta. They took part in Hood's Tennessee campaign and the few who remained in 1865, including Harrison and Tuggle, ended up with Joe Johnston in North Carolina. In 1863 Harrison was a 28-year old farmer who owned 11 slaves (Tuggle was not one of them) on a 320-acre farm in Shelby County. He was wounded at Chickamauga. After the surrender he returned to his farm to find his wife had passed away. He remarried and later became a prosperous planter and held minor public offices. Of the original 85 in his company only four were living in 1923 and "so far as I know only one of the faithful colored servants, Dick Tuggle of Germantown, Tenn."[72] Harrison described the prewar social relations in his area as egalitarian, with no distinctions between slaveowner and non-slaveowner.

Sam Cullom's application is also thin. He was born in 1841 and went off to war at age 20 with Private, later Captain, Calvin E. Myers of the 4th and 8th Tennessee.[73] Myers did not own Cullom, but did own 20 slaves. He was born in 1830 and his parents owned 300 acres of prime bottom land on the Cumberland River, worth in all about $10,000 in 1861. Like Harrison, Myers believed that his corner of the Old South had been marked by friendly relations between white and black, slaveowner and non-slaveowner.[74] The latter two categories mingled freely and "all were on an equal [basis]." Myers wrote a letter in support of Cullom's pension application. The 8th Tennessee fought at Corinth, where Myers was shot in the leg, and with the Army of Tennessee from Murfreesboro to Atlanta, with Hood in Tennessee, and ended up in North Carolina.

George Washington Yancey, whose story of being captured three times was told above, went to war with Private Joe Nailling, also of the 4th Tennessee. Nailling's grandparents owned about 100 slaves and his parents owned 20. He ran away from home to join the army in early 1863.

This comparison of white and black questionnaires, brief and limited though it is, points out the diversity of the experiences of Tennessee's servants. All three masters came from slaveowning families, even though they may not have been slaveowners themselves. When compared to Fred Bailey's in-depth study of the whites' questionnaires, they were not poor, but not rich either.[75] The masters went off to war as two privates and one captain, the servants as one free-born, one hired-out, and one owned.

Perhaps the story of Coleman Davis Smith will serve as a means bringing this essay to an end, for his tale is both representative of the group but also unique in its particulars. He filled out one of the questionnaires, but did not apply for a pension from Tennessee as a servant.[76] Born in Virginia in 1844, he had been purchased, along with his mother and father, by Lewis Davis and taken to Tennessee as a child. He had grown up with, and been a playmate of, the Davis children, including Sam Davis. As they grew into manhood, Sam and Coleman continued their close friendship, the latter recalling that "Sam Davis and I worked together plowing and hoeing, doing such work as comes up on a farm, until the war." When Sam joined the army and became a soldier, Coleman went with him. And when Sam Davis became a spy, Coleman remembered that he and Sam "scouted mostly. I remember we burned a wagon train of ammunition for the Yankees and __ more guns. We slept anywhere and ate anywhere."[77] The two stuck together; they were master and servant, but clearly also friends. "When he ate, I ate," recalled Coleman, "when he slept, I slept."

When Sam Davis was captured near Pulaski, Tennessee, in 1863, so was Coleman. When Sam was charged as a spy, Coleman was not held, and it is fair to assume that Northerners couldn't imagine or understand the relationship between them, nor the role Coleman played in the army or in Sam Davis' life. Though jailed with Sam at first, Coleman was not charged. When they were in jail together, Coleman put some "important papers" that Sam had secreted away into a slit in the sole of his shoe. Coleman also begged Sam to tell what the Yankees wanted to know, but Sam refused. Coleman pleaded with Sam to let him tell the secrets, but Sam again refused.

After the execution of Sam Davis as a spy, Coleman Davis

made his way back to the Davis farm near Smyrna, where he was warmly greeted by the rest of the family. He stayed there until long after the war ended.

Appendix A
Year of Birth of Tennessee's Black Confederates

1853: 1
1852: 2
1851: 2
1850: 9
1849: 10
1848: 18
1847: 22
1846: 21
1845: 24
1844: 19
1843: 15
1842: 11
1841: 10

1840: 12
1839: 7
1838: 5
1837: 6
1836: 6
1835: 6
1834: 2
1833: 4
1832: 1
1831: 0
1830: 1
1829: 1
1828: 0
1827: 1
1826: 1
1825: 0
1824: 2
1823: 2

Appendix B
Units In Which Black Confederates Served

Tenn. Infantry	Tenn. Cavalry	
1st.......7	1st....5	1st Confederate Infantry...2
2nd......1	2nd...3	12th Kentucky Infantry....1
3rd......5	3rd....1	6th Kentucky Infantry......1
6th......2	4th...3	2nd Kentucky Cavalry.....4
7th......2	6th...1	
8th......4	7th...10	5th Alabama Infantry...1
9th... ..2	8th...1	12th Alabama Infantry...1
12th....4	9th Battn...1	31st Alabama Infantry...1
13th ...2	11th...2	11th Alabama Cavalry...1
14th....5	14th...1	
15th....3	21st...1	10th Georgia Infantry...1
16th....4	48th...1	46th Georgia Infantry...1
17th....4		Forrest's HQ..................8
18th....2		Gen. Hoke's HQ.............1
19th....1		6th Mississippi Inf........1
20th....5		9th.Mississippi Inf........1
23th...2		14th Mississippi Inf......2
24th..11		15th Mississippi Inf......1
27th...1		29th Mississippi Inf......1
28th...1		3rd Mississippi Cav......1
30th...2		1st Miss. Light Arty......1
31st...3		
42nd...1		5th No. Carolina Cav. 1
43rd...1		
45th...1		17th Texas Inf. 1
46th...1		
47th...1		White's Battery 1
48th...2		Manley's Battery 1
50th(Old)...1		
51st...1		
54th...2		

Notes

1. Pension application of Wiley Sutton Ivie, Confederate Servants Pension Applications, Tennessee State Library Archives, Nashville. Hereafter individuals will be noted with just the person's name and a number indicating their place in order. Wiley's is #51.

2. For an exception, see the gravesite of a member of the 1st Virginia Cavalry described in Carl Cahill, "Note on Two Va. Negro Civil War Soldiers: One Union, One Confederate," *Negro History Bulletin*, November, 1965, 39-40.

3. Quoted in Eugene Genovese, *Roll, Jordan, Roll: The World The Slaves Made* (New York: Pantheon Books, 1974), p. 347.

4. [An English Observer], *Battlefields of the South* (New York: John Bradburn, 1865), Vol. I., p. 58.

5. Quoted in Isaac W. Heysinger, *Antietam and the Maryland and Virginia Campaigns of 1862* (New York: Neale Publishing Company, 1912), 122-123.

6. Jay S. Hoar, "Black Glory: Our Afro-American Civil War Old Soldiery," *Gettysburg Magazine* January, 1990, 125.

7. United States War Department, *The War of the Rebellion: A Compilation of the Official Records of the Union and Confederate Armies.* 70 Volumes in 128 parts. (Washington, D.C.: Government Printing Office, 1880-1901), Series IV, Volume 2, page 86.

8. (New York: Cambridge University Press, 1982).

9. C. Peter Riley, *Slaves and Freedmen in Civil War Louisiana* (Baton Rouge: Louisiana State University Press, 1976).

10 . (New York: W.W. Norton, 1966). See also Lenwood G. Davis and George Hill, *Blacks in American Armed Forces, 1776-1983* (Westport, Conn.: Greenwood Press, 1985) and Jay David, *The Black Soldier: From The American Revolution to Vietnam* (New York: William Morrow, 1971).

11. Joseph Glathaar, *Forged in Battle: The Civil War Alliance of Black Soldiers and White Officers* (New York: The Free Press, 1990).

12. Bell I. Wiley, *Southern Negroes, 1861-1865* (Baton Rouge: Louisiana State University Press, 1938) and Robert Ewell Greene, Ed., *Black Defenders of America, 1775-1973* (Chicago: Johnson Publishing Co., 1974).

13. James Brewer, *The Confederate Negro: Virginia's Craftsmen and Military Laborers, 1861-1865* (Durham, N.C.: Duke University Press, 1969.

14. Leon F. Litwack, *Been In The Storm So Long: The Aftermath of Slavery* 2nd Edition (Glenview, Ill.: Scott, Forsman and Company, 1979). See also Randall C. Jimerson, *The Private Civil War: Popular Thought During The Sectional Conflict* (Baton Rouge: Louisiana State

University Press, 1988), and *The Confederate Veteran*, passim.

15. Reid Mitchell, *Civil War Soldiers: Their Expectations and Experiences* (New York: Simon and Schuster, 1988)

16. J.G. Randall and David Donald, *The Civil War And Reconstruction* (Lexington, Mass.: D.C. Heath, 1969) and James M. McPherson, *Ordeal By Fire: The Civil War and Reconstruction* (New York: Alfred Knopf, 1982).

17. John Boles, *Black Southerners, 1619-1869* (Lexington: The University Press of Kentucky, 1983).

18. Arthur W. Bergeron, Jr., "Free Men of Color in Gray," *Civil War History* XXXII(1986), 247-255. See also Mary F. Berry, "Negro Troops in Blue and Gray: The Louisiana Native Guards, 1861-1863," *Louisiana History* 8(1967), 165-190. Most of the latter is devoted to the Native Guards who were Union troops, not the Confederates. See also Alexia J. Helsley, "Black Confederates," *South Carolina Historical Magazine* 74(July, 1973),184-187.

19. J.K. Obatala, "The Unlikely Story of Blacks Who Were Loyal To Dixie," *Smithsonian* 9(1979), 94-101;Wayne R. Austerman, "Virginia's Black Confederates," *Civil War Quarterly* VIII(1987), 46-54; Greg Tyler, "Rebel Drummer Henry Brown, *Civil War Times Illustrated* February, 1989, 22-23;Scott E. Sallee, "Black Soldier of the Confederacy," *Blue and Gray* 1990, 24-25; Greg Tyler, "Article Brings Notice To A Unique Rebel, *Civil War Times Illustrated* May/June 1990, 57, 69; Edward C. Smith, "Calico, Black and Gray: Women and Blacks in the Confederacy," *Civil War* XXIII(1990), 10-16; and Jeff Carroll, "Dignity, Courage and Fidelity," *Confederate Veteran* November/December 1990, 26-27; Richard Rollins, "Black Confederates at Gettysburg," *Gettysburg*, VI(January, 1991).

20. H. C. Blackerby, *Blacks in Blue and Gray: Afro-American Service in the Civil War* (Tuscaloosa, Ala.: Portals Press, 1973); Ervin Jordan, Jr., is working on black Confederates in Virginia and Charles K. Barrow, of Atlanta, is researching a wider topic.

21. Sam Collier #257.

22. Alex Porter #38.

23. James Reeves #33.

24. Lee Webber #84.

25. Brewer, *Confederate Negro.* For more examples, see James E. Newton and Ronald L. Lewis, *The Other Slaves: Mechanics, Artisans and Craftsmen* (Boston: G.K. Hall and Co., 1978).

26. Sam Newsom #271.

27. Bell Wiley, *Southern Negroes*, p. 22.

28. *Satistical Abstract of the United States, 1991: The National Data Book* 111th Edition (Washington, D.C.: Department of Commerce, Bureau of The Census, 1991).

29. Charles Murray #224.

30. Henry Neal #130.

31. William Easley #10.

32. Taylor Kinnard #227.
33. Henry Gore #132.
34. Bob McClarson #180.
35. Alexander Ransom #201.
36. Wade Watkins #270.
37. Ned McCullough #137.
38. Monroe Jones #41.
39. Lee Fuller #85.
40. Ike Anderson #95.
41. Alfred Brown #233.
42. Jacob Coleman #2.
43. See the essay by Bergeron cited above.
44 . See for example the story of two servants who picked up muskets and fought in Capt. Thomas Nelson, *The Confederate Scout* (Washington, D.C.: The Neale Publishing Company, 1957), p. 122.
45. Henry Yourie #12.
46. David Jarnigan #31.
47. George Matthewson #37.
48. R.H. Bradley #104.
49. Ben Jones #106.
50. Sam Kirk #125
51. James Maney #164.
52. George Washington Yancey #206.
53. Dawson Pugh #192.
54. Clay Hickerson #79.
55. Dave Burns #123.
56. Henry Church #19.
57. James Reeves #33.
58. Harrison Mayes #43.
59. Rush McNeely #172.
60. Charles Wilkerson #58.
61. Charles Cannon #217.
62. Quoted in Gilbert Osofsky, *"Puttin' On Ol' Massa:" The Slave Narratives of Henry Bibb, William Wells Brown, and Solomon Northrup* (New York: Harper & Row, 1969), p.9.
63. Ibid, 26-27.
64. Henry Nelson #23.
65. William Bibb #136.
66. Sam Collier #357.
67. George Sewell #129.
68. Wiley, *Southern Negroes*, p. 134.
69. Two variables occurred in calculating these numbers. Forty served more than one master, and we counted only the first . In the cases of promotion, the master's original rank was counted.
70. Gustavus W. Dyer and John Trotwood Moore, Compilers, *The Tennessee Civil War Veterans Questionnaires* Five Volumes (Easley, S.C.: Southern Historical Press, 1985).

71. Richard Tuggle #176

72. *Questionaires*, Vol. 3, p. 1032-3.

73. Sam Cullom #57.

74. *Questionnaires*, Vol. 4, 1619-21. Myers' file is somewhat confusing. He was a veteran of the Mexican War and answered the questions with information about his service in that conflict.

75. Fred Bailey, *Class and Tennessee's Confederate Generation* (Chapel Hill: The University of North Carolina Press, 1987)

76. *Questionnaires*, Volume 5, pp. 1973-1975. He did, however, apply for a pension from Mississippi.

77. The burning wagon trains may be a reference to the burning of the Federal supplies at Holly Springs in 1863, in which Davis participated.

J.B. White and John Terrill, 6th Tennessee Cavalry

"Better Confederates Did Not Live:" Black Southerners in Nathan Bedford Forrest's Commands

Thomas Y. Cartwright

In late August 1868, General Nathan Bedford Forrest gave an interview to a reporter. Forrest said of the black men who served with him:

. . . these boys stayed with me . . . and *better Confederates did not live.*[1]

Black Confederate Nim Wilkes once said:

I was in every battle General Forrest fought after leaving Columbia ... I was mustered out at Gainesville(Alabama, May 1865).[2]

The story of black Southerners in Confederate armies is essentially an untold story just starting to come to the attention of historians and the general public. Why have their experiences been forgotten until recently? Perhaps one small reason is that during the post-war era the Federal government refused to furnish grave markers for black Confederates. The Federal government would only furnish grave markers for Union, Confederate, and black Union soldiers.[3] Some individuals might feel these black Confederates were only teamsters, cooks, nurses, and valets; these positions are now considered a part of the modern military forces.

Among the black southerners who served in Confederate armies were many who served in General Nathan Bedford Forrest's commands. Both slaves and Free Men of Color served with Forrest's Escort, his Headquarters and many other units under his command.

General Forrest and his men were products of the world in which they lived. They had many of the the racial attitudes held by the entire society, north and south. The south was a biracial, caste society, yet within that context a full spectrum of interpersonal relationships and racial attitudes existed, from brutally savage to respect, honor, dignity, and even love. General Forrest made his living before the war as a cotton planter, raising livestock, and trading in slaves. Like many other slaveowners, he had a paternalistic attitude toward his slaves, one that was comparatively humane and benevolent.[4] Within the restrictions imposed by the slaveholding society in which he lived, Forrest managed to treat the black Southerners with whom in came in contact as well as he perhaps could do. Judging by the comments and actions of some of the people he owned, and emancipated, he treated them with a level of respect respect and human dignity that went significantly beyond the requirements of his profession. Many of the black Southerners he dealt with, in turn, recognized his friendship and returned it many times over, during and long after the war.

General Forrest (and others like him) broke through the overwhelming pressure of the world, and the conventions of the social relationships of the day, to treat black Southerners in a way that resulted in strong bonds of loyalty and friendship, from both sides, which lasted through the war and the rest of their lives.

Black southerners participated in the Southern war effort all across the South in various ways, and the black Southerners under Forrest were probably representative, though they may well have had better relationships with him than some had with others. They normally served in some type of support role and sometimes saw combat. There were a large number of black Southerners who were allowed to attend United Confederate Veterans meetings during the post-war era. This shows that black Confederates were held in high esteem by Confederate veterans because their application for membership had to be approved by whites.

General Forrest took 45 slaves to war in 1861. He told a Congressional committee after the war:

> I said to 45 colored fellows on my plantation that I was going into the army; and that if they would go with me, if we got whipped they would be free anyhow, and that if we succeeded and slavery was perpetrated, if they would act faithfully with me to the end of the war, I would set them free. Eighteen months before the war closed I was satisfied that we were going to be defeated, and I gave those 45, or 44 of them, their free papers for fear I might be called. [5]

Another source that documents the truth of his statement came from a Confederate soldier named George W. Cable from New Orleans who served for a time as a clerk in Forrest's Headquarters. One of his tasks was to help make out some of these "manumission" papers.[6] It is clear from the end of 1863 to the close of the war these 44 black men served as free men under the flags of the Confederacy.

I used many sources for this essay, one being the Colored Man's Pension Applications in the Tennessee State Archives. The applicants needed two witnesses who would support their claims. In many cases no one remained living to verify these claims; special considerations were sometimes made in these instances. There were 285 black Tennesseans who applied for these pensions. The State of Tennessee honored most of these claims. The Federal government would not acknowledge their service with the Confederacy. All of the applicants were old men when they applied for pensions. These 285 black men can be only a fraction of the black Tennesseans who served the Confederacy. These relationships before, during, and after the war will be examined in detail. The ties between Forrest's troopers and the black men they brought from home will also be examined.

Forrest's relationships with black Southerners are well documented. In 1877 a reporter named Lacadio Hearn had written:

It is said Forrest was kind to his negroes; that he never separated members of a family, and that he always told his slaves to go out in the city and choose their own masters. There is no instance of any slave taking advantage of the permission to run away. Forrest taught them that it was to their own interest not to abuse the privilege... There were some men in town to whom he would never sell a slave because they had the reputation of being cruel masters.[6]

Col. George W. Adair in the post-war era stated:

> Forrest was kind, humane, and extremely considerate of his slaves. He was overwhelmed with applications from a great many of this class, who begged him to purchase them. He seemed to exercise the same influence over these creatures that in a greater [manner?] he exercised over the soldiers who in later years served him as devotedly as if there were a strong personal attachment between them. When a slave was purchased for him his first act was to turn him over to his Negro valet, Jerry, with instructions to wash him thoroughly and put clean clothes on him from head to foot. Forrest applied the rule of cleanliness and neatness to the slave which he practiced for himself... The slaves were thus transformed and proud of belonging to him. He was always very careful when he purchased a married slave to use every effort to secure the husband and wife, as the case might be, and unite them, and in handling children he would not permit the separation of a family. [7]

Another account of Forrest's relationship with his slaves is from a former slave named Mary Herndon. In 1933 she was living in Memphis, Tennessee. Mary was born near the Indian Nation line. At a very early age she was taken from her mother. At the time of this interview Mary was 104 years of age:

> I was born among Indians. My mother lived with them and my grandmother was nearly an Indian. I was

> bought by a white man and carried to Cameron, Missouri, where as a young girl, I became a family nurse and later grew to be a sewing girl for the family.

Her first master acquired some debts which he could not pay. The sheriff of Springfield, Missouri, foreclosed on her first master and took all the slaves to settle the debt:

> Maybe it was a gamblin' debt for all I know, because my first master used to gamble. But Sheriff Metlock had nothing to do with the debt acept to sell all us and I was bought by General Forrest and Mr. Simmons at Springfield, Missouri, and with 100 more, loaded into wagons and taken to St. Louis. We came on a steamboat from St. Louis to Memphis. Forrest had a slave yard enclosed by a high brick wall on Adams St. near Third. There we was kept until late fall, when I was sold to Louis Fortner a rich planter with a big place near where Mason, Tennessee... I say this in respect to General Forrest; he bought and sold slaves but he was kind to them. He treated me mighty well, bought me new clothes, fed all of us far better than we had been fed by old masters. One time after General Forrest sold me to "Massa" Fortner, he came out to see about selling more slaves, saw me and spoke to me. General Forrest was a good man.[8]

FORREST'S HEADQUARTERS

Thornton Forrest

Thornton Forrest filed his pension application on July 5, 1921. He was living in Collierville, Tennessee, Fayette County, at the time he submitted his application. Thornton Forrest was owned by General Nathan Bedford Forrest. Thornton was a member of General Forrest's Headquarters staff, and was a steward.

Thornton left Memphis in 1861 with General Forrest and served until the surrender at Gainesville, Alabama, in May 1865. On the pension application Thornton stated that he "lived in Tennessee all my life except for the two years on General Forrest farm, Hernando, Mississippi, immediately following the war."[9]

This statement seems to be confirmed by a *Memphis Bulletin* article published May 30, 1865:

> General Nathan Bedford Forrest was at Grenada until

> the middle of last week. He acted honestly and fairly in his negotiations with the Federal authorities. He turned over all the property in his position. He remarked that he was now as good a Union man as anybody—that the South was whipped and he was going to support the Federal government as heartily as anyone could. When General Forrest left Grenada for his plantation on the Mississippi River about 20 of his former slaves stayed with him.[10]

Thornton was one of the 20 former slaves that went home with General Forrest. Home was Sunflower Landing in Coahoma County, Mississippi, a plantation of some 3,000 acres.[11] One source states that "the negroes who had gone to Georgia during the war, and others whom he had set free before the war, returned to him and became an integral part of his plantation."[12] Other sources indicate the 20 former slaves were part of the original 45 that left with Forrest in 1861.[13]

Another negro who went home with Forrest was his former valet and body servant, Jerry. In August 1866 Federal cavalry was riding by General Forrest's plantation. As the cavalry filed into the lot on the way up to the house, King Phillip (Forrest's old war horse) charged at the Yankees. When some of the Union cavalry struck at the animal Forrest's war-time body servant, Jerry, whom the other blacks in Forrest's command referred to as the "Ginral," rushed out to defend the horse. The Federal captain said "General now I can account for your success. Your negroes fight for you, and your horse fight for you."[14]

Ben Davis

Ben Davis was born March 4, 1836 in Fayette, Tennessee. He was owned by Hugh Davis of LaGrange, Tennessee. In 1861 Ben Davis was given to General Forrest as a personal body servant by Hugh Davis. He remained in this position through the war. At the time he applied for pension on July 12, 1921 he was living in Memphis. A letter from Mr. Hargrove to the pension board stated:

> Now, General Hickman, it is impossible to find men living in Memphis that knew Ben Davis, when he was in the army. He said all has since died. But he gave the name of the following gentlemen that knew him personally, and will vouch for him if they are still living; Col. Hugh Street, Meridian, Miss; Col. Ashberry, Oklona, Miss; Col. Henderson; Oklona Miss.[15]

Colonel Thomas Henderson was chief of scouts for Gen. Forrest. Henderson's scouts played important roles in many campaigns, including the raid on Memphis.[16] No information has been found on Colonel Hugh Street and Colonel Ashberry. It is assumed Ben Davis was with Forrest at Gainesville, Alabama in 1865.

Nim Wilkes

Nim Wilkes was born in Maury County, Tennessee, date unknown. He was owned by Jim Wilkes. Nim served as a personal servant for General Forrest and was a teamster. Nim Wilkes stated on his pension application:

> I was in every battle General Forrest fought after leaving Columbia (Tennessee) until the surrender. Generally, driving an ordnance wagon. Got hurt at Como, Mississippi after the battle of Ft. Pillow. Mule fell on me and hurt my right ankle. Was laid up in the hospital at Corinth. I think the Dr. was Cowan. Mustered out at Gainesville. Took the oath of allegiance.[17]

Dr. James B. Cowan served as Chief Surgeon on Forrest's staff. In October 1863 Dr. Cowan witnessed General Forrest calling General Braxton Bragg a coward when they were in the Chattanooga area.[18] Forrest's Headquarters was stationed at Como, Mississippi from January 1, 1864 to the early part of February 1864.[19]

There were three periods in the early to middle part of the war era when Forrest was in Columbia. The command left Columbia on December 10, 1862 on the raid into West Tennessee.[20] The raid captured many small garrisons. Trenton surrendered with over 700 men.[21] On December 31, 1862 the battle of Parker's Crossroads was fought. The raid received official congratulations from the Confederate congress.[22]

Forrest was back in the Columbia area around January 3, 1863. On January 10, 1863 several of Forrest's regiments were used on an expedition to Harpeth Shoals, on the Cumberland. The transports *Hartsing*, *Trio*, and *Parthenia*, and gunboat *Major Slidell* were captured.[23]

On January 26, 1863 General Forrest was ordered to General Bragg's headquarters at Shelbyville. There he was informed of the expedition to capture Fort Donelson.[24] General Forrest's command returned to the Columbia area on February 17, 1864.[25] Out of this general area (Columbia, Spring Hill) they fought the battles of Brentwood, Thompson Station and the first battle of Franklin.[26] On April 23, 1863 Forrest's command was sent in pursuit of Colonel Abel D. Streight. Somewhere between December 1862 and April 1863 Nim Wilkes joined Forrest. On Nim's pension application, J. E. Usher, M. D. and James Crowe served as witnesses. The two gentlemen stated that "Nim suffered from senility, rheumatism of right leg, said to be result of service in war."[27]

Another former Confederate soldier swore on an affidavit:

> State of Tennessee, Lawrence County, R. V. Gagle appeared before me his date and made oath as follows: I was a soldier in the Confederate army and met Nim Wilkes (colored) at Corinth, Mississippi, at which time he was with Forrest's Brigade. I knew him from that time to surrender at Selma, Alabama, and he was still with Forrest in the Confederate service. I knew him almost two years in Confederate service with General Forrest.

In August 1915 when his pension application was submitted Nim Wilkes was living near Crestview, Tennessee.[28]

The duties of the Headquarters staff included organizing General Forrest's personal material such as food, horses, and clothes. They were also used as couriers. Using black Southerners as couriers was a favorite Confederate trick. They deceived the Federals into thinking they were dumb or pro-union (which of course the Northern assumed anyway, not being willing to believe that black Southerners could be pro-Confederate), and thus manipulated unsuspecting Federals.

FORREST'S ESCORT

Forrest's Escort was organized September, 1862, in Middle Tennessee. This company was recruited for General Forrest by Captain Montgomery Little, a native of Bedford County. Captain Little, Captain John C. Jackson, and Captain Nathan Boone commanded Forrest's Escort during the war.[29] Most of the ninety members were Middle Tennesseans. They joined Forrest in October 1862.[30] Some of the duties of the escort were to protect General Forrest and his staff and to serve as an honor guard during reviews, parades, etc. They also ran messages.

Captain Little was killed at Thompson Station, Tennessee, March 1863. In Gainesville, Alabama, May 9, 1865, they mustered a strength of 119 men. The Escort, from the beginning of the war to the end, had a very high morale. General Forrest's Escort fought with him through most of the battles of the war. They saw action around Lavergne on October 7, 1862. On November 6th, they participated in a demonstration against Nashville. The West Tennessee raid was next with the battles of Humboldt, Trenton, and Parkers Crossroads. In the early spring of 1863 the Escort participated in action around Spring Hill, Thompson Station, College Grove, Franklin, and Brentwood. In the early summer of 1863 they were involved in the capture of Streight's command in Rome, Georgia. They then moved south and east, covering Bragg's withdrawal in the Chattanooga Campaign. After the battle of

Chickamauga the escort was transferred as a part of General Forrest's new command to West Tennessee. The command was concentrated in West Tennessee in time to see action at Brice's Crossroads, Harrisburg, and were on the raids of Paducah and Memphis. Following the destruction of Johnsonville, Forrest's command provided the screening action for Hoods' Tennessee campaign. Forrest's command was a part of the rear guard on the retreat from December 16, 1864 to January 1865. The escort was with General Forrest for the battle of Selma and the surrender at Gainesville, Alabama.[31]

Polk Arnold

Polk Arnold was born in Shelbyville, Bedford County, Tennessee in 1844. His owner was Pleasant Arnold. Polk joined the Confederate army in 1863 and served with General Forrest, Captain J. C. Jackson and Captain Boone. Polk stated on his pension application that "I was with Pleasant Arnold and F.F. Arnold, who were with General Forrest under Captain J. C. Jackson."

A witness, Caddie Arnold Wallis, stated on the application:

> He was a slave of Pleasant Arnold, Applicant served in the Confederate Army from 1863 to the close of the war as a servant to said Pleasant Arnold and F. F. Arnold with General N. B. Forrest's Escort. Captain John C. Jackson and Capt. Nathan Boone, applicant returned to my fathers home after the surrender. Where upon the return of F. F. Arnold. . . , remained until the death of the latter whose widow, Mrs. Caldonia Arnold, is upon the pension role.[32]

It has been said that Forrest's Escort were "ever ready to undertake what their chief so often looked to them to do; the fighting of a full regiment."[33] Pleasant Arnold served as a private in General Forrest's Escort. Arnold was killed at the battle of Harrisburg, Mississippi, July 17, 1864.[34]

Jones Greer

Jones Greer was born in Lincoln County, Tennessee in 1844. His owner was Alex Greer. Jones Greer stated on his pension application: "In 1863, or 1864", he served with Captain Boone, John Jackson, Sam Donaldson, and George Cowan.[35]

Captain Boone, Captain John Jackson, and Lieutenant George Cowan were a part of Forrest's Escort.[36] Lieutenant Samuel Donaldson served as aide-de-camp on Forrest's staff.[37] Greer was a servant for Lieutenant George Cowan.[38] Lt. George Cowan commanded the escort in their last battle of the war. Cowan also had the honor to lead the escort in General Forrest's funeral procession.[39]

J. B. Person stated on Jones' pension application:

> I was with Forrest's Escort and applicant was with us at Gainesville, Alabama in May 1865. He was a servant I know for George Cowan, George Gilespie, and McEwen.

A. A. McEwen served with Forrest's Escort. McEwen stated on the pension application that "I, A. A. McEwen, state that applicant was my personal servant and was with us at close of war. I was discharged at Gainesville, Alabama in May 1865."

Jones Greer was living in Marshall County, Belfast, Tennessee, at the time he filed for pension. He owned about 10 acres of land that was valued at $250. He had 3 acres of corn valued at $50.00.[40]

Frank Russell

Frank Russell was born in Bedford County, Tennessee. In 1921 he was living in Williamson County, Franklin, Tennessee. He stated that in 1862 "I was with my master R. C. Garrat[,] Forrest['s] Escort."

R. C. Garret and Nancy Farmer were witnesses for Frank:

> The applicant Frank Russell was his servant and was with him when the war closed and was faithful and true to him the whole time.[41]

Frank Russell was one of the few pensioners that had substantial assets. In 1921 he owned 60 acres of land valued at $1,080 and had about $300 in cash. The records show a Pvt. R. C. Garrett who served in Forrest's Escort.[42] This is an example of a private with a servant.

Preston Roberts

Preston Roberts enlisted at the first call for volunteers in 1861. Roberts' functioned unofficially as Quartermaster under the command of General Nathan Bedford Forrest. It is more than apparent that General Forrest had a great deal of confidence in Roberts. Roberts was in charge of all funds for the food and was in command of 75 cooks.[43] C. S. Severson served as General Forrest's Chief Quartermaster from November 20, 1861 until late 1864. Major R. M. Mason served in that position from that time to the end of the war.[44] In the post-war era Roberts was awarded the Southern Cross of Honor by the United Daughters of the Confederacy.[45] Preston Roberts died in June 1910.[46]

There are still many questions concerning Roberts. Did he go off to war with General Forrest in 1861? What state was he from? Where did he live after the war? When was he born? Where is he buried?

Was he a free man at the beginning of the war? Unfortunately, there seems to be no documentation that will allow us to answer these questions.

3RD TENNESSEE CAVALRY

Alfred Duke

Alfred Duke was born in Yalobusha County, Mississippi, in 1848. His owner was William Duke. Alfred left for war in 1861 with Wiley Duke (William Duke's son). Alfred stated on his application:

> At the beginning of the war I was with General Forrest['s] regiment. Near Mobile, Alabama on the line of Georgia and Alabama the Yankees captured my master, Mr. Wiley Duke. I took his horse and Mr. Bersers and went home with Mr. Bersers. Mr. Bersers then knew the way to my master's home from there. I arrived at home just two months before the surrender in 1865. I was in the Confederate service almost the entire period of the war.

William Terry & Henry G. Evans were witnesses for Alfred Duke. [47]

George Hanna

George Hanna was born in Cheatham County, Tennessee, September 10, 1847. His owner was George Washington Hanna. George Hanna stated on his application: "Enlisted December 2, 1861. I served with Captain Sam Mays, Colonel Bill DeMoss, and Lieutenant Colonel N. B. Forrest."[48]

Through consolidations a portion of the 3rd Tennessee Cavalry became a part of the 10th Tennessee Cavalry. Colonel Edward B. Trezevant was killed March 5, 1863 at the Battle of Thompson Station, Tennessee. William E. DeMoss became Lieutenant Colonel, and finally Colonel.[49]

Two men testified:

> I, J. P. Starnes, swear that I was a member of same company and regiment with said G. W. Hanna the owner of George Hanna and saw him driving supply wagon for his master in C. S. Army during war.
>
> I, W. K. Hanna, swear that I am son of George Hanna (white) and know that Uncle George as we call him belonged to my father. During his life time and that applicant is worthy and was in army with my father.[49]

1ST TENNESSEE INFANTRY AND 3rd TENNESSEE CAVALRY

Ned Gregory

Ned Gregory was born in Lincoln County in 1843. He was owned by Mr. Brown Gregory until his death in 1858 at which time his widow inherited ownership of Ned.

On June 10, 1921 Ned filed for pension. He was living in Winchester, Franklin County, Tennessee. Mr. W. F. Gregory and Mrs. Eliza G. Murrell were witnesses for Ned:

> Personally appeared before Geo. Mosely Clark of the county Court Clerk of Franklin County, Tennessee. W. F. Gregory and Mrs. Eliza Murrell who made oath in due form of the law that Ned Gregory went in the Confederate Army with T. D. Gregory in January 1863 and remained with him until April 1864 when Captain T. D. Gregory sent him home to make a crop, and in the same fall at that time Forrest made his raid into Tennessee the said Ned Gregory went out with William Chick who was the overseer of Ned, and Mrs. Mary Gregory. The said Wm. Chick being a member of Forrest's old regiment and remained until after the battles of Franklin and Nashville in which he served and came home with the said Wm. Chick and attempted to return with the said Chick but was forbidden by his mistress Mrs. Mary Gregory in my presence and I heard my mother tell him there was no use in going as it [the war] was about over, and told Ned, If he did go he could not have the mule to ride.[50]

Ned Gregory, like many others, served under two or more men.

William (W. D.) Chick served in the 3rd Tennessee Cavalry, Company C. This was Forrest's first regiment. There is no Captain T. D. Gregory in the records. However, there is a Private T. D. Gregory that served in the 1st Tennessee Infantry, (Turney's).[51]

The 3rd Tennessee Cavalry regiment has a very complex history. Lt. Col. Nathan B. Forrest was the unit's first commander. It was organized as a battalion in Memphis, October 1861, then increased to a regiment in January 1862. The 3rd Tennessee Cavalry was consolidated with many units during the war. In February 1865 they were consolidated with the 12th Tennessee Cavalry. They were surrendered and paroled at Gainesville, Alabama, May 1865.[52]

4TH TENNESSEE CAVALRY

Robert Bruce Patton

Robert Patton was born in Williamson County, Tennessee on January 4, 1846. Robert Patton served with Lieutenant Sam C. Tulloss. Patton appears to have served as a "free man of color." His father, Jerry Patton, was born a free man. His father lived in Nolensville and rented from Miss Lou Rerrive Owens. Robert stated that "in October 1862, I was with Dr. J. W. Starnes and after that was with Colonel W. S. McLemore."[53]

4TH TENNESSEE CAVALRY AND 11TH TENNESSEE CAVALRY

Marshall Thompson

How could a ten year old boy be in the Confederate army? Marshall Thompson was in that position. He was born April 10, 1852. His owner was Captain Arron Thompson who served in the 4th Tennessee Cavalry, Co. A. Marshall Thompson stated on his application: "I served with Colonel Starnes, and Charles Temple." Two witnesses stated on the pension: "that they knew him (Marshall Thompson) was a porter for Colonel Starnes in the Confederate Army." Marshall also said: "In 1862 I was with Colonel Starnes of the 4th Tennessee Cavalry."[57]

Colonel J. W. Starnes was a physician, and one of Forrest's best officers.[55] Charles Temple was a private in Co. I, 11th Tennessee Cavalry.[56] Company I was a part of the original Douglas' Tennessee Partisan Ranger Battalion. They were organized August 10, 1862 in Williamson and Davisdson Counties. Thomas F. Perkins was their Captain. Four of the companies were consolidated February 25, 1863 with Holman's Partisan Ranger Battalion to form the 11th Tennessee Cavalry.[57] Col. J. W. Starnes was commanding a brigade on June 30, 1863 when he was killed by a sharpshooter during the Tullahoma Campaign.[58] It is assumed that Marshall served with Private Charles Temple after Colonel Starnes death. This is another excellent example of a private having a servant. What does this say for the number of black Southerners with the Confederate Army? It is possible that there were many, with no documentation.

Hardin Starnes

There was another black confederate who served with Colonel Starnes. His name was Hardin Starnes. Hardin stated on his pension application, dated March 15, 1929, that he was with "Colonel J. W.

Starnes until his death in 1863." Dr. Y. M. Haley of Nashville stated on the application:

> This is to tell you I have known Hardin Starnes colored for the past 40 years and believe he is worthy of trust. He will I believe give you an exact account of his activities during the conflict between the North and South and am sure needs any help you may see fit to give him. Any courtesy shown him will be a favor to me. With personal regards and best wishes, Sincerely Yours, Y. M. Haley.[59]

The 4th Tennessee Cavalry was organized as Starnes' 8th Battalion at Camp Cheatham in Robertson County, Tennessee on December 11, 1861.

On February 24, 1862, Brig. General John B. Floyd took command of Wharton's and McCavland's Regiments, Starnes' and E. S. Smith's Battalions and marched with them to Chattanooga. There Starnes's battalion was transferred to the command of Maj. Gen. E. Kirby Smith. In April the battalion skirmished with the enemy at Wartrace, Bedford County. The battalion was increased to a regiment on May 26, 1862 at Camp Roberts, Bledsoe County, Tennessee. In June they were in a skirmish at Readiville.

On July 3, 1862 the regiment was assigned to Brig. General Heth's division. On September 27th the 4th Tennessee Cavalry was screening Maj. Gen. E. Kirby Smith's command in a battle near Richmond, Kentucky. The regiment served with General Forrest in the demonstration on the outskirts of Nashville and on the expedition into West Tennessee, ending with the Battle of Parkers' Crossroads on December 31, 1862. In the spring of 1863 the regiment fought at the battle of Thompson Station, Brentwood, and the battle of Franklin. Colonel Starnes was commanding a brigade during this period. The 4th Tennessee Cavalry was a part of his brigade and was commanded by Colonel McLemore. Colonel Starnes was killed in June 1863. On August 31 the unit was in Dibrell's Brigade under Forrest's command. The unit was transferred to Wheeler's Command on October 31, 1863.

The 4th served in the Atlanta Campaign until August 20, 1864. General Wheeler's command was ordered on a raid into Tennessee to destroy Sherman's railroad communications. On this raid the regiment became separated and did not get back together until early 1865. Part of this regiment joined Brig. Gen. John Stuart Williams who had moved into East Tennessee and Virginia. They were engaged in the Battle of Saltville, Virginia on October 2, 1864. These units later joined General Wheeler in the Savannah, Georgia campaign in late 1864. The other part of the unit (4th) was ordered to join Forrest on the Tennessee Campaign of 1864. They stayed with Forrest until January 1865.

Detachments of the 4th were with General Dibrell in South Carolina. The 4th Tennessee Cav. surrendered at Greensboro, North Carolina on April 26, 1865.[60]

GENERAL CHALMER'S ESCORT AND 6th TENNESSEE CAVALRY

John Terrill

John Terrill was the personal servant and aide to J. B. White. Legend says John Terrill served with J. B. White to the end of the war, and became a Doctor for the black community in the post-war era.

J. B. White, the son of William White, was born in 1844 at the old White homestead near Franklin, Tennessee. As a boy of sixteen he went to Mississippi and joined General Chalmer's escort. He later rode with General Forrest.

The photograph accompanying this essay shows the two men wearing United Confederate Veterans uniforms, belt buckles, and reunion medals.[61] Records list a "J. B. White" in the 6th Tennessee Cavalry, Co. D. This regiment served a portion of the war in Forrest's Command.[62] J. B. White became a doctor after the war. He practiced medicine for a time, but a greater part of his life was spent in the pharmaceutical business.[63]

It appears Terrill attended U.C.V. meetings during the post-war era. The Confederate Veterans would not have allowed Terrill to wear this uniform just for a photograph. A man could not attend United Confederate Veterans meetings unless he had served with honor in the war. It was a privilege to attend these meetings.

16TH TENNESSEE CAVALRY

Wright Whitlow

Wright Whitlow was born in Kentucky on December 25, 1836. He was brought to Tennessee when he was five years old. Wright's owner was a man named Jim Pat Whitlow.[64] J. P. Whitlow served in Company G, 16th Tennessee Cavalry.[65]

Wright stated on his application:

> I was with my master, J. P. Whitlow, until after the battle of Ft. Pillow. I witnessed the battle of Ft. Pillow and at one time during the battle I held the horse of General Forrest while he mounted his new one after the first one had been shot from under him. After Ft. Pillow I was sent with some important letters but was cap-

> tured on my way home by Federal[s] and was searched and after being held prisoner for some time I was finally paroled upon giving oath not to rejoin the Confederate Army and on that account I never returned to said army.[66]

Forrest had three horses shot at the battle of Ft. Pillow. Two of these animals died. The first horse was mortally wounded, reared up then fell upon Forrest and badly bruised him. Captain Anderson strongly suggested he continue the reconnaissance on foot. Forrest felt his chances were about the same either way and he could see better from the saddle.[67]

The son of J. P. Whitlow stated in an affidavit attached to the pension application:

> My name is Bernard Whitlow. I am 42 years old and live in Haywood County, Tennessee. I have known the applicant, Wright Whitlow, all my life. During the Civil War he belonged to my father's father. My father was a Confederate soldier and honorably discharged. It is part of family tradition that Wright Whitlow was my father's body servant during the war [all] of my father's service, or a part of it. Personally, I know nothing of the matter, owing to my youth, nor do I know of anyone who does but I would say from what I have heard, that Uncle Wright is correct in his assertion as to his service.[68]

How did Wright Whitlow feel about the battle of Ft. Pillow? What did he feel about the black Union soldiers in the Fort? Unfortunately, we have no answers to this question. What type of important "letters" was he was given? We don't know that either, but entrusting him with them reveals a high level of trust that Forrest's troopers had for Wright.

The 16th Tennessee Cavalry was also called the 21st (Wilson's) Tennessee Cavalry. The unit was organized February 4, 1864 as a consolidation of several organizations. The regiment was organized into eleven companies. Company G was organized July 13, 1863 by Lt. Col. Williams with men from Madison County.

On February 20, 21, 22, 1864, the regiment took part in the battle with Maj. General William "Sooy" Smith's forces near Okolona, Mississippi. On April 11, the regiment was a part of Chalmers Division in the battle of Ft. Pillow.

The unit saw action at the battle of Brice's Crossroads, Harrisburg, Athens, Johnsonville, and the Tennessee Campaign of 1864. The regiment was paroled at Gainesville, Alabama.[69]

20TH TENNESSEE CAVALRY

Lewis Muzzell

Lewis Muzzell filed his pension application on October 13, 1921. There is no birth date given on the pension. His owner was William Daniel Muzzell, and went by the name of Daniel.[70] Records show that Daniel Muzzell was a Private in Company E, 20th Tennessee Cavalry. One source spells the name "Muzzlen."[71] Lewis Muzzell stated on his application:

In the spring of 1864 Daniel Muzzell obtained from General Forrest a furlough to return to Henry County to hear the funeral of his Mother preached. We came as far as Jackson, Tennessee when we were intercepted by a runner with a message from General Forrest ordering him back to the army at Gallensburg, Mississippi. He then wrote me a pass and sent me to Steve Muzzell at Mainsfield, Henry County, Tennessee. I came on to Henry County and did not return but stayed with Steve Muzzell in accordance with the instructions of my young master who told me to stay until he returned. This he never did, being killed at Gallensburg, Mississippi about the 1st day of May 1864.

Mr. A. J. Walters, whose statement is filed on the application, stated that Daniel Muzzell was killed at Okolona. Lewis stated that "This is a mistake as I was in the battle of Okolona with my master and it was afterwards that he was killed."[72]

This is another example of the trust whites had in black Southerners. They would never put their lives in the hands of those who might betray them. This is also another example of a private with a servant. These men, Daniel and Lewis, probably grew up together. They went off to war together as friends, as well as servant and master.

There is no mention of Gallensburg in any source on Forrest's Cavalry. The 20th Tennessee Cavalry was in Buford's Division, Bell's Brigade of Forrest's Cavalry.[73] Furloughs were given to Bell's Brigade during the middle of May.[74] No records show a battle of any kind fought May 1, 1864.

On May 2, 1863, there was a sharp skirmish with 2,000 Federal Cavalry under Sturgis. The 20th Tennessee Cavalry was no where near that fight.[75]

An ex-Confederate soldier with the 20th Tennessee Cavalry stated on his pension application:

> I, William S. Bomar, make oath that I knew Daniel Muzzell during this time. I also knew Lewis Muzzell, colored. I was a member of Colonel[Captain] Bomar's

> Company, Colonel Henry Greer, Colonel Forrest's Cavalry, joining September 18, 1863 the day after my 18th birthday staying with same until February or March 1864. When I was detailed having been sent to Henry County from Jackson, Tennessee to gather up clothing when captured. After this Captain Bowman's Company and Captain William Hallum's Company and Greer's regiment, and Russell's regiment consolidated. I was in same mess with Daniel Muzzell and Lewis Muzzell (colored) was the cook. Lewis stuck to his master Daniel at all times and under all circumstances. I remember one instance in particular; we were fording the Tennessee River below Mussell Shoals when Daniel Muzzell's horse got his foot hung in the rocks. Lewis was told to go on with the Company to fall back but Lewis stood crying and said he wasn't going away until Mas' Dan got out. He was regarded, and is now regarded, well by all who knew him and deserves a pension.[76]

Lewis Muzzell's pension application was accepted, as were all the men that are covered in these sketches. He died on April 8, 1932. His family wanted a Confederate headstone for his grave. Their wish was not granted. The Federal Government would not supply headstones for black confederates.[77]

Alex Porter

Alex Porter was born in Henry County, Tennessee. The date is unknown. He was owned by Dr. James. Porter, the brother of a future Governor of Tennessee. Alex stated that he served with General Forrest in Col. Russell's regiment and was a servant for Captain Killis Clark.

H. E. Fraizer stated on Alex Porter's application:

> That he (Fraizer) was a member of Co.F. 20th Tennessee Cavalry, Bell's Brigade, under General Forrest from the beginning to the close of the war. . . Alex Porter, colored man, was with Captain Clark from the battle of Brices Cross Road until I (Fraizer) left the Company after being wounded at Athens, Tennessee. Captain Clark was carried off the battlefield at Athens. . . . Alex Porter, colored, was with Captain Clark all the time, waiting on him during the time I was with Captain Clark from the fight at Brices Cross Roads to Athens, and I understood waited on him when he was wounded. Alex made a good servant and stuck to Captain Clark

> like a brother. He has lived a correct life since the war, and [is] a member in good standing of the [U. C. V.] Fitzgerald Kendall Camp.[78]

These are important statements indicating trust, loyalty, and even love. This is also another example of a black man being a member of a U.C.V. Camp.

Forrest fought the battle of Athens, Alabama, on September 24, 1864. Forrest attacked Athens, destroying the railroad tracks, cutting the telegraph wires, and capturing a corral of horses and mules. He forced the Federals to surrender by using the old trick of deploying his 4,500 to appear to be 10,000.

Forrest reported to General Taylor:

> My force captured this place (Athens) this morning, with 1,300 officers and men, fifty ambulance and wagons, five hundred horses, two trains of cars loaded with quartermasters' and commissary stores, and a large quantity of small arms and two pieces of artillery... My loss five killed and twenty-five wounded.[79]

Records show a Captain A.V. Clark in the 20th Tennessee Cavalry. Colonel Russell commanded this regiment.[80] Alex Porter was an honorary member of the United Confederate Veterans, Fitzgerald Kimball Camp #1284. He died in the city of Paris, Henry County, Tennessee on July 8, 1932.[81]

The 20th Tennessee Cavalry was also called the 15th Tennessee Cavalry regiment. The unit was organized on order of Major General N. B. Forrest after his February, 1864 appointment to the command of the cavalry forces in West Tennessee and North Mississippi. Many of the men were members of Greer's Tennessee Cavalry, which had been raised within the Federal lines in West Tennessee during the fall of 1863.

The regiment was in Buford's Division, T. H. Bell's Brigade, where the unit fought in the battles of Okolona, Paducah, Ft. Pillow, Brice's Crossroads, Harrisburg, Athens, Johnsonville, and the Tennessee Campaign of 1864. It was paroled at Gainesville, Alabama.[82]

4TH ALABAMA INFANTRY

James Jefferson

There was a black Southerner who had the honor to fight in one of the first and last battles of the war. His name was James Jefferson, from Summerfield, Alabama. He was owned by Dr. Samuel Watkins Vaughn and went by the nick name of "Jim Jeff."

The state of Alabama voted to secede from the Union on January 11, 1861. The Magnolia Cadets (later known as Co. C, 4th Alabama Infantry), left for Virginia on April 24, 1861. Dr. Vaughn's son Paul Turner Vaughn left Selma with the cadets. A few months later Dr. Vaughn decided to visit his son. Dr. Vaughn and Jim Jeff arrived as the 1st Battle of Manassas was starting.[83]

The commanders were two West Point classmates; Brig. Gen Irwin McDowell for the Union Army and General P. G. T. Beauregard for the Confederate Army.[84] All students of the war know that on the morning of July 21, 1861 the Federal's attacked driving the Confederates back. The Southerners were pushed back to their now famous stand on Henry House hill.

The 4th Alabama Infantry suffered 305 casualties during the heavy fighting. During the battle a couple of Confederate soldiers were wounded near Dr. Vaughn and Jim Jeff. Dr. Vaughn picked up one of the wounded men's muskets and joined the 4th Alabama. Jim Jeff grabbed a musket and joined the ranks beside Dr. Vaughn. In time, the Union forces were driven from the field.

Paul Turner Vaughn was promoted to Lieutenant for gallantry on the battlefield. James "Jim Jeff" Jefferson had the honor to be personally congratulated for his loyalty and courage by, none other than, President Jefferson Davis. After the battle Dr. Vaughn and Jim Jeff went back to Alabama. The Selma area was protected from the Union forces until the end of the war.[85]

Selma was the last important arsenal left in the South by 1865.[86] General Nathan Bedford Forrest was in command of protecting the city. Selma lies upon the west bank of the Alabama River, and stands upon a bluff nearly one hundred feet above high water level. The city was fortified by a double line of works. The works required a great many more men that Forrest had under his command. Armstrong's Brigade had about 1,400 men to hold the left and western portions of the line. Roddy's Brigade had about 1,700 men to hold the center and Eastern positions of the line.[87] Many of the local citizens joined the defense of Selma in the center of the lines.[88] Three recruits who joined General Forrest in the defense of Selma were 61 year old Dr. Vaughn, thirteen old David Vaughn, and Jim Jeff. They joined Captain Benjamin Harrison Summerfield's militia on the breastworks.[89] The Confederate forces were outnumbered by Major General James Wilson's Union forces by more than 3 to 1.[90] In many places there were 10' intervals between the Confederate, defenders.[91]

On April 2, 1865 the Union forces broke through both lines of defense. The Vaughns and Jim Jeff spent the night in Mrs. Margie Peters' garden. They later hid in the home of a relative. A week later Jim Jeff acquired three horses for them to ride to Summerfield.

In the post-war era James Jefferson ran a small grocery store on the Summerfield road. The Vaughns made sure that James Jefferson received a Confederate pension, which they said was an expression of gratitude from the Confederacy.[92]

Regiment Unknown
Cal Sharp

Cal Sharp was born September 12, 1841 in Lewis County, Tennessee. Cal filed an application for pension January 3, 1931. Willis Sharp and Silas Stockard stated on Cal's pension application:

John Sharp served under General Forrest and that claimant Cal Sharp was a slave belonging to the father of John Sharp, Mires Sharp, and that Cal Sharp, the claimant served with his master under General Forrest and did black smith work and that he would go back and forth from the front to his home and look after the horses and would care for the family of Mires Sharp and cont. in the service of his master in the army until the war ended.

This is another example of the feelings whites and black Southerners held for each other. No one could have forced Cal to do these things for the Sharp family. Many families would have starved to death were it not for these black Southerners. These men were more than servants. In many cases they were considered family. Cal Sharp died on January 26, 1935 at the age of 93.[93]

SUMMARY

The war ended for General Forrest, his command, and most of the South in May 1865. General Forrest's relationships with black Southerners continued for the rest of his life, and was consistent, before, during and after the war. They stayed with him until his death, and he did what he could for them, within the context of the racial attitudes of the post-war United States.

There were many examples of Forrest promoting racial harmony after the war. In an area of eastern Mississippi he prevented a racial riot in 1868. Forrest made speeches to both sides and calmed the situation.[94]

At Brownsville, Tennessee, on August 10, 1868, Forrest spoke to a political rally and said: "I wish distinctly to state I am not against colored man, neither have I ever been against the colored man. . ."[95]

Two months later in Jackson, Tennessee, Forrest addressed another political rally:

> I beg leave to make the following statement. We have no feeling of unkindness to freed men. In seeking their freedom, they have only done what every human being

similarly situated would do. . . .[96]

In late August Forrest gave an interview to a reporter named Woodward who wrote for the *Cincinnati Commercial.* General Forrest later repudiated most of the article concerning the Ku Klux Klan, Ft. Pillow, and other political items. Forrest said of the black men who served with him, and this seems to be a direct quote:

> . . . these boys stayed with me, drove my teams and better Confederates did not live.[97]

Forrest gave another interview in 1869, to a reporter from the *Louisville Courier Journal*:

> Those [black Southerners] among us during the war behaved in such a manner that I shall always respect them for it... I have always felt kind towards them and always treated them kindly.[98]

The key word is "respect." No man deserves the respect of another man. These men earned the respect of General Forrest and his troopers.

The rural west Tennessee town of Trenton saw racial trouble in 1874. Two white men made themselves uninvited guests at a barbecue hosted by black residents. The hosts were insulted when the two men refused to pay for their dinner. It appears the two white men were fired on by the angry crowd. Sixteen of the barbequers were arrested by the Sheriff of Trenton. The posse had to defend itself from two attacks by groups of masked whites. At approximately 1:00 a.m. a group of masked men took the black citizens from the jail. They killed six on the edge of town. The others were never seen again.

Forrest's response to this incident was typical of the man and the attitudes he held throughout his life:

> If I were entrusted with proper authority I would capture and exterminate the white marauders who disgraced their race by this cowardly murder of negroes.[99]

On July 4, 1875, the city of Memphis, by general consent, observed the anniversary of American independence. The festivities were held in one of the parks or at the fair grounds. General Forrest, General G.J. Pillow, and others were asked to make speeches by the Jubilee of Pole Bearers (a political and social organization in the post-war era comprised of black Southerners) at the fairgrounds. Miss Lou Lewis, a member of the organization, was introduced to General Forrest then presented him with a bouquet of flowers and said: "Mr. Forrest -

allow me to present you this bouquet as a token, of reconciliation, and offering of peace and good will."

General Forrest received the flower with a bow, and replied:

> Miss Lewis, ladies and gentlemen - I accept these flowers as a token of reconciliation between the white and colored races of the South. I accept them more particularly, since they come from a lady, for if there is any one on God's great earth who loves the ladies, it is myself. This is a proud day for me. Having occupied the position I have for thirteen years, and being misunderstood by the colored race, I take this occasion to say that I am your friend. I am here as the representative of the Southern people - one that has been more maligned than any other. I assure you that every man who was in the Confederate army is your friend. We were born on same soil, breathe the same air, live in the same land, and why should we not be brothers and sisters. When the war broke out I believed it to be my duty to fight for my country, and I did so. I came here with the jeers and sneers of a few white people, who did not think it right. I think it is right, and will do all I can to bring about harmony, peace and unity. I want to elevate every man, and to see you take your places in your shops, stores and offices. I don't propose to say anything about politics, but I want you to do as I do - go to the polls and select the best men to vote for. I feel that you are free men, I am a free man, and we can do as we please. I came here as a friend and whenever I can serve any of you I will do so. We have one Union, one flag, one country; therefore, let us stand together. Although we differ in color, we should not differ in sentiment. Many things have been said in regard to myself, and many reports circulated, which may perhaps be believed by some of you, but there are many around me who can contradict them. I have been many times in the heat of battle - oftener, perhaps, than any within the sound of my voice. Men have come to me to ask for quarter, both black and white, and I have shielded them. Do your duty as citizens, and if any are oppressed, I will be your friend. I thank you for the flowers, and assure you that I am with you in heart and hand.[100]

Notes

1. Quoted in William S. Fitzgerald, "We Will Stand By You," *Civil War Times Illustrated*, Nov-Dec, 1993, 71-72. Emphasis added.

2. Nim Wilkes, Black Confederate Pension Applications, #111 Tennessee State Library and Archives, Nashville, Tennessee. Hereafter pension applications will be cited with a name and number.

3. Shadrick Searcy #235. Searcy served with the 46th Georgia Infantry. His family requested a Confederate headstone for his grave and was denied.

4. For an analysis of relationships between whites and blacks in slavery that emphasizes the role that capitalism played in shaping the paternalistic attitudes of slaveowners toward their slaves, see Eugene Genovese, *Roll, Jordan, Roll: The World The Slaveholders Made* (New York: W. W. Norton, 1976).

5. Quoted in Robert Selph Henry, *Nathan Bedford Forrest; First with The Most* (New York: Mallard (Mallard Press, 1991), 14.

6. *Ibid*, 15.

7. Quoted in John Allen Wyeth, *That Devil Forrest* (New York: Harper & Brother, 1959), 18.

8. J. H. Curtis, in the *Memphis Commercial Appea*l, April 28, 1933.

9. Thornton Forrest #48

10. *Memphis Bulletin*, May 30, 1865

11. Quoted in Henry, *Forrest,* 439.

12. Capt. J Harvey Mathes, *General Forrest* (Memphis: D Appletoy and Co., 1902), 359

13. Wyeth, *That Devil Forrest,* 546, Henry, *Forrest,* 439.

14. Quoted in Henry, *Forrest,* 441

15. Ben Davis #15.

16. Henry, *Forrest,* 280.

17. Nim Wilkes #11.

18. Wyeth, *That Devil Forrest,* 242-3.

19. Henry, *Forrest,* 213-4.

20. *Ibid.*, 108-9.

21. Mathes, *General Forrest,* 84.

22. Henry, *Forrest,* 116-121.

23. General Thomas Jordan and J. P. Pryor, *The Campaigns of Lt. General N. B. Forrest and of Forrest's Cavalry* (Dayton: Morningside Bookshop, 1977), 224.

24. Jordan and Pryor, *Campaigns,* 224-225. The expedition was under the command of Major General Joseph Wheeler. Wyeth, *That Devil Forrest,* 127-132. On February 3, 1862 the command attacked Ft. Donelson. The attack ended in failure. Forrest refused to

serve under Wheeler again.

25. Jordan and Pryor, *Campaigns,* 230-231.
26. *Ibid.*, 231-248.
27. *Ibid.*, 249.
28. Nim Wilkes #11.
29. "History of Forrest's Escort," *Tennesseans In The Civil War* Pt. 1, (Nashville: Civil War Centennial Commission, 1964), 17.
30. Jordan and Pryor, *Campaigns,* 235
31. *Tennesseans in the Civil War*, 16-17.
32. Polk Arnold #5.
33. Jordan and Pryor, *Campaigns,* 369-370.
34. Lt. Gen. N. B. Forrest's Escort Reunion Books, Collection of Carnton Plantation; Carnton Association, Franklin, TN.
35. Jones Greer #61.
36. *Tennesseans in the Civil War*, Part I,. 16.
37. Jordan and Pryor, *Campaigns,* 685.
38. Jones Greer #61.
39. Henry, *Forrest,* 461.
40. Jones Greer #61.
41. Frank Russell #17.
42. *Tennessee In The Civil War*, Part 2, 166.
43. Preston Roberts #416.
44. Jordan and Pryor, *Campaigns,* 685.
45. Jimmie Robinson, *Metro Forum News*, Nashville, Tennessee.
46. Preston Roberts #416.
47. Alfred Duke #190.
48. George Hanna #252; *Tennesseans in the Civil War*, Pt. 1, 76.
49. George Hanna #252.
50. Ned Gregory #3.
51. *Tennesseans in the Civil War*, Pt. 2, 88-179.
52. *Tennesseans In The Civil War*, Pt. 1, 55-59.
53. Robert Bruce Patton #24.
54. Marshall Thompson #229.
55. Mathes, *General Forrest,* 133.
56. *Tennesseans In The Civil War*, Pt. 2, 396.
57. *Ibid.*, Part l, p. 40.
58. Wyeth, *That Devil Forrest,* 210.
59. Hardin Starnes #238.
60. *Tennesseans In The Civil War*, Pt. I, 62-64.
61. Carter House Archives, Franklin, Tennessee, and *Confederate Veteran*, October 1910, 578.
62. *Tennesseans In The Civil War*, Pt. 2. 66,428.
63. *Confederate Veteran*, October 1910, 578
64. Wright Whitlow #236.
65. *Tennesseans In The Civil War*, Pt. 2, 430.
66. Wright Whitlow #236.

67. Wyeth, *That Devil Forrest,* 317.

68. Wright Whitlow #236.

69. *Tennesseans in the Civil War*, Pt. I, 99-100.

70. Lewis Muzzell #65.

71. *Tennesseans in the Civil War*, Pt. 2,. 299.

72. Lewis Muzzell #65.

73. *Tennesseans in the Civil War*, Pt. I, 98.

74. Jordan and Pryor, *Campaigns,* 456. Bell's and Neely's brigades had reentered West Tennessee, and their regiments were situated at points that were favorable for recruitment, granting furloughs to officers and men to visit their families, renovate their clothing, and obtain remounts, as far as needed, by the end of the month.

75. *Ibid*, p. 457.

76. Lewis Muzzell #65.

77. *Ibid.*

78. Alex Porter #38.

79. Wyeth, *That Devil Forrest,* 428-434.

80. *Tennesseans In The Civil War*, Pt. 1, 97.

81. Alex Porter #38.

82. *Tennesseans in the Civil War*, Pt. 1, 97-99.

83. *Selma Times-Journal*, April 23, 1992, 221.

84. Lt. Col. Joseph B. Mitchell, *Decisive Battles of the Civil War* (New York: Ballantine Books, 1955), 27.

85. *Selma Times Journal*, 221.

86. Jordan and Pryor, *Campaigns,* 676.

87 *Ibid.*, 672-673.

88. Mathes, *General Forrest,* 346. Selma had been up to that time one of the chief centers in the west for arsenals, depots, and ordnance foundries for the Confederate army and navy. The city was protected by a double line of works in the shape of a horseshoe, the point touching the river north and south. The exterior line had a trace of nearly four miles with bastions, ditches, and palisades, requiring a strong force for proper defense. There was an interior line not finished or tenable.

89. *Selma Times Journal*, 221.

90. Henry, *Forrest,* 432.

91. Wyeth, *That Devil Forrest,* 534.

92. *Selma Times Journal*, 221.

93. Cal Sharp #248.

94. Jack Hurst, *Nathan Bedford Forrest: A Biography* (New York: Alfred A. Knopf, Inc., 1993, New York), 319.

95. Quoted in William S. Fitzgerald, "We Will Stand By You," *Civil War Times Illustrated*, November-December, 1993, 71-72.

96. *Ibid.*, 72.

97. *Ibid.*

98. *Ibid.*, 88.
99. Hurst, *Nathan Bedford Forrest,* 361.
100. *Memphis Daily Avalanche*, July 6, 1875, 1.

Black Confederates In Lincoln County, North Carolina

Rudolph Young

African-American authorities on African-American history have, in one way or another, failed to emphasize the role of black Confederate soldiers. John Hope Franklin and others say little on the subject.[1] Some authorities state flatly that there were no Confederate soldiers, or that there were too few to mention.[2] *Colliers Encyclopedia*, as late as thirty years ago, said that "the Confederate army used many Negro servants and laborers, but did not employ combat troops."[3] Yet one author believes that a conservative estimate is that there were over 40,000 Black Confederates.[4]

The question usually comes up about why a black man would, slave or free, serve in the Confederate Army? To answer that question, we must go to 1861 and read the newspaper.

On January 1, the *Charleston Mercury* recorded that "153 colored men of the city offered their services to work on redoubts, defense and where necessary for the protection of the coast."[5] On April 24, the same paper noted that "a group of colored men offered to aid in building defenses and was put to work" by the Confederates."[6] On April 28, "a Virginia meeting of colored persons expressed a willingness to aid Virginia's cause to the utmost of our abilities."[7] A mass meeting of black residents of New Orleans, resolved to organize *two* regiments of the Native Guards, a black unit, "to fight shoulder to shoulder with other citizens."[8] On April 30, the *Mercury* reported that "a company of colored men offered their services in Nashville, Tennessee."[9]

The question about why blacks served can be answered by the appeal of the *Memphis Avalanche* in May 9, 1861. To "Patriotic free colored men of the city of Memphis for the service of our common defense."[10]

Students of African American history should have been able to predict with a great degree of certainty that some, if not most, black Southerners would support their country, as did most white Southerners. During the Revolutionary War black and white fought together, on both sides.[11] In 1861, most blacks found themselves as residents of a country called the Confederate States of America, a country that on February 4, in Montgomery, Alabama, adopted a Constitution guaranteeing the recognition and protection of slavery. Slavery was a terrible thing and is to this day a blot on American history as well as Confederate history. Most blacks served because of loyalty to their country or loyalty to an individual; in doing so, they have demonstrated that it is possible to hate the system of slavery and love one's country.

Lincoln County, N. C.

Lincoln County, North Carolina, was not a place of great Civil War battles. Only one shot was fired when Col. Palmer's troops of the Union Army occupied the county for five days in April 1865. Yet 8 Confederate generals had ties to Lincoln County. Five of them were born there. The others married women who were born in Lincoln County, including Stonewall Jackson.[12]

In 1861, the population of the rural Western North Carolina County was about 6,000 people; over 20% of the population served in the Confederate Army. There were about 1,500 black people in the county; most were slaves. About 75 were classified as free persons of color. At least two free blacks served in the Confederate Army.[13]

All blacks who aided the Confederacy did not serve in the army. Most of them served in the county's iron industry. There were several iron furnaces which employed about 400 slaves. One of these furnaces, the Stonewall Furnace, supplied iron to make cannons at Richmond, Virginia.[14]

An old Baptist preacher, Isaac Cansler, grew poppy for the Confederate Medical Laboratory located near Lincolnton, the County seat.[15]

Black Confederates such as Benjamin Franklin Hunter, and Adam Miller Moore were typical of those who served with the army. Both men were community leaders after the Civil War. As of late 1993, both of them had children still living. There was no stigma attached to having served in the Confederate army among African Americans in the years following the war, but as time passed, attitudes changed. In interviews with the Moore and Hunter family members in August 1993 these attitudes reflected the views of Black Historians:

1. The role of blacks in the Confederacy was minimized by suggesting that only a few blacks served.

2. Some family members expressed "shame." They believed that their ancestors served to keep their fellows in slavery.

3. Some of them acted as if they had a Confederate skeleton in their closet.[16]

BENJAMIN FRANKLIN "FRANK" HUNTER

The Hunter family, like many black American families, especially in the South, have a strong tradition of oral history. Family stories are often passed on from generation to generation. In the case of Frank Hunter, family history has it that Frank was sent to serve George W. Hunter as a personal servant. When George W. Hunter was wounded, Frank served as a nurse and later he served as a messenger. After G. W. Hunter died, Frank was sold by the Hunter family. No record of such a sale was ever found.[17]

Most of the people I interviewed in both families had no knowledge of their Confederate past. They knew only that their ancestors were slaves, but when they were told the truth, they expressed interest and pride in an aspect of their history which had been hidden.

Benjamin Franklin Hunter enlisted on June 22, 1861 under the name Frank Hunter. The roster of North Carolina Troops gives only his enlistment date, race and name. Based on what his daughter, Odessa Hunter McCracklin, stated in 1993 at the Reunion of the Descendants of Frank Hunter, we are able to reconstruct a service record.[18]

Frank Hunter was born a slave to Adam and Mary Hunter who were the property of Dr. Cyrus L. Hunter of Lincoln County, North Carolina. On June 22, 1861, Frank and George W. Hunter, the son of Dr. Cyrus L. Hunter enlisted in Company K of the 23rd Regiment of the North Carolina Troops. This unit was formed in eastern Lincoln County and became known as the Beatties Ford Riflemen. Beatties Ford was the name of a village which was at the ford of the Catawba River along the road from Charlotte, North Carolina to Lincolnton, North Carolina.[19]

There was a third man called Henry L. Hunter who also enlisted with George and Frank. It has not been determined if this Henry Hunter was the Henry Hunter who was an older brother of George W. Hunter. Mrs. McCracklin stated that Frank Hunter was sent as a servant of George W. Hunter who was a law student when the war started. George W. Hunter was elected 3rd Lieutenant in the unit and promoted to 1st Lieutenant before being wounded at the Battle of Seven Springs. He recovered from his wounds and was transferred to Company B of the same regiment, where he became Captain and commander. Frank was transferred with him. George Hunter was again wounded at the Battle of Chancellorsville in Virginia; Frank Hunter carried the wounded officer back to North Carolina; George W. Hunter died in a Charlotte Hospital in July, 1863.[20]

There is no documentary record of what happened to Frank Hunter from 1863 to 1865. He does appear on the pension rolls. North Carolina required that black Confederates meet the same requirements as other veterans. Records show that after the Civil War (1869) Frank married a women called Elvira and moved to a farm near Cherryville. Elvira died in 1880, and he married Milo Davenport and lived near Stanley, North Carolina. Frank Hunter purchased about 300 acres of land and engaged in farming.[21]

ADAM MILLER MOORE

The oral tradition of the Moore family states that Adam Moore was caught by a Union patrol near Chancellorsville. He had visited a farm foraging for food with no success. Adam told the patrol that he was a runaway from the plantation he had just left, since the patrol had been instructed not to take-up "contraband Negroes." They told him that he could make it to the main union force by traveling in a certain direction. After the patrol left, Adam returned to his unit informing the commander of the exact location for the Federal forces.[22]

Adam Miller Moore and Adam Miller Roberts were the best of friends. They grew up together on a farm on Indian Creek which was once owned by Tory John Moore. Adam Moore was the older of the two by almost eight years. Both of them had ancestors who were at the Battle of Ramseur's Mill.[23] At the beginning of the Civil War, Miller Roberts enlisted in the Army of the Confederacy and Adam Moore, who was then thirty years old, remained on the farm. Miller Roberts soon rose to the rank of Lieutenant in Company M, of the 16th Regiment of North Carolina Troops. He was wounded and spent some time in a Richmond hospital. Early in 1862, Roberts returned to Indian Creek.

It was then that Adam Moore was asked to serve the Confederacy. He could have been ordered because he was a slave. When asked in 1938 why he served, Adam replied, "If the South won my master promised Freedom and if the North won the Yankees promised Freedom".[24]

The two men left what later became Cherryville in 1863. They joined their company just before the Battle of Chancellorsville, Virginia. Adam Moore was put in charge of building breastworks. It was soon learned that Moore had "a way" with horses so his next job was taking care of the horses.

In 1863, black servants in the Confederate Army could not officially carry weapons, but many did. Miller Roberts gave Adam a pistol which he carried under his shirt. On the first day of battle, the men were separated again. Adam Miller Roberts was killed. Adam Moore recalled that it rained very hard for the next several days. In later years, rain reminded Adam of Chancellorsville.[25]

Adam M. Moore was born to Abram and Jenny Moore in 1831. He served in the Confederate Army from May 1863 until April 1865 as builder of fortifications, keeper of horses, forager, and as an unclassified soldier. After the Civil War, he went to work for the Seaboard Railroad and then as a farmer until he went blind at age 97. When he returned from the war he was not able to find his wife. She was reported to have followed a Federal Army unit in search for Jefferson Davis which passed through Dallas, North Carolina in the spring of 1865. In 1880, he married Eliza Rendleman, the daughter of an African called Hanibal Smith. Adam divorced Eliza in 1898, and married Betty "Nannie" Magness.[26]

Adam Moore established his family in Iron Station, North Carolina, Lincoln County, where he co-founded a church and a school. He died in 1941 at 109 years old.[27]

[Editor's note: The author has additional information regarding the experiences of other black Confederates from Lincoln and York counties including Thad Archer, J. Hanibal Beatty, George Bird, Daniel Brooks, Erwin Watson and Dan Witherspoon. George Bird and Dan Witherspoon both served as cooks with the Palmer Rifles, which became Company A, 12th South Carolina Infantry. George Bird was a Free Man of Color who joined in 1861 and served until 1865. The publishing deadline for this book did not allow enough time to develop the information into essay form.]

Notes

1. John Hope Franklin, *From Slavery To Freedom* (New York: Knopf, 1980) Third Edition, 288-89: "some even took part in combat." Franklin has few words for black Confederates, and none are named. Lerone Bennett, *Before The Mayflower* (Chicago: Johnson Publishing, 1991). This is a chronological listing of events, with one paragraph on black Confederates. Bennett estimates that there were 38,000 black Confederates.

2. The Encyclopedia Britannica's *The Negro In American History* Vol. II *A Taste of Freedom* (London: Encyclopedia Britannica Education Corp., 1969), 359, says "a *few* slaves were forced to accompany their masters to war on the Confederate side." Harry A. Ploski and James Williams, Eds., *The Negro Almanac: A Reference Work Of The Afro-American* (New York: Wiley, 1983), 836, says "no definite records exist to determine how many black soldiers fought for the Confederacy." No black Confederate combat troops are mentioned in any of the encyclopedias published before 1964 consulted by the author. For example, *Collier's* Vol. 6, under the heading "The Civil War" 518-555, fails to address the issue of black support for the Confederacy.

3. *Collier's Encyclopedia*, Vol. 7, (New York: MacMillan Education Company), 1988, 144, "Comparative Manpower, The Confederate States of America," says "the slaves carried on the work of agriculture and in building military defenses."

4. Judge John Friday, Lincoln County Historical Association, Speech on the Confederate Flag, 1993. The author's own estimate, based primarily on Bennett's and Friday's, is that there were approximately 40,000 black Confederates.

5. *Charleston Mercury*, January 1,1861, Reprint *Negro History Bulletin*, 1961, Vol. 24, Issue 1-8, Pages 143-147, October 1960-May 1961

6. *Ibid,* April 24, 1861.

7. *Ibid*, April 28, 1861.

8. *Ibid.*

9. *Ibid*. April 30, 1861.

10. *Memphis Avalanche*. May 9,1861.

11. *The Negro Almanac*, 789-826, "The Revolutionary War." Bennett, *Before The Mayflower*, 48-69.

12. *Annals of Lincoln County*. (Charlotte: Sherrill, 1938), 175, 337.

13. U.S. Census of Lincoln County, North Carolina, 1861, National Archives. Copy in Lincoln County Library, Lincolnton, N.C.

14. Letter, July 1868, From William Bernie, Agent of the Bureau of Freedmen, Refugees and Abandoned Lands in Lincolnton,

North Carolina to Headquarters in Raleigh. The Records of the Freedman's Bureau, North Carolina State Archives, Raleigh; also in the National Archives, Washington, D.C.

15. *Annals of Lincoln County, North Carolina*, 102-103, 130. Interview with Frank Tomlin, a descendant of Isaac Cansler, Iron Station, N.C. Date of original interview unknown; reinterviewed January 18, 1994. *The City Register of Lincolnton,* 1867; *Gaston County Marriage Bonds, 1848-1888* Abstracted and Compiles by Libby Watt Goodnight, Linda Bell and Robert Carpenter (Ozark, Mo.: Yates Publishing Co., 1986), 145; "Co-Habitation Records of Lincoln County, North Carolina," Excerpted by Rudolph Young from *Freedom Marriages* (Microfilm) Raleigh: North Carolina Department of Archives.

16. Interview with various members of the Hunter family in August 1993.

17. *Ibid.* Interview, Odessa Hunter McCracklin, 1992 in Denver, North Carolina.

18. *Roster of North Carolina Troops.*(Raleigh: North Carolina Department of Archives & History) Vol. VII, 239, Item 15 - Frank Hunter, 16 Henry G. Hunter, 17, Henry Hunter. George W. Hunter, *Ibid.*, p. 238, Item 7: "Capt. George W. Hunter, Company B, 23rd Regiment of N.C. Troops; transferred from Company K. Wounded at Chancellorsville, Virginia, May 3, 1863. Died in hospital at Charlotte, N.C., on or about July 14, 1863, of wounds."

19. Interview with various members of the Hunter family in August 1993. Interview, Odessa Hunter McCracklin, 1992 in Denver, North Carolina. She was one of 20 children of Frank Hunter and one of three living in 1993.

20. See note 19.

21. Pension Roll - Lincoln County, by Beatties Ford Riflemen, Lincolnton Public Library; Adam Moore, Page 88, Item 158, Frank Hunter, Page 87, Item 120.

22. Speech by Pearlie Moore Watts, 1962. Mrs. Watts, the daughter of Adam Moore, is now over 90 years of age. She lives in the Hog Hill Community which is in Vale, North Carolina. The speech was delivered at the annual Busy Bee Day, always held on the last Sunday in May, to raise money to maintain three cemeteries in the area of Iron Station. The Busy Bee Club was founded at Mt. Vernon Baptist Church which was co-founded by Adam Moore.

23. Miller Roberts, Roster of North Carolina Troops, Company M, 16th Regiment North Carolina Troop. Division of Archives & History, Raleigh, North Carolina. Ramseur's Mill was named for the ancestors of Major General Stephen Dodson Ramseur. Miller Roberts was a descendant of John Moore. John Moore had a slave named Emanuel who was with John Moore at the Battle of Ramseur's Mill. Emanuel was an ancestor of Adam Moore. Conversations with Ella Magness Smith, the step-daughter of Adam Moore. Mrs. Ella Smith (1885-1961), lived next door to the author.

She became his baby-sitter in 1947 and they had a close relationship until her death. The dates of these conversations cannot be ascertained. Mrs. Smith not only talked about Adam Moore, but about the history of the Mt. Vernon Community in Iron Station, North Carolina.

24. Interview with Nathaniel Oates, Sr., Iron Station, North Carolina, 1993. Mr. Oates, 79, was neighbor of Adam Moore. Date of original interview unknown; reinterviewed January 18, 1994. Interview with Edith Lomax, a resident of Iron Station, North Carolina, 1993. Edith is a retired school teacher and the daughter of Wellington Lomax, a distant relative of Hiram Rhodes Revels, and the granddaughter of Bishop Thomas H. Lomax, co-founder of Livingston College in Salisbury, North Carolina, and Lomax Hannon College in Greenville, Alabama. Miss Lomax is a lifelong resident of Iron Station. She related this story: “Adam Moore was a cook in his company. Once the men did not have enough meat to eat, so Adam caught and cooked a camp dog. Some of them said to Adam, 'Adam this is good meat, where did you get it?' Adam answered, 'the good Lord will provide.' Later, some of the men asked Adam where the dog was that was always around during mess call. Adam answered 'the Lord knows.' ”

Additional information found in a grave marker, Mt. Vernon Church Cemetery, Mt. Vernon Church Road, Iron Station, Lincoln County; U.S. Census, Lincoln County; North Carolina Marriage Records.

25. *Ibid.*

26. Pearlie Moore Watts, “Busy Bee” speech, 1962. *Lincoln County, North Carolina Marriage Records, 1868-1886* Extracted and copyrighted by Paul Dellinger, 1986. *Marriage Bonds of Lincoln County, North Carolina*, 1898: “Adam Moore, 57, Black to Bettie Magness, 37.” Parents of Adam Moore listed as Abram and Jennie Moore of Gaston County, North Carolina. *Marriage Records [Lincoln County], 1887-1900* Extracted and copyrighted by Paul H. Dellinger, P.O. Box 5153, Lincolnton, N.C., 28092, (April, 1987), 81.

27. Edith Foster, interview with the author and Joe Depriest of the *Charlotte Observer*, September 1993. Miss Foster is the granddaughter of Adam Moore. She remembered the house and produced a photograph of a rambling, two-story home. The deed book of Lincoln County shows the purchase of land by Adam and Bettie Moore. Grave marker, Adam Moore, Mt. Vernon Church Cemetery, Mt. Vernon Church Road, Iron Station, Lincoln County, N.C.; U.S. Census, 1900, Lincoln County, Enumeration District 109, 16, National Archives, copy in Charlotte Public Library, Charlotte, N.C.; the Census shows Will Deck as the next-door neighbor. Will Deck was the father-in-law of Nathaniel Oates, one of the sources for this essay. North Carolina Marriage Records.

Black Confederates At Gettysburg
Richard Rollins

By 9 o'clock on the evening of July 2nd, Colonel E. Porter Alexander, of Longstreet's artillery recalled, "the field was silent. It was evident that we had not finished the job and would have to make a fresh effort in the morning." The fighting had hardly ceased when Charley, one of his two body servants, came looking for him, "with a fresh horse, affectionate congratulations on my safety, and , what was equally acceptable, something to eat. Negro servants hunting for their masters were a feature of the landscape that night."[1]

Indeed, black Southerners were a feature of any landscape dominated by Confederate armies. The Old South was a biracial, caste society, and the armed forces it fielded reflected that social reality. They were an extension of the social structure. Within this peculiar historical context, blacks supported the Confederacy in a variety of ways, from labor to actual combat, on virtually every major battlefield of the war, including Gettysburg.

Black support for the Confederacy, and armed participation in gray and butternut uniforms, has been largely overlooked or ignored by historians and the general reading public. One can read through nearly the entire mountain of literature on the military side of the Civil War without discovering that some blacks sided with the South.[2] The same can be said for the literature on the "common soldier," and it can be added that it also largely ignores blacks who fought for the Union.[3] The best of the latter category, Bell Wiley's *The Life of Johnny Reb*, acknowledges their presence but said little about them, glossing over their service to the South. After outlining the role of body servants he said that there were "several instances on record of servants thus engaged killing and capturing Federals." He also noted that the largest number of Negroes in Confederate service were engaged in manual labor, usually on fortifications or in transportation. Wiley mentioned, in an aside, that a black regiment was raised in New Orleans but rejected by the Confederate government, then discussed the history of the debate in the Confederacy over the arming of blacks, noting they were officially excluded until March of 1865, when the Confederate government finally recruited them. Wiley incorrectly says that "no assurance of freedom was given" and that "the ironic spectacle of Negroes fighting for the cause of Southern independence and the perpetuation of their own bondage was prevented from materializing by Lee's capitulation."[4]

Scholars writing on black life during the war also have usually ignored black Confederates. Wiley again serves as a useful spokesman.

"There seems to be no evidence that the Negro soldiers authorized by the Confederate government ever went into battle," he wrote in 1938, and added that if any other black Confederates ever saw battle "the per cent of Negro blood was sufficiently low for them to pass as whites."[5] Both of those statements are incorrect.

In fact some black Confederates did "see the elephant" with the support of the Confederate government. Even more to the point, thousands of black Southerners found their way into battle beneath the "starry cross" of their own volition, in spite of being officially prohibited by the Confederate government.[6] Despite being enslaved, or severely discriminated against when free, there were many whose motivations were strong enough to propel them to overcome major obstacles and fight for the South. Some clearly must have had the support of the white Southerners who served with them in locally-raised companies and regiments. And, judging by the letters preserved in the *Official Records*, many more would have joined them had they the opportunity.[7] They became an integral, important part of Southern armies. An English observer estimated there were 30,000 black servants in the Army of Northern Virginia in 1862.[8] Dr. Lewis Steiner, a member of the Sanitary Commission who happened to be in Frederick, Maryland, in the days just before Sharpsburg, noted their presence in the Army of Northern Virginia in 1862. The description he recorded in his diary probably could have been written in June of 1863. According to Steiner, about 5% of the combat troops were black.

> Wednesday, September 10
>
> At 4 o'clock this morning the Rebel army began to move from our town, Jackson's force taking the advance. The movement continued until 8 o'clock P.M., occupying 16 hours. The most liberal calculation could not give them more than 64,000 men. Over 3,000 negroes must be included in the number. . . . They had arms, rifles, muskets, sabers, bowie-knives, dirks, etc. They were supplied, in many instances, with knapsacks, haversacks, canteens, etc., and they were manifestly an integral portion of the Southern Confederacy army. They were seen riding on horses and mules, driving wagons, riding on caissons, in ambulances, with the staff of generals and promiscuously mixed up with all the Rebel horde.[9]

This historical blindness is easily understood. The numbers of armed black Confederates was always small, and they had little if any significant impact on the war. Most were not regularly enlisted, so the official documentation of their service is extremely thin. Most could not write; only a few letters or other accounts of the war by black Southerners exist. There are no famous incidents of black Confederates turning the tide of battle, no histories of their units. The largest body of evidence consists largely of anecdotes recorded in obscure places and pension applications filed half a century after the war and now tucked away in various state archives. Black Confederates fought, as they so often lived, with little visibility. Whites assumed their inferiority as well as their participation and support, and felt little need to describe or document it. Speaking of this lack of written records, black historian James Brewer has said, "the omission of the Confederate Negro from the pages of history seems like a striking instance of the death of the unfit in the struggle for historical survival."[10] It is also easy to understand the reluctance of Northern writers, both during and after the war, to admit that all blacks did not see them as liberators, or to be unable to comprehend their motivations. The current emphasis among black writers on the struggle for equality seems quite naturally to make black Confederates unattractive, and their motivations suspect.[11] Yet even the little information about these people that survives does fall into certain patterns and reveals at least a small part of their participation in the Confederate war effort and at Gettysburg.

This lack of interest in black Confederates began to change just a few years ago. Two scholarly articles have appeared, the best of which, Arthur W. Bergeron's "Free Men of Color in Gray," graced the pages of *Civil War History*.[12] A few articles have also been published in magazines aimed at a larger general reading public.[13] One book has already been written and at least two others are in the works.[14]

One scholar has estimated that up to 25% (65,000 out of 261,000) of free Negroes in the South and 15% (600,000 out of 4 million) of slaves sided with the South at one time during the war.[15] Whatever the actual figures, it will be difficult to conclusively prove any estimate.

Black Southerners found their way into Confederate armies in three ways. They served as body servants, taking up arms or in other ways demonstrating their support for the war. There were many individuals who enlisted in regular units on their own. Finally, there were several all-black or predominately-black units in Confederate armies or local defense forces. All three categories of black Confederates appeared at Gettysburg.

Probably the largest numbers were the ubiquitous "body servants." At Fort Mill, South Carolina there is an unusual monument, with the following inscription:

Dedicated to
the faithful slaves
who, loyal to a sacred trust
toiled for the support
of the Army with matchless
devotion and with sterling fidelity guarded
"Our Confederate States of America.[16]

Black servants seemed to be everywhere, especially early in the war. In 1861 the 3rd Alabama Infantry marched to war with 1,000 white soldiers in the ranks, and almost as many blacks. No one knows how many accompanied the regiment into Pennsylvania with Rodes' Division, or what role they played in the regiment's fights on July 1st.[17] This black presence was not unusual. It was strong enough in the Southern armies that one author has estimated that 12% of the Confederates' laboring manpower was black, while the North's was just 10%.[18] Samuel Cooper, Adjutant and Inspector General, issued an 1862 order that "the adjutants of the regiments throughout the Army will inquire into and report all cases of slaves serving with their respective regiments without written authority from their masters."[19] In other words, the Confederate government recognized that black Southerners had run off to join the army: the Southern army.

Body Servants were not officially part of the army, and therefore were rarely listed on muster rolls, and were never listed on hospital roles. Very little of the work they performed, much less how they lived, what they ate, and so on, was ever recorded, and precious little documentation has survived. Yet thousands upon thousands now lie beneath Southern soil, often nameless, with little or no recognition ever having been given to their role in the Confederacy. Few headstones lie over their graves in Southern soil with Confederate memorial markers decorated with the "Stars and Bars" on Confederate Memorial Day. In fact, even during the war, many had only first names. In the army they not only cooked the food and cleaned up the mess, but often drove and butchered the herds of beef and hogs. For their masters, and often for many others, they set up and struck tents, cleaned clothes, cared for the sick and wounded; in the Navy they stoked the fires in steamships and tended the sails on older ships. In the Cavalry, and for officers in the other branches, they fed and cared for the horses. In short, they performed virtually every act of labor one can imagine.

There are numerous accounts of servants performing medical duties and saving lives in other ways. A body servant of a Confederate soldier named Robertson, related to Confederate General Beverly Holcombe Robertson, found his wounded master on the battlefield at Gettysburg, given up for dead. He took care of him and took him to Virginia, thereby saving his life.[20] Robert W. Morgan, A Virginia private, was wounded during the early stages of Pickett's Charge. He had been shot in both feet, so he grabbed a second musket and hobbled to the rear where he was "taken care of by the faithful negro servant, Horace, who had been with us from the beginning and remained faithful to the end." Horace carried Robert on his back to an ambulance, then stayed with him all the way back to Virginia.[21] Another Virginian, Dr. Matt Butler, Assistant Surgeon of the 37th Virginia, had his horse shot out from under him and was wounded in the foot on July 2nd. He limped along with the help of a black helper, Jim. They passed a woman baking cornpone over an open fire, and both men were extremely hungry. They asked the woman for some but she refused, saying she was baking it for a Yankee Colonel, and named him. They left her and eventually found a place to hide from the Yankees. The negro said "Now Doctah, you got a gold dollah, give it to me, I'se gwine out to git some eatins." He soon returned with a large serving of pone, dripping in butter and also carrying a gallon of buttermilk. When the doctor asked how he had gotten it, Jim replied "I des told dat lady, de kunnel am waitin' for his pone."[22]

Not all body servants were slaves owned by whites. Many were free Negroes with attachments—economic and otherwise—to the people they served. Robert Greene, in *Black Defenders*, lists several who were hired, not owned, and who served for three or four years.[23] Stonewall Jackson's servant, Jim Lewis, was "inconsolable" at Jackson's death. He led Jackson's horse in the funeral procession, then returned to the army and served Colonel "Sandie" Pendleton at Gettysburg and after, until Pendleton died at Fisher's Hill in 1864.[24] Robert E. Lee's cook, William Mack Lee, was a free Negro who served the General throughout the war and until the General's death in 1870.[25]

It seems that nearly every Confederate officer who wrote an account of his exploits at Gettysburg had at least one servant, and often two. E. Porter Alexander hired two servants, Charley and Abram, in early 1862. He describes Charley as being 15 years old, "medium tall & slender, ginger-cake colored, & well-behaved & good dispositioned boy." Charley stayed with him through the entire war and Alexander said "I had to give him a little licking but twice—once for robbing a pear tree in the garden of the Keach house, in which we were staying on the outskirts of Richmond below Rocketts, & once in Pa. just before Gettysburg, for stealing apple-brandy & getting tight on it."[26] This was the same Charley who brought him food at the close of July 2nd. Surgeon Spencer Welch of the 13th South Carolina of McGowan's Brigade had at least two. On the march into Pennsylvania one of them remarked that he "don't like Pennsylvania at all" because he "sees no black folks." When one got lost in Maryland, he sent home for another, who brought with him most welcome stories of life at home.[27] More typical than Alexander's and Welch's accounts, Moxley Sorrel simply noted that he had sent "my man" to an abandoned farm house for food on the morning of July 3rd.[28]

Resourceful servants like Alexander's Charley became excellent and important foragers. One such individual was dubbed "General Boeyguard" in honor of his ability to find and capture food. He was a cook who often left the line of march into Pennsylvania at daybreak and did not reappear until the column had halted for the night. He always returned laden with hams, chickens, fruit and other produce from the local farms. "No one ever bothered to inquire too closely about how he had obtained such choice viands in enemy country" wrote one officer.[29]

Another, Dick Poplar, was a well-known caterer and cook in Petersburg before the war. He was taken prisoner at Gettysburg and sent to Pt. Lookout, where he resisted Federal entreaties to take an oath of allegiance. He spent 20 months in prison.[30] Like Poplar, many of these cooks found their way into combat. Perhaps some of their enthusiasm come through in a story related in terms common to the Civil War era if not to ours. One veteran remembered that the cooks of his company often joined in the fight:

> You might as well endeavor to keep ducks from water as to attempt to hold in the cooks of our company, when firing or fighting is at hand. In fact, an order has been frequently issued to keep darkies in the rear in time of battle, but although I lectured my boy about it, I was surprised to find him behind me at Manassas, rifle in hand, shouting out: "Go in, Massa! give it to 'em, boys! Now you've got 'em, and give 'em H-ll."[31]

On the way to Gettysburg some of the men of Kershaw's Brigade had dismantled and burned some rail fencing, thereby breaking orders against destroying Yankee property. Their punishment was to march for a time under the command of the company's black cooks, much to the merriment of other white troops.[32]

Black Southerners found their way into combat units in the Confederate armies as body servants but a few also enlisted in regular units as individuals. Any estimate of the numbers involved will be merely guess-work, though one reliable historians believes there were 3,000 from Louisiana alone.[33]

At least three, and probably more, fought at Gettysburg. Charles F. Lutz was born in St. Landry Parish in 1842, the son of a white father and mulatto mother. He enlisted in Company F, 8th Louisiana Infantry in 1861 and went to Virginia with the brigade commanded by Gen. Richard Taylor. These men came to be known as the Louisiana Tigers, one of the fiercest, most notoriously aggressive units in all the South, both on and off the field of battle. They were "wharf rats," workers and toughs from the docks of New Orleans. They fought at Winchester, Cross Keys, and Port Republic with Stonewall Jackson in the Valley campaign of 1862 and in the Seven Days, Second Manassas, Sharpsburg, and Fredericksburg with Lee and the Army of Northern Virginia. Lutz was captured at Chancellorsville along with about 100 men from the 8th. He spent two weeks in prison, was released and back in the Army of Northern Virginia in June. On the evening of July 2nd he charged up Cemetery Hill with Hays' Louisiana Brigade. The Confederates overran and captured three Federal lines and several cannon. They paused to regroup and were soon attacked by several brigades of Federals who held their fire until within twenty feet of the

Louisianans. The volley killed or wounded many Southerners, including Lutz. He took a bullet in the left arm and was captured for a second time. He was eventually exchanged again, but went home to recuperate from his Gettysburg wound and never returned to Virginia. He was discharged in May, 1865, and received a Confederate pension in 1900.[34]

William Colen Revels was 20 years old when he volunteered for Confederate service, and was one of the first men of any color in Surry County, North Carolina, to march off to war. He spent the greater part of the war in the 21st North Carolina infantry, and is listed on the rolls as a "negro." He was wounded in the leg at Winchester, and caught a bullet in the right thigh at Gettysburg, probably on East Cemetery Hill on July 2nd. According to research by Richard Manning of Winston-Salem, North Carolina, Revels was one of at least 5 black Confederates in the 21st, although the only one that can currently be documented as having served at Gettysburg.[35] Finally, at least one bit of oral history exists that indicates that Federal soldiers spotted two or more black Confederate soldiers in the Culp farm on the evening of July 2nd.[36]

A third black Confederate was described by Colonel Arthur Fremantle, a British officer of the Coldstream Guards, observing the Army of Northern Virginia in 1863 and taking part in the Gettysburg campaign. On the retreat to Virginia he spotted a black Southerner, "dressed in full Yankee uniform, with rifle at full cock, leading along a barefooted white man, with whom he had evidently changed clothes. General Longstreet stopped the pair, and asked the black man what it meant." He replied that two white Confederates had captured the Yank, then had a bit too much brandy, whereupon they turned the prisoner over to him. Fremantle was impressed with the man's earnestness and seriousness, as well as the "supreme contempt with which he spoke to his prisoner."[37]

A fourth probably marched with the 14th Tennessee Infantry. They came up with Archer's Brigade and helped open the battle on July 1st. On the third they formed the center of the line led by Col. B.D. Fry. Stories have circulated for years about a "black Corporal" who picked up a flag near Emmitsburg Road on July third, climbed over the fences and charged up the ridge, only to be shot just before reaching the stone wall.[38] He has not been positively identified.

In addition, the *New York Herald* reported that on July 1st a group of armed black Confederates was captured: "Among the rebel prisoners who were marched through Gettysburg there were observed seven negroes in uniform and fully accoutered as soldiers."[39]

Black musicians were so common that the Confederate Congress passed an act in 1862 providing that "whenever colored persons are employed as musicians in any regiment or company, they shall be entitled to the same pay now allowed by law to musicians regularly enlisted."[40] Several of these were at Gettysburg. "Old Dick" Slate was a veteran of the Mexican War who enlisted as a drummer with the 18th

Virginia Infantry in 1861. Along with fellow drummer George Price and fifer Austin Dix, all were listed as "free men of color." Their regiment served in Garnett's Brigade of Pickett's Division. There is no documentation indicating where they were on the afternoon of July 3rd. General John B. Gordon had Josepheus Black and two other musicians in his entourage.[41]

Black Southerners supported the Confederate war effort not only as servants, as individuals in regularly enlisted white units, but also in units that were composed entirely, or almost entirely, of blacks, both free and bonded. These fall naturally into three categories. The first group are units about which little is known. Sightings of unnamed units of black Confederates occurred several times in both the Eastern and Western theaters.[42] The second were units of regularly-enlisted Negroes who were usually free. There were at least four in Louisiana, including the Louisiana Native Guards, a 1,300-man regiment raised in 1861 and who participated in the defense of New Orleans.[43] There were at least five similar units active in the defense of Mobile and several others around the South.[44] The all-black units of slaves and former slaves raised by the Confederate government in March and April 1865 make up a third category.[45]

Most of the black Confederate musicians enlisted as individuals on their own, but at least one larger unit may have appeared at Gettysburg. McGowan's (Gregg's) Brigade of South Carolina infantry had an all-black or predominately-black band. It's interesting to picture them in gray uniforms, crossing the Potomac on a hot June afternoon, flags flying over their heads as they played "Dixie" on fife and drum. There were at least 14 black musicians in the Brigade during the war. All were listed as "free persons of color" except one, William Rose, a slave who apparently ran away from his master to join the army.[46] They were listed on the muster-rolls of each company; two of them who enlisted in 1861 in this group were blind, and one served six months before he dropped out.[46] The Band marched with McGowan's Brigade through the entire war with the Army of Northern Virginia, including Gettysburg.[47]

The wagon train that carried the wounded back the Virginia, 17 miles long and taking 34 hours to pass a given point in southern Pennsylvania, was driven in part by black teamsters. Some of these men also drove cattle through the woods and thickets to feed Lee's army from Virginia to Gettysburg and back.[48] In the wagons black servants fed and cared for white wounded Confederates like the ones named Robertson and Morgan cited earlier, and probably a few wounded black ones too. One resident of Greencastle described the army on its retreat and recorded that "the common soldiers seemed to be either too stupid to speak, or else forbidden to give a true account of the battle, but all the way through the colored portion declared that they were badly whipped."[49] One Confederate officer recalled that while the wagons were massed at Williamsport waiting for the water to recede, the Yankees approached and began shelling the area. Another officer was amazed to observe that not a single teamster was to be seen. He could not account for it, until he happened to look toward the river, and there saw hundreds of black heads just showing above the water. The negro teamsters with one accord had plunged into the river to escape the shells, and were submerged to the neck![50]

When Yankees appeared on July 5th, however, these same teamsters were probably the 500 "wagoners" that another officer says were organized "into companies, and armed . . . with the weapons of the wounded men found in the train." Slightly wounded officers, quartermasters and commissaries were pressed into service as officers. With about 2100 regular soldiers they stood off a Yankee force of much larger numbers headed by Buford and Kilpatrick. "This came to be known as 'the wagoner's fight' in our army," recalled one officer, "from the fact that so many of them were armed and did such gallant service in repelling the attack made on our right. . ." [51]

As he observed the retreat Col. Fremantle wrote about the role that black Confederates might play in the war if only the Confederate government might grasp the potential. One does not have to agree with the assumptions he made about the motivation of black Southerners to agree with the basic concept expressed by Colonel Fremantle in his last sentence:

> I am of the opinion that the Confederates could, if they chose, convert a great number [of the black population] into soldiers; and from the affection which undoubtedly exists as a general rule between the slaves and their masters, I think that they would prove more efficient than black troops under any other circumstances. But I do not imagine such an experiment will be tried, except as a very last resort.[52]

And of course, his last sentence was correct, for in March of 1865 the Confederate government officially enlisted black Confederates in its armed forces.[53]

Gettysburg did not end with the retreat. Just as the war lingered on well into the twentieth century in the memories of the white soldiers who fought at Gettysburg, so it also remained a significant event in the minds of black Confederates. Two examples will illustrate the point. A Major from South Carolina died on the retreat, and after the war his widow, brother-in-law, and former servant returned to Pennsylvania to recover the remains. The servant had stayed with the officer until the end, was with him when he died, and buried him. "Under the guidance of the colored man" the family dug up the remains and took them home.[54] Captain William McLeod of the 38th Georgia was mortally wounded in the action around Barlow's Knoll n July 1st.

His servant Moses went on the battlefield, retrieved McLeod, and carried him to a temporary hospital at the Jacob Keim farm, where McLeod died. Moses wrapped him in a blanket and buried him, remained with the men of Gordon's brigade during the retreat to Winchester, then took Mcleod's personal effects back to the family plantation near Swainsboro, Georgia, where he remained after the war. In 1865 Moses and Mcleod's brother-in-law drove a wagon from Georgia to Gettysburg, exhumed the remains, and carried them home.

Notes

1. Quoted in Richard Wheeler, *Witness to Gettysburg* (New York: Harper and Row, 1987), 219.

2. The large number of books that might be cited here prohibits listing them. It would include nearly every book ever written on military aspects of the War.

3. Again, many works could be cited here, but two will suffice: Bell Irvin Wiley, *The Life and Times of Johnny Reb* (Baton Rouge: Louisiana State University Press, 1978) and James I. Robertson, *Soldiers In Blue and Gray* (Columbia: South Carolina University Press, 1988).

4. Wiley, *Johnny Reb*, 330.

5. Bell Irvin Wiley, *Southern Negroes, 1861-1865* (Baton Rouge: Louisiana State University Press, 1938), 160-161. See also C. Peter Riley, *Slaves and Freedmen in Civil War Louisiana* (Baton Rouge: The Louisiana State University Press, 1976).

6. For the details of the debate within the Confederacy over the use of black troops, see Robert F. Durden, *The Gray and the Black* (Baton Rouge: Louisiana State University Press, 1972).

7. See, for example, *The War of the Rebellion: A Compilation of the Official Records of the Union and Confederate Armies Three Parts* (Washington, 1899), hereafter cited as *OR*, Series IV, 3, 1193; IV, 3, 693; I, 49, 1193; I, 49, 1277.

8. [An English Observer], *Battlefields of the South* (New York: John Bradburn, 1865), Vol. I., p. 58.

9. Quoted in Isaac W. Heysinger, *Antietam and the Maryland and Virginia Campaigns of 1862* (New York: Neale Publishing Company, 1912), 122-123.

10. James Brewer, *The Confederate Negro: Virginia's Craftsmen and Military Laborers, 1861-1865* (Durham, N.C.: Duke University Press, 1969.

11. For example, see Ira Berlin, *Freedom: A Documentary History of Emancipation* (New York: Cambridge University Press, 1982). Berlin includes many documents illustrating Southern racist attitudes, but none revealing that Southern blacks served the

Confederacy.

12. Arthur W. Bergeron, Jr., "Free Men of Color in Grey," *Civil War History* XXXII(1986), 247-255. See also Mary F. Berry, "Negro Troops in Blue and Gray: The Louisiana Native Guards, 1861-1863," *Louisiana History* 8(1967), 165-190. Most of the latter is devoted to the Native Guards who were Union troops, not the Confederates. Alexia J. Helsley, "Black Confederates," *South Carolina Historical Magazine* 74(July, 1973), 184-187.

13. J. K. Obatala, "The Unlikely Story of Blacks Who Were Loyal To Dixie," *Smithsonian* 9(1979), 94-101; Wayne R. Austerman, "Virginia's Black Confederates," *Civil War Quarterly* VIII(1987), 46-54; Greg Tyler, "Rebel Drummer Henry Brown, *Civil War Times Illustrated* February, 1989, 22-23; Scott E. Sallee, "Black Soldier of the Confederacy," *Blue and Gray* 1990, 24-25; Greg Tyler, "Article Brings Notice To A Unique Rebel, *Civil War Times Illustrated* May/June 1990, 57,69; Edward C. Smith, "Calico, Black and Gray: Women and Blacks in the Confederacy," *Civil War* XXIII(1990), 10-16; and Jeff Carroll, "Dignity, Courage and Fidelity," *Confederate Veteran* November/December 1990, 26-27.

14. H. C. Blackerby, *Blacks in Blue and Gray: Afro-American Service in the Civil War* (Tuscaloosa, Ala.: Portals Press, 1973); Ervin Jordan, Jr., is working on Black Confederates in Virginia and Charles K. Barrow, of Atlanta, is researching a wider topic.

15. Ervin L. Jordan, Jr., quoted in the *Richmond Times-Dispatch*, "Virginia' section, November 5, 1990, 1,7.

16. Blackerby, *Black and Gray*, ii.

17. Wiley, *Southern Negro*, 134.

18. Jay S. Hoar, "Black Glory: Our Afro-American Civil War Old Soldiery," *Gettysburg Magazine* January, 1990, 125.

19. OR, IV, 2, 86.

20. Blackerby, *Blacks in Gray*," 22.

21. William H. Morgan, *Personal Reminiscences of the War of 1861-1865* (Freeport, N.Y.: Books for Libraries Press, 1911), 167-168.

22. Quoted in Coco, *Bloodstained*, 54.

23. Robert Greene, Ed., *Black Defenders of America* (Chicago: Johnson P:ublishing Co., 1974).

24. Austerman, "Black Confederates," 51.

25. William Mack Lee, *History of the Life of Rev. Wm. Mack Lee* (Norfolk, Va.: Beale Publishing Co., 1916).

26. E. Porter Alexander, *Fighting For The Confederacy: The Personal Recollections Of General Edward Porter Alexander* Edited By Gary W. Gallagher (Chapel Hill: University of North Carolina Press, 1989), 76-77.

27. Spencer Glasgow Welch, *A Confederate Surgeon's Letters to His Wife* (New York: The Neale Publishing Company, 1911), 58.

28. Moxley Sorrel, *Reflections of a Confederate Staff Office*r Ed.

Bell Wiley (Jackson, Tenn.: McCowat-Mercer Press, 1958), 152.

29. Austerman, "Black Confederates," 50.

30. Francis W. Springer, *War for What?* (Nashville, Tenn: Bill Coats Ltd, 1990), 175.

31. *Battlefields*, 282.

32. Gregory A. Coco, *On the Bloodstained Field II Gettysburg* (Gettysburg: Thomas Publications, 1989), 16-17.

33. John D. Winters, *The Civil War in Louisiana* (Baton Rouge: Louisiana State University Press, 1963), 21.

34. Bergeron, "Free Men of Color," 248-249. See also Andrew Booth, *Records of Louisiana Confederate Soldiers and Louisiana Confederate Commands* (New Orleans, 1920), Volume III, Book I, 815; Compiled Service Records of Confederate Soldiers Who Served in Volunteer Organizations From Louisiana, State Archives.

35. Hester Bartlett Jackson, Ed., *Surry County Soldiers in the Civil War*(Charlotte: Delmar Printing, p. 148; Weymouth T. Jordan, Jr., Comp., *North Carolina Troops, 1861-1865, A Roster* (Raleigh: Division of Archives and History, 1977), VI, 608; Agnes Moseley Wells, *1860 Census of Surry County, North Carolina* (Mt. Airy, N.C.: Privately Printed, 1983), p. 103. I thank Richard Manning for this information. He has identified numerous black North Carolinians who served as servants and soldiers.

36. Dr. William Ridinger, a Licensed Battlefield Guide at Gettysburg since the 1940s, remembers W. C. Storrick, Park Historian in the 1920s and 30s, telling him that Union veterans who visited Gettysburg told Storrick that they saw black Confederate soldiers at the Culp Farm on the evening of July 2nd. Conversation with William Ridinger, July 3, 1993.

37. Walter Lord, Ed., *The Fremantle Diary, Being the Journal of Lieutenant Colonel James Arthur Lyon Fremantle, Coldstream Guards, on His Three Months in the Southern States* (Boston: Little, Brown, 1954), 225.

38. Wallace Cross believes his name was George B. Powell, who is recorded as having picked up the flag and been wounded just short of the stone wall. C. Wallace Cross, Jr., *Ordeal By Fire: A History of the Fourteenth Tennessee Volunteer Infantry Regiment, C.S.A.* (Clarksville: Clarksville Montgomery County Museum, 1990), 72. My thanks to Wallace Cross for this citation. There is room for disagreement here. Barry Crompton of East Brighton, Australia, believes the black corporal and colorbearer shot down might have been Boney Smith, who was not carried on the rolls. He cites R. T. Mockbee, "Historical Sketch of the 14th Tennessee Regt of Infantry, CSA, 1861-1865," William McComb Papers, Eleanor S. Brockenbrough Library, The Museum of the Confederacy, Richmond. My thanks to Barry Crompton. The 14th apparently had several blacks in their ranks, and these may have been the men captured on July 1st, described below. Over 1,300 men served

in the 14th during the war. So far I have checked 300 of their records without finding information that would shed light on the name of the individual in question.

39. *New York Herald*, Quoted in Coco, *Bloodstained*, 30. Thanks to Patrick Massengill for this citation.

40. *OR*, IV, I, 1059.

41. Obatala, " Unlikely," 98.

42. Rollins, "Black Confederates."

43. Berry, Bergeron.

44. Rollins, "Black Confederates."

45. Ibid., and Burke Davis, *To Appomattox: Nine April Days.*

46. *South Carolina Troops In Confederate Service*, A. S. Salley, Jr., Comp. (Columbia: The R. L. Bryan Co., 1913), I, 218, n. 17. 219. The precise number present at Gettysburg cannot be calculated. The rolls are incomplete, but several indicated in their pension applications service as late as 1864.

47. See *Black Defenders*. Also Blackerby, *Blacks In Gray*, 18, and *South Carolina Troops*.

48. J. F. J. Caldwell, *The History of A Brigade of South Carolinians, known first as "Gregg's" and subsequently as "McGowan's Brigade* (Philadelphia: King and Baird Printers, 1866).

49. Blackerby, *Blacks in Gray*, 30.

50. Quoted in Jacob Hoke, *The Great Invasion of 1863, Or, General Lee in Pennsylvania* (Dayton, Ohio: W. J. Shuey, 1887), 501.

51. Quoted in Coco, *Bloodstained*, 96.

52. Hoke, *Great Invasion*, 489-490.

53. Fremantle, *Diary*, 225.

54. Durden, *The Gray and the Black.*

54. Hoke, *Great Invasion*, 495-496.

55. Conversation with Michael Hofe, June 11, 1994. This is but one fragment of a long, fascinating story. See Michael Hofe, *With No Stain Upon My Stone* (Gettysburg: Thomas Publications, forthcoming).

Section II

Reviews

Professor James Brewer, 1917-1974

Clio's Forgotten Son: James H. Brewer and *The Confederate Negro*

Ervin L. Jordan, Jr.

The Confederate Negro: Virginia's Craftsmen and Military Laborers, 1861-1865. By James H. Brewer. (Durham, North Carolina: Duke University Press, 1969. xvii +212 pp. Map, illustrations, tables, notes, bibliography, and index.)

On the morning of March 9, 1974, James and Zadye Brewer were having breakfast at their home. As Brewer read the morning newspaper, he playfully teased his wife while sipping from a cup of coffee. Suddenly, he slumped over in his chair. Mrs. Brewer thought it a continuation of his joking, but she quickly realized something was horribly wrong. An ambulance was summoned but James Brewer, a professor of Afro-American history and co-director of Afro-American and African studies at the University of North Carolina at Chapel Hill for less than a year, was dead from a massive heart attack at age 56. His funeral, held at Durham's B. N. Duke Auditorium three days later, was attended by faculty and students of North Carolina Central University, the University of North Carolina and Virginia State College, as well as representatives of Sigma Pi Phi and Omega Psi Phi fraternities, the Durham Committee on Negro Affairs and other organizations, friends, relatives and neighbors. The *New York Times* praised him as a eminent scholar in the field of black history. He was buried in Beechwood Cemetery, a short distance from his home.[1]

Throughout his academic career, Brewer sought to integrate blacks into the American mainstream through scholarly reexaminations of all aspects of their history. He metaphorically described blacks as forgotten casualties of yesterday in unmourned graves, victims of historians' indifference, distortions and neglect: "Robert Vann and his controversial political philosophy have become a casualty of history" (1958); "In a lonely grave . . . forgotten and unknown, lies John Mitchell, Jr., a casualty of history" (1958); "Today, in a lonely unmarked grave, forgotten and unknown, lies the Confederate Negro—a casualty of history."[2]

Ironically, nearly 20 years after Brewer's death, he too, has suffered the same fate: obscurity. The purpose of this historiographical essay is threefold: to define James Howard Brewer, to analyze and evaluate his work, and to reassess the impact and influence of his acclaimed classic, *The Confederate Negro.*

Clio's Forgotten Son
AN HISTORIAN AND HIS TIMES

The passage of time, the number of books and articles a scholar produces and his or her professional memberships does not necessarily guarantee future generations will remember one's writings as contributions to an understanding of the past. In three studies of black historians, Brewer is briefly mentioned or not at all. The most recent of these monographs, published in 1986 and considered the foremost study of professional black historians, does not include him despite his association with black historians such as Luther P. Jackson and John Hope Franklin.[3]

One likely cause for this exclusion is that *The Confederate Negro* is Brewer's only book (it remains the sole book-length study of black Virginians during the war) and his small output of published articles. Long out of print, his book surprisingly has never appeared in paperback, yet is recognized and favorably mentioned by reputable historians for its continuing value in a variety of historical studies: Civil War, Southern, Confederate, African-American and slavery.[4]

Nine months prior to his untimely death, Brewer outlined the black experience in the South: "The building of the Southern civilization . . . is the result of our brawn, our sweat, our tears, and dexterity. We were not brought here as the result of an act of goodwill; we were brought here for purposes of exploitation. We as a people are the most massive artificial transplant of living organisms outside our native habitat in human history. By the laws of Darwin and Spencer we ought to be extinct."[5]

His scholarly interests included slavery in Virginia and North Carolina and black newspapers and their editors. One of his articles broke new ground with its examination of 17th century black property owners and was subsequently cited by other scholars. His reviews and essays (for which he applied and received research grants), objective and meticulously researched, concise and edifying, appeared in *The Journal of Southern History, The Negro History Bulletin, The North Carolina Historical Review, The Journal of The Association of Social Science Teachers* and *The William and Mary Quarterly.* The North Carolina Mutual Life Insurance Company issued Brewer's *Negro Progress Calendar* in 1968. He lectured widely and was respected by his peers, as demonstrated by his memberships in the Association for the Study of Afro-American Life and History, the Association of Social Science Teachers, the North Carolina Historical Society, the Organization of American Historians and the Southern Historical Society.[6]

James Howard Brewer was born in Pittsburgh, Pennsylvania, on September 18, 1917, the son of Bertha and Henry Brewer. In 1917, there were approximately nine million black Americans. The last surviving Confederate general, Felix Huston Robertson of Texas, would live for another eleven years. It was the year of birth for four African-Americans who would make outstanding contributions in the areas of poetry, drama and music: Gwendolyn Brooks, Ossie Davis, Dizzy Gillespie and Lena Horne. It was also a bloody and violent year, one which saw the United States' entry into World War I, race riots in Houston and East St. Louis and 38 blacks lynched.[7]

After a public school education and graduation from Peabody High in 1936, Brewer and his twin brother, John, attended Virginia State College (now University) in Petersburg from 1936 to 1940; he received a baccalaureate degree in history. James attended the University of Pittsburgh and obtained a master of arts degree in history in 1941, but World War II interrupted his graduate education. He served in the army from 1942 until 1946, receiving an honorable discharge with the rank of captain of military intelligence. He then returned to graduate school and received a doctorate degree from Pittsburgh in 1948 for his dissertation on antebellum North Carolina slavery.[8]

African-American recipients of advanced academic degrees were relatively rare during the 1940s and 1950s and desperately sought after by black institutions. Brewer taught history in Pittsburgh public schools and at Fayetteville State Teachers College, North Carolina, from 1946 to 1949. He returned to Virginia State College as an associate professor of history and taught there until 1963. Doubtless, he was delighted to come back to his alma mater and renew his acquaintance with Luther Porter Jackson (1892-1950), a Kentucky native who devoted his life to teaching, community service and Afro-Virginian history. "Your coming is welcome to us," Jackson said to him, "inasmuch as it will serve to relieve us of some very large classes. I will gladly give you at least one of my classes. Perhaps you would like to teach my course on the slave system."[9]

Jackson was a disciple of Carter G. Woodson (1875-1950), who founded the Association for the Study of Negro Life and History (now the Association for the Study of Afro-American Life and History) in 1915 to educate the public, sponsor research and promote the achievements of American blacks. Woodson dedicated his life to ensuring an accurate historical record of black achievement; he established *The Journal of Negro History*, a quarterly which published scholarly articles and documents on the African-American experience and served as its editor until his death. Woodson organized Negro History Week (which evolved into Black History Month during the 1960s) in 1926; eleven years later he founded *The Negro History Bulletin*, designed for secondary school teachers, students and the general public.

The workaholic Jackson was a role model for Brewer and other young black scholars; nearly twenty years after his premature death (both he and Brewer died while in their fifties) Brewer wrote a laudatory preface for a reprint of a Jackson monograph: "In this book, my former history professor is content to be a scholar. His style is simple, and his tone is measured. He has presented the facts as they are, believing that facts properly set forth will speak for themselves." These words paralleled Brewer's own philosophy of scholarly research.[10]

In addition to Jackson's influence, Brewer had his own ideas about an academic teaching career and rejected what he considered as stereotypical occupations for educated black men: "I had the choice of being a black lawyer, a black doctor, a black preacher, a black mortician, or a black professor. Those were the existing realities. I didn't like medicine or law. I didn't want to fool with dead bodies. And I wasn't particular about preaching."

His teaching career continued at North Carolina Central University (1963-1973) with a joint appointment as visiting professor of Afro-American history and acting co-director of the University of North Carolina at Chapel Hill's Afro-American and African studies curriculum (1972-1974). Appointed a full professor at the University of North Carolina in May of 1973, Brewer was its first black history professor and taught Afro-American history classes beginning with the fall semester. He served on educational and advisory committees and as a consultant for public school systems and colleges in Florida, Georgia, Nebraska, New York, North Carolina, Pennsylvania and Wisconsin. He found the time and energy to serve as a visiting professor at Duke University and as a scholar-in-residence at the Smithsonian Institute during 1965-1966.

Brewer's daily schedule was active and full. He chaired the athletic committee and served as announcer for North Carolina Central's football games, but as a teacher he truly was in his element. An advocate of black history long before African-American studies became fashionable in academic circles, Brewer believed the teaching of African-American history had a constructive effect on black students longing for role models and white students indoctrinated in the American myth of whites-only history-makers as worthy of recognition and study.[11]

Students fought to enroll in his classes for he was widely regarded as a master teacher. Frequently, they were invited to the Brewer home for socials. They looked up to him, and in turn he spoke well of and defended them: "I find one of the unfulfilled needs of black students . . . is ego models in the world of academia. . . . When a black kid comes to this campus where does he find black adults? Right with a pick and shovel. These kids need black professors. . . . A lot of these kids come to talk to me. It's kind of a catharsis for them." Brewer taught two classes each semester but worked at his university office daily and maintained regular hours for students who needed to see him. Once, his wife enrolled in one of her husband's courses to renew her teaching certificate and described him as the best teacher she ever had. When Mrs. Brewer earned a final grade of "A" and expressed suspicion about favoritism, Brewer insisted she rightfully earned her grade.[12]

With the passage of time, Brewer became the father of three, an uncle of thirteen nieces and nephews and a grandfather. He boxed as a young man and while at Virginia State was an all-conference football player; he remained a lifelong fan of basketball and football. As a working historian, Brewer made numerous trips to archival repositories accompanied by Mrs. Brewer and trusted her research on his behalf. At home, he helped with household chores and worked in a study which he shared with her as a sewing room because he enjoyed having her near him.

Brewer typed with two fingers, his favorite pipe unlit and clenched between his teeth. Brewer always sought Mrs. Brewer's critique of his writing, consulted her about his research and introduced her to visiting historians and prominent guests; he considerately included her during his conversations with them. He dedicated *The Confederate Negro* to "the women in my life": his wife Zadye, daughter Bertha, and sisters Anna and Isabell.

A many-dimensioned man with a straightforward personality, Brewer was an excellent bridge player who also enjoyed fishing. He willingly cleaned his catch because he did not know how to cook, yet disliked eating fish because of the bones. The Brewers vacationed at Virginia Beach where they owned a vacation home and visited Haiti. He liked dogs (Great Danes) and collected swords, pistols and rifles. An avid reader, Brewer preferred black history and constantly took notes; he was a gregarious host who relished inviting guests to his home for an evening of conversation, usually about history.[13]

A scholar must balance scholarship and professional activities with public service and civic commitment. While Brewer never matched the intensity of civic activism of Luther P. Jackson or the publication output of Carter G. Woodson, he nevertheless took part in the growing civil rights movement. Certain social and legal customs were hard for him to easily repudiate; Mrs. Brewer once shocked him by boldly drinking from a public whites-only water foundation. The Brewers participated in civil rights marches and even put up their home as bail money on behalf of Virginia State College students arrested during a Richmond desegregation march.

Professional awards and recognition were scarce for Brewer during his lifetime. He was appointed in 1960 by Virginia State's president to represent the college on the Virginia Civil War Commission University Board to plan commemorations of the war's centennial. Other honors included the 1970 Mayflower Award for *The Confederate Negro* as the best non-fiction book published in North Carolina and a plaque for outstanding contributions to black history. He was the posthumous recipient of the University of North Carolina's 1974 Nicolas Salgo Distinguished Teaching Award for "excellence in inspirational teaching of undergraduate students" and the university established a scholarship in his honor.[14]

THE WRITING OF *THE CONFEDERATE NEGRO*

As early as 1950, Brewer was acutely aware of the necessity for a new look at American slavery. He believed "slavery varied from state to state, and often within sections of the same state" and that further study of slave labor patterns would enable a clearer knowledge "into the overall picture of slavery and the work and management of human chattel."[15]

Before Brewer, few scholars were interested in blacks as consenting Confederate allies, Charles Harris Wesley and Bell Irvin Wiley among the exceptions. Wesley, an African-American, published *The Collapse of The Confederacy* in 1937. He briefly outlined the utilization of black military laborers, laws and other facets affecting them. His study provided little analysis and basically mentioned the practice with a few examples and dismissed the entire effort as "the last desperate measure of the Confederacy." Wesley's book was published by a black publishing firm, therefore, he may not have been inclined to praise or objectively contemplate blacks as acquiescent Confederate volunteers.

The following year saw publication of Wiley's *Southern Negroes, 1861-1865*, a detailed, subject-oriented analysis of blacks in the Confederacy which, unfortunately, reflected the racial mores of the 1930s by its use of contemporary derogatory terms for blacks. The chapter on military laborers, ostensibly clinical in its assertion that they were chiefly employed in building defensive works and fortifications, dehumanized blacks as things not persons. Wiley's paternalistic tone and broad generalizations essentially concentrated on white Confederate attitudes and reactions; individual blacks were named, typically in comic anecdotes at their expense.[16]

Also in 1938, Walter Adolphe Roberts (1886-1962), a native of Kingston, Jamaica, published a well-received and laudatory biography of Confederate Admiral Raphael Semmes, commander of the *Alabama*, the South's most famous merchant shipping raider. Roberts, a journalist who published more than twenty books of poetry, plays, fiction and history, lived and worked in the United States between 1911 and 1956 before returning to Jamaica. He was the first black to write a history of a Confederate military officer and though not a trained historian, contacted the Semmes family and conducted detailed research in Jamaica, Alabama, Louisiana and Washington, D. C. Roberts' reasons for writing the Semmes biography are a mystery as he did not include a preface or introduction. He also noted that Semmes "believed the white man must dominate at all costs."[17]

Any understanding of *The Confederate Negro*'s scope and theme requires cognizance of the period during which it was written. Brewer began his quest during the beginnings of the black civil rights movement.

During his preliminary research trips in 1958 and 1962, black Americans were beginning to organize for their civil rights to demand an end to legalized racial segregation. Willing to seek the advice and assistance from a variety of sources, Brewer wrote to scholars and so-called race leaders. He corresponded with James J. Kilpatrick, the conservative editor of the *Richmond News Leader* and at the time a defender of the "massive resistance" backlash against desegregation. After a Kilpatrick lecture entitled "A View of The Conflict," Brewer, while disagreeing with Kilpatrick, pointed out that he had been treated respectfully by black members of the audience even though they did not wholly share Kilpatrick's points of view.[18]

The Confederate Negro was researched during the waning remnants of Jim Crowism. Blacks who sought to conduct research usually faced a predicament in staff who could not believe any black had the intellect to comprehend 19th century documents nor modern techniques of historical analysis. Mrs. Brewer diplomatically recalls that during research trips, she and her husband sometimes encountered "racial problems" at "white" archives. In the South of the 1960s it was unconventional, if not potentially hazardous, for an African-American academic to undertake a quest to highlight *black* contributions on behalf of the Confederacy. At the National Archives, the Library of Congress and elsewhere, Brewer employed a discreet technique: he would quickly make friends with black archival employees and they in turn provided him with greater assistance than he would have otherwise received. Considering the times and availability of materials, his accomplishment is all the more remarkable.[19]

Brewer's main objective was to ascertain the extent of Afro-Virginian service to the Confederacy in field and factory. His initial working titles were "The Negro in The Virginia Confederacy" and later, "Shadows of the Confederacy: Virginia Negroes in the Southern War Effort." But by May of 1962 he had finally chosen *The Confederate Negro* because he wanted to emphasize the Old Dominion as the South's most important state politically, economically, industrially and militarily. She had a greater population of blacks (548,907) than any other place in the United States; the majority of the war's battles were fought on her soil.[20]

Initially, Brewer himself believed "Confederate Negroes" were "invidious . . . repugnant, a thing to be used, not a person to be respected." Yet he later complained to a fellow historian that:

> Historical opinion assures one that the Confederate Negro was docile but irresponsible, loyal but lazy, humble but a liar and a petty thief. Then too, his behavior was described as childish and silly, and his relationship with his master was portrayed as one of utter dependence and attachment. Historical opinion

> also states that he viewed slavery not as degrading, but routine. And from such a portrayal there arose erroneous generalizations concerning his exhibited behavior in support of the Confederate war effort.[21]

But if this were true, Brewer wondered, why did the South in 1865 accept black soldiers, a sacred right and trust normally considered appropriate only for white men? As his research continued, he began to comprehend the character and legacy of black Southerners. Afro-Virginians, in Brewer's estimation, were representative of "Confederate Negroes," typified by paradoxes and contradictions. He defined them as involuntary allies, historical enigmas, integrated components and extensions of Confederate armies and overlooked participants. Although vilified, degraded and constrained by racial prejudice, "though enslaved in a land of freedom, the negro quickly responded to the rebel yell." Calls for assistance were answered by forcibly enrolling or accepting volunteers eager to prove their loyalty. He considered their loyalty as sincere but an illogical response to what blacks perceived as increasing racial tolerance. In my view, his findings do not necessarily prove this, and place too much acceptance of the expansion in the number of black workers in the war effort as a legitimate manifestation of white acceptance. The phenomenon of black volunteerism may have in large part represented individuals anxious to improve their economic situation.

A senior research associateship at the Smithsonian and grants from the Richmond University Center and Virginia State College between 1958 and 1965 enabled Brewer to consult a maze of Confederate, federal and state documents, free black registers, tax and pension records, city council minutes, state newspapers and journals.[22] The combination of fresh primary materials and contemporary scholarly literature enabled the preparation of a painstaking, fact-based narrative based on sound research. The Virginia State Library, city and county clerk offices and the Confederate Museum (Museum of The Confederacy) were canvassed; fewer sources were consulted at the Southern Historical Collection (University of North Carolina at Chapel Hill), the Virginia Historical Society and the Library of Congress. (It may be that Brewer examined collections at other repositories but found nothing relative to his topic.)

Over 500 copious and pragmatic endnotes of 30 pages accompany the text and are in themselves worthy of a second book. Thirty-one intriguing tables, an average of five per chapter, complement the narrative flow to provide additional information, though some are repetitive or offer information already provided by the text. Brewer is not guilty of minutia padding; he obviously sought to present Afro-Virginian history in a new light and clearly preferred to provide as many facts as possible rather than neglect significant details.[23]

Instead of detailing his findings in a chronological narrative,

Brewer presents evidence in a broad, descriptive and topical framework. His chapters define and identify black occupations and experiences, interwoven with well-documented examples, of the experiences of free black and slave workers.

Brewer evaluates their duties and the policy decisions and type of paperwork involved in their management, supervision and regulation; chapters three, four and five are exceptionally detailed in this respect. He notes the practice of slave hiring as "undoubtedly prolong[ing] the war by preventing Federal invasions from seriously affecting the resources of the state."[24]

Afro-Virginians built defensive works, produced ships and ordnance; cared for the wounded and sick at military hospitals; built and repaired railroads, bridges and canals; grew and harvested crops and transported food, troops and materials. Among their skilled occupations were blacksmiths, boatmen, bricklayers, canal workers, carpenters, caulkers, cooks, drillers, engineers, hospital orderlies and nurses, laundresses, machinists, masons, mechanics, miners, railroad firemen, shoemakers, smelters, stevedores, tanners, teamsters, wagonmakers and wheelwrights. Regrettably, relevant first-person details and reminiscences by blacks are scarce. Judiciously citing blacks by name, thanks in part to surviving though limited private manuscript collections and official Confederate records, Brewer's research began to restore these previously invisible, nameless men and women to the historic record.

For example, John Updike and Richard Parsons, free black owners of ships and slaves, who worked for Confederate victory; slaves Cyrus, James, Samuel and Laura, Danville hospital workers; George, John, Jim and Beverly, blacksmiths who each earned annually one thousand dollars. The variety of skilled occupations indicates a need for further study on Virginia's free black community, its potential resources, self-help mechanisms and ability to survive in the South's largest slaveholding state. Brewer criticized the exclusion of Afro-Southerners:

> Historians today are far from acknowledging [the Confederate Negro's] essential importance . . . nor do they claim that his brawn and skill enhanced the fighting potential of Southern armies. Yet, looking through existing war records, one finds something else. The Negro was an inseparable part of the economic machinery which supported and sustained the Southern forces. . . . Behind the fighting lines he bore a multitude of burdens.[25]

He concisely explores the subject of Afro-Virginians as Confederate soldiers and suggests 27,771 free black males of military age were available by 1864 and characterized black employment as a force which revitalized the gray navy. His evidence contradicted earlier black historians who unanimously denied or denounced black Confederate soldiers as nonexistent imaginings of nostalgic Southerners and neo-Confederates (extremist supporters and defenders of the Old South). But black Southern soldiers existed and Union soldiers died by their hands.[26]

The book received considerable praise. One of the nation's most distinguished historians, John Hope Franklin (whose book *From Slavery To Freedom* is considered the best history of African-Americans ever written) noted that Brewer's analysis showed how invaluable blacks were to Virginia's military effort. Eugene Genovese, another award-winning scholar, hailed it as "a careful study showing ... that compulsory black labor effectively sustained the Confederate war effort in all phases.[27]

A reviewer for *The Journal of Southern History* commended the book because "the scholar and general reader will both appreciate the author's ability to explain complicated economic and technological problems in plain English." Vanderbilt University's Jacque Voegeli applauded Brewer's "statistical evidence showing blacks were comprehensively and effectively employed as skilled craftsmen and unskilled laborers for the Virginia war effort." Another commentator pointed out that because Brewer obtained much "statistics materials" this meant "other aspects of Negro life may be similarly documented" and recommended the book to college and university libraries.

A *Journal of American History* commentator hailed Brewer for correcting "a serious omission while delivering a telling blow to the destruction of the stereotypical southern Negro" and for reminding us that slavery was a system of exploitation, broken promises and denial of equality or freedom. "A long overdue chapter in Southern historiography . . . with much information akin to case histories, make this a most readable book," opined a University of North Carolina librarian, who perceived parallels between Afro-Confederate labor battalions and labor armies utilized by the Soviet Union during World War II.[28]

Although Brewer received letters of congratulation and the accolades of family, friends and academic colleagues who took pride in his accomplishment, black attitudes toward *The Confederate Negro* ranged from indifference to disapproval. The sixties decade saw a rise in black self-pride and group consciousness. Black history was to be used as one of many weapons against racism, to make whites feel guilty (even to the point of securing from them financial restitution for sufferings caused by slavery and discrimination) while highlighting the achievements and idolization of famous and obscure African-American heroines and heroes. In the year of its publication, James Earl Ray was sentenced to 99 years imprisonment for the assassination of Martin

Luther King, Jr.; race riots broke out in Hartford, Connecticut, Baton Rouge, Fort Lauderdale, and Springfield, Massachusetts; the Supreme Court ordered end to public school segregation "at once"; psychologist Arthur Jensen claimed blacks were genetically less intelligent than whites, and Harvard University established its first African-American studies program.[29]

Some academics and civil rights activists were embarrassed or piqued that Brewer would presume to classify Afro-Southerners' forced labor as indicative of black support of the slaveholders' rebellion, not to mention indirectly praising blacks in traditional, subservient roles. The book was regarded as an insensitive, simplistic betrayal of the suffering of slaves during an era of which the less said, the better. Black nationalists questioned the motivations and racial loyalty of black scholars whose writings seemed to praise or otherwise speak favorably of the Confederate States of America. Any African-American academic who objectively discussed the Confederacy was not only considered its defender but an advocate of white supremacy and a betrayer of blacks.

Carter G. Woodson condemned such viewpoints: "To write on the Confederacy is like invading a forbidden field. Negroes are supposed to talk and write about affairs which are peculiarly their own history. While the history of the Confederacy is history influenced by the Negro, white men, we are told, can handle that satisfactorily." In spite of their founder's axiom, neither *The Journal of Negro History* nor *The Negro History Bulletin* ostensibly reviewed the book. A bibliographical essay published in the *Journal* shortly after Brewer's death described his research as "conceptual ambivalence" beset by a "constant theme of inner tension" and a reluctance to "interpret black motivation for supporting a cause dedicated to slavery."[30]

Brewer was criticized for concentrating on black men as military, industrial and agricultural workers while ignoring black women, runaway slaves and black resistance, Afro-Virginians and the Union army, education, black Confederate soldiers, the Emancipation Proclamation, miscegenation and similar consequential subjects. Critics complained the study only analyzed Southern blacks who voluntarily and loyally served the South while neglecting black dissent and testimony in previous publications, such as Works Progress Administration (WPA) interviews with ex-slaves conducted between 1920 and 1940. Others took him to task for what they alleged as a misleading primary title, an "awkward and repetitive style" and dismissed the book as inferior to Bell Irvin Wiley's 1938 study.[31]

Such criticisms are undeserved. One searches in vain for an overt defense of the South by Brewer. He had no ax to grind nor was he a Confederate apologist. His stated purpose was to provide a topical assessment of Afro-Virginian involvement in the Confederate struggle for independence and show how they were "used to close a huge gap in Virginia's technological needs." This meant a narrowly defined group of slaves and free blacks. Second, Brewer wanted his book to become "a sound basis for wholesome race relations" to give Confederate and contemporary blacks historical respectability and dignity. Third, while a few contemporary published sources of black eyewitnesses existed at the time, many were not relevant to Virginia. In WPA interviews, several of the state's surviving slaves indicated they were never directly employed by the Confederacy or else briefly noted such experiences in passing. The majority of Virginia slave reminiscences were made available *subsequent* to the publication of *The Confederate Negro*. One such study, *Weevils in the Wheat*, did not appear until four years after Brewer's death.[32]

Another problem beyond Brewer's control was the state of archival finding aids for manuscript collections during the 1960s. At several Deep South archival repositories, detailed card catalogs and guides, if they existed, either overlooked or ignored direct references to antebellum and wartime Southern blacks except as a caste of faithful personal slaves or random and irregular troublemakers. As one black Virginia historian explained: "Black workers . . . are seldom mentioned in diaries, letters, and newspaper accounts of the period. Whites treated them as invisible inferiors for as slaveowners many were used to black servility. It was a subject that was as superfluous to daily conversation as the numbers of breaths a person had taken on a given day."[33]

Brewer's book is an innovative beginning to understanding the full story of black Southerners; without bias or favoritism, he is content to tell their story, present the evidence and urge others to explore and expand scholarship on this subject. He perceives Afro-Virginians as players, not spectators; to ignore them is to disregard a significant perspective of the South's historiography. It is the duty of every historian to compile evidence which offers fresh perceptions on old enigmas. Under any circumstances, this slim, thought-provoking volume of six chapters is a uncommon accomplishment and a "thoughtful and moving account" of the Afro-Virginian contribution and value to the Confederacy. Brewer hoped his book might prevent blacks from becoming casualties of history and serve as a catalyst for similar African-American research.[34]

Brewer witnessed some of America's most profound changes in race relations. He was 20 years old when Joe Louis became the world heavyweight boxing champion, 30 years old when Jackie Robinson became the first black major league baseball player of the century, 40 years old when Congress passed the first civil rights act since 1875 to protect the rights of blacks, and 50 years old when Thurgood Marshall became the first black justice on the U. S. Supreme Court. At Brewer's death, the black American population had increased from nine to 24 million.

In the twenty-three years since the publication of *The Confederate*

Negro, similar state studies of Afro-Southerners have appeared. Despite their titles and claims to evaluate the black experience, they tend to focus on whites, particularly slaveholders. Brewer, ever mindful that African-American contributions to the American national experience have yet to be equally emphasized, warned against exclusionary knowledge of the past as leading to racial animosity. He was of the opinion that by looking at history with an unprejudiced spotlight "this would put things in a more reasonable focus." The black presence Americanized the South, Brewer believed, and he predicted the United States would become a multicultural nation with the biracial South as its model.[35]

James Brewer probably would not have described himself as a Civil War scholar. He was first an African-American and second a historian. He did not believe historical revisionism could in itself solve four hundred years of racial problems. As a pioneer, not a polemicist, he objectively examined and assessed the life and times of Afro-Virginians as laborers and craftsmen in Civil War Virginia. He impartially interpreted the black community's durability within a slave society and brought to light their contributions and activities. As one of the most extraordinary monographs ever written about blacks, Brewer's book is an unique, enduring and indispensable contribution to our understanding of African-American and Civil War history.

Notes

1. Mrs. James Brewer interview, Durham, North Carolina, November 17, 1990; funeral program and miscellaneous James H. Brewer papers in her possession (hereafter cited as Brewer Papers-Durham); *New York Times*, March 11, 1974, 32, col. 2 (erroneously lists his age as 64); "Death," *The Journal of Southern History* 40, no. 4 (November 1974): 692 (which erroneously lists his age as fifty-three). At the time of his death Brewer was completing *The Black Ethos*, a study of the psyche of twentieth-century blacks and their migration from the South. My own monograph, *Black Confederates And Afro-Yankees: The History of The African-American Experience In Civil War Virginia* (forthcoming, University Press of Virginia) will supplement *The Confederate Negro*.

2. James H. Brewer, "Robert Lee Vann, Democrat or Republican: An Exponent of Loose Leaf Politics," *Negro History Bulletin* 21, no. 5 (February 1958): 103; James H. Brewer, "The Ghosts of Jackson Ward," *Negro History Bulletin* 22, no. 2 (November 1958): 27; James H. Brewer, *The Confederate Negro: Virginia's craftsmen and military laborers. 1861-1865* (Durham, North Carolina: Duke University Press, 1969), 167.

3. Earle E. Thorpe, *Negro Historians In The United States* (Baton Rouge: Fraternal Press, 1958), 145; Earle E. Thorpe, *Black Historians: A Critique* (New York: William Morrow and Company, Inc., 1971), 186; August Meier and Elliot Rudwick, *Black History And The Historical Profession, 1915-1980* (Urbana: University of Illinois Press, 1986). Occasionally, Brewer is confused in various sources with John Mason Brewer (1896-1975), a noted black folklorist.

4. Author's telephone conversation with Duke University Press, fall 1990. Recent studies mentioning *The Confederate Negro* include: Edward D. C. Campbell, Jr., and Kym S. Rice, eds., *Before Freedom Came: African-American Life In The Antebellum South* (Richmond: Museum of The Confederacy and Charlottesville: University Press of Virginia, 1991), 18, 177-178, 203; James M. McPherson, *Battle Cry of Freedom: The Civil War Era* (New York: Oxford University Press, 1988), 881; Randall M. Miller and John David Smith, eds., *Dictionary or Afro-American Slavery* (New York: Greenwood Press, 1988), 787; Philip Morgan, ed., *"Don't Grieve After Me": The Black Experience in Virginia 1619-1986* (Hampton, Virginia: Hampton University Press, 1986), 58; James S. Olson, *Slave Life In America: A Historiography and Selected Bibliography* (Lanham, Maryland: University Press of America, Inc., 1983), 94; David C. Roller and Robert Twyman, eds., *The Encyclopedia of Southern History* (Baton Rouge: Louisiana State University Press, 1979), 266; J. K.Obatala, "The Unlikely Story of Blacks Who Were Loyal To Dixie," *Smithsonian Magazine* 9 (March

1979), 100.

5. Pittsburgh Boxer Brings "Soul Teaching" To UNC," *The Chapel Hill Newspaper*, June 3, 1973.

6. Funeral program, Brewer Papers-Durham; Mrs. Brewer interview, 1990; James H. Brewer, "Negro Property Owners in Seventeenth Century Virginia," *William and Mary Quarterly*, 3rd. series, 11, no. 4 (October 1955): 574-580; T. H. Breen and Stephen Innes, *"Myne owne ground": Race and Freedom on Virginia's Eastern Shore 1640- 1676* (New York: Oxford University Press, 1980), 1, 8, 11, 115-117; Brewer to E. W. Gregory, October 20, 1960, James A. Brewer Papers, Special Collections, University Archives, Johnston Memorial Library, Virginia State University, Petersburg (hereafter cited as VSU). Brewer's article was reprinted in August Meier and Elliot Rudwick, Eds., *The Making of Black America: Essays In Negro History*, vol. 1 (New York: Atheneum, 1969), 201-205.

7. Lerone Bennett, Jr., *Before The Mayflower: A History of Black America*, 5th Ed. (Middlesex, England: Penguin Books, 1984), 517-519; Ezra J. Warner, *Generals In Gray* (Baton Rouge: Louisiana State University Press, 1959), xiv, 260-261; Peter N. Bergman and Mort N. Bergman, *The Chronological History of The Negro In America* (New York: Harper & Row, 1969), 359, 382-383.

8. Mrs. Brewer interview, 1990; James H. Brewer, "An Account of Negro Slavery In The Cape Fear Region Prior To 1860" *University of Pittsburgh Bulletin*, vol. 46, no. 10 (June 15, 1950), 3; James Howard Brewer, "Robert Lee Vann and *The Pittsburgh Courier*" (Masters thesis, University of Pittsburgh, 1941); James Howard Brewer, "An Account of Negro Slavery In The Cape Fear Region Prior To 1860" (Ph.D. dissertation, University of Pittsburgh, 1948).

9. Brewer Papers-Durham; Mrs. Brewer, telephone conversation with Ervin Jordan, August 25, 1992; "Death," *The Journal of Southern History* 40, no. 4 (November 1974): 692; Brewer, "An Account of Negro Slavery" (*University of Pittsburgh Bulletin*), 3; Jackson to Brewer, June 11, 1949, and, Brewer to Jackson, June 18, 1949, Luther Porter Jackson, Sr., Papers, Folder 247, Box 12, VSU.

10. Meier and Rudwick, *Black History And The Historical Profession*, 85-88; Professor Lucious Edwards, University Archivist, Virginia State University, Petersburg, telephone conversation with Ervin Jordan, September 3, 1992; Luther Porter Jackson, *Free Negro Labor & Property Holding in Virginia. 1830-1860*, with a new Preface by James Brewer (New York: Atheneum, 1969).

11. *The Chapel Hill Newspaper*, June 3, 1973.

12. *Ibid.*; Mrs. Brewer interview, 1990.

13. Funeral program, Brewer Papers-Durham; Mrs. Brewer interview, 1990.

14. Brewer Papers-Durham; Mrs. Brewer, telephone conversation, 1992; Brewer to Gregory, October 20, 1960, Brewer

Papers, VSU.

15. Brewer, "An Account of Negro Slavery" (*University of Pittsburgh Bulletin*), 1.

16. Charles Harris Wesley, *The Collapse of The Confederacy* (Washington, D. C.: The Associated Publishers, Inc., 1937), 134, 140-151, 156; Bell Irvin Wiley, *Southern Negroes, 1861-1865* (New Haven: Yale University Press, 1938), chapter viii, passim.

17. W. Adolphe Roberts, *Semmes of The Alabama* (Indianapolis and New York: The Bobbs-Merrill Company, 1938), 261.

18. Brewer to Kilpatrick, November 20, 1961, Brewer Papers, VSU.

19. Mrs. Brewer interview, 1990. Brewer was not the only black historian who encountered racial discrimination at archival repositories. See John Hope Franklin, *Race and History: Selected Essays 1938-1988* (Baton Rouge and London: Louisiana State University Press, 1989), 304-305.

20. E. W. Gregory to Brewer, November 23, 1960; Brewer to James J. Kilpatrick, November 20, 1961; Brewer to Dr. F. D. Patterson, May 22, 1962, Brewer Papers, VSU.

21. Brewer to Dr. F. D. Patterson, May 22, 1962, Brewer Papers, VSU .

22. Brewer, *Confederate Negro*, xvii; E. W. Gregory, chairman, Research Council, University Center In Virginia, Inc., to Brewer, November 23, 1960, Brewer Papers, VSU. He also attempted to secure funding from the Phelps-Stokes Fund; see Brewer to Dr. F. D. Patterson, May 22, 1962, Brewer Papers, VSU.

23. Brewer, *Confederate Negro*, ix-x, xvii, 169-199, 201-204.

24. Ibid, xvi, 163-165, 167. For examples of black Confederate loyalty see Ervin L. Jordan, Jr., *Charlottesville And The University of Virginia In The Civil War* (Lynchburg, Virginia: H. E. Howard, Inc., 1988), 28 & 55.

25. Brewer, *Confederate Negro*, 11, 13, 21, 34-35, 76, 102-103, 126, 162-167, 186, 198.

26. George Washington Williams, *History Of The Negro Race In America From 1619 To 1880* (New York: G. P. Putnam's Sons, 1882), 278; Joseph T. Wilson, *Black Phalanx: A History Of The Negro Soldiers of The United States In The War of 1775-1812, 1861-'65* (Hartford, Connecticut: American Publishing Company, 1888) 483, 495, 499; Benjamin Brawley, A *Short History Of The American Negro*, revised edition (New York: The Macmillan Company, 1924), 113; W. E. Burghardt Du Bois, *Black Reconstruction* (New York: Russell & Russell, 1935), 119-120; Wesley, *Collapse Of The Confederacy*, 42; Carter G. Woodson, "Charles H. Wesley Unmasks The Confederacy" (book review), in *The New York Age*, February 5, 1938, 6.

27. John Hope Franklin, *From Slavery to Freedom: A History of Negro Americans*, 5th Ed. (New York: Alfred A. Knopf, 1980), 218 &

528; Eugene Genovese, *Roll. Jordan Roll: The World The Slaves Made* (New York: Random House, 1974), 150.

28. F. N. Boney review, *The Journal of Southern History*, 36, no. 1 (February 1970): 114; Jacque Voegeli review, *American Historical Review* 75, no. 4 (April 1970): 1191; unsigned review, *Choice* 6, no. 10 (December 1969): 1470; Roland C. McConnell review, *The Journal of American History*, 57, no. 2 (September 1970): 442-443; William Stevens review, *Library Journal* 94, no. 20 (November 15, 1969): 4137.

29. Bennett, *Before The Mayflower*, 587; Laurence Urdang, *The Timetables of American History* (New York: Simon and Schuster, 1983), 395; Alton Hornsby, Jr., *Chronology of African-American History* (Detroit: Gale Research, 1991), 136.

30. Mrs. Brewer interview, 1990; Woodson, "Charles H. Wesley Unmasks The Confederacy," p. 6; Clarence L. Mohr, "Southern Blacks in the Civil War: A Century of Historiography," *The Journal of Negro History* 59, no. 2 (April 1974): 193-194. Mohr's article does praise Brewer: "[He] has produced by far the most through study of wartime black labor available for any Southern state." My review of available indexes for *The Journal of Negro History* and *The Negro History Bulletin* failed to locate any mention of Brewer or his book.

31. McConnell review, 442; Voegeli review, 1191; Boney review, 113-114.

32. Brewer, *Confederate Negro*, xv; Brewer to Dr. F. D. Patterson, May 22, 1962, Brewer Papers, VSU; Charles L. Perdue, Jr., Thomas E. Barden, and Robert K. Phillips, *Weevils in the Wheat: Interviews With Virginia Ex-Slaves* (Charlottesville: University Press of Virginia, 1976).

33. Jordan, *Charlottesville And The University of Virginia*, 55.

34. Brewer, *Confederate Negro*, ix, 167. The first chapter of *The Confederate Negro* was reprinted in full in Robert V. Haynes, *Blacks In White America Before 1865: Issues and Interpretations* (New York: David McKay Company, Inc., 1972), 490-503.

35. *The Chapel Hill Newspaper*, June 3, 1973. See also John Cimprich, *Slavery's End in Tennessee, 1861-1865* (University, Alabama: University of Alabama Press, 1985); Barbara J. Fields, *Slavery and Freedom on the Middle Ground: Maryland During The Nineteenth Century* (New Haven: Yale University Press, 1985); Clarence L. Mohr, *On The Threshold of Freedom: Masters And Slaves In Civil War Georgia* (Athens: University of Georgia Press, 1986); and, Randolph B. Campbell, *An Empire For Slavery: The Peculiar Institution In Texas, 1821-1865* (Baton Rouge: Louisiana State University Press, 1989).

Robert Durden's *The Gray and the Black*

Arthur W. Bergeron, Jr.

Robert F. Durden, *The Gray and the Black: The Confederate Debate on Emancipation.* (Baton Rouge: Louisiana State University Press, 1972. 305 pp. Preface, index.)

This book consists of a collection of documents or excerpts from documents dealing with the arguments for and against both arming slaves to fight for the Confederacy and granting them their freedom for having done so. The focus, as Durden states in his preface, is on the plan advanced by Jefferson Davis in late 1864. Durden argues that previous historians ignored this plan or had not given Davis credit for it. He says also that the writers who have talked about the proposal "have largely missed Davis' point," that is, Davis and other Confederate leaders "attempted to force the South to face the desperate alternative of sacrificing one of its war aims—-the preservation of slavery— in order to make a last-ditch effort to achieve the other— an independent southern nation" (vii).

The increasing number of black soldiers in the Union armies caused some Confederates in 1863 to urge a policy of emancipation. Editors of such newspapers as the *Jackson Mississippian* and *Montgomery Weekly Mail* called for freeing and arming male slaves in the fall of 1863. The latter paper argued "it is better for us to use our negroes for our defense than that the Yankees should use them against us" (34). Major General Patrick R. Cleburne and some of his subordinate officers advanced a proposal in January of 1864 to enlist slaves into the Confederate army and to offer them their freedom after the war. Davis quickly suppressed this idea when it came to his attention.

Later in that year, however, he changed his mind, and his message to Congress on November 7 called for enlisting slaves as combat soldiers. Secretary of State Judah P. Benjamin added his voice to Davis' in a speech on February 9, 1865, in which he advocated joint action by the Virginia legislature and the Confederate government to free and arm slaves. Nine days later, General Robert E. Lee wrote a letter to Congressman Ethelbert Barksdale in which he supported the idea, saying it was "not only expedient but necessary" (206). The force of Lee's reputation helped push the Congress into action. In March, it passed a bill that authorized Davis to call as many as 300,000 slaves into military service. That law did not, however, hold out any hope of emancipation, but Davis decided to add that incentive in carrying out the provisions of the act. As many Civil War scholars and buffs know, a few companies of slaves were enlisted. The war was practically over by this time, and none of these men saw any fighting.

Durden concludes his book with two answers to the question of why the Confederacy failed "to achieve an effective and timely change in its own policy." First, he says, many Confederate leaders realized in late 1864 that the war was going against them and rejected a scheme that would only have protracted "the bloody ordeal," not have reversed its outcome. Secondly, too many Southerners could not "force themselves to agree to any tampering with the cornerstone of the Confederacy." Durden writes, "in the final analysis, the South as a whole could not summon the intelligence, imagination, and moral courage to begin voluntarily to abandon the peculiar institution" (287).

Several criticisms can be, and have been, made of Durden's book. He argues for "a reservoir of good will between the white and black races in the South"(viii) but his documents do not support that contention. This is not to say that his argument has no validity, only that he fails to quote enough sources to bolster his claim. Durden admits that there is "only indirect evidence" of how blacks would have "reacted to the possibility of their playing a larger, or more military, role for the Confederacy"(47). The only document he offers in support of his feeling "that if freedom were anywhere in prospect, some blacks were indeed willing to become Confederates" is a brief story carried by the *New Orleans Bee* in November 1863. That article quotes a *New York Tribune* correspondent's conversation with an English doctor who had served as a surgeon in several Confederate military hospitals. The Englishman stated that he had talked with a number of slaves who were willing to fight for "Master Jeff" in exchange for their freedom and a small plot of land.

Other criticisms relate to Durden's choice of documents and his introductions to them. The vast majority of sources are letters printed in the *Official Records*, newspaper articles and editorials and printed correspondence and speeches. He includes only seven documents from archival collections. Perhaps a more thorough investigation into the holdings of archives and libraries around the country would have located more pertinent manuscripts. Some of the documents Durden quotes really seem to have no place in his book, for example, the Emancipation Proclamation. Because of the nature of *The Gray and the Black*, it lacks the in-depth analysis some readers may wish it contained. A narrative rather than a collection of documents would have made a much stronger publication. Even more lengthy introductions to or comments on the documents might have improved the book.

The Gray and the Black will disappoint many readers. Durden has some interesting and controversial opinions but does not sufficiently support them. He has given us a collection of documents rather than a well-argued and well-documented monograph.

Louisiana Office of State Parks — Arthur W. Bergeron, Jr.

Glimpses of Invisible Men: A Review of Essays in Professional Journals and Popular Magazines

Richard Rollins

The literature on black Southerners in Confederate military service is both limited in scope and thin in depth of research. The few works in book form will be covered by other authors. In this review I will concentrate on those essays appearing in either professional scholarly journals or the more popular Civil War magazines.

Black Confederates have been nearly invisible to both scholarly and public eyes. When historians have written about them, it has almost always been with a "gee-whiz" attitude; since virtually no one has known their story, the specific subject seemed unique or extremely unusual. The essayists have usually narrowed their scope to a single individual or a few individuals, setting them in the context of individual lives rather than larger social movements. The authors' lack of knowledge of the larger patterns of life among black Southerners during the war prohibited them from making connections to other slaves and free people of color and their experiences in the Confederacy. In this manner they have rarely recognized that the entire South faced the same issues and conditions, and therefore larger patterns of experience existed throughout the region.

These essays have in a sense been shaped by the popular view among Northerners of what the South was like and what the lives of black Southerners was like. As Reid Mitchell has shown in his recent book on *Civil War Soldiers: Their Expectations and Their Experiences*, the overwhelming popular belief, carried South by white Federal soldiers and held with equal conviction by most white Northerners was that black Southerners knew what the war was about and automatically sided with the North. This led Northerners, in some cases, to disbelieve what they saw, and to interpret their experiences in terms of their expectations. It blinded most Northerners to the reality of the diversity of black Southern culture.

The landmark essay that caught many readers' attention and brought the subject into contemporary public consciousness was Ed Smith's "Calico, Black and Gray: Women and Blacks in the Confederacy," appearing in *Civil War: The Magazine of the Civil War Society* in 1990. In it Smith speculated on the reasons why black Southerners sided with the South and then cited several specific examples. It was a provocative piece written from the perspective of a black Southern academician, and it set off quite a debate within the "Civil War community." He showed that blacks had indeed supported the Confederacy, and speculated on their motivations. He also talked about the role of blacks in the union and the experiences of women in the war.

In fact the earliest scholarly glance at black Confederates was Charles Wesley's essay in the *Journal of Negro History* in 1919. That's not a journal normally read by Civil War historians, so it has gone largely unnoticed. Wesley began by noting that in the early days of the war most black Southerners saw it as an attack on independent states in the same manner as did white Southerners. He then traced the Confederacy's use of black labor on defense projects and wrote a state-by-state examination of the policies of each state toward the role of blacks in the war. His work foreshadowed Robert Durden's *The Gray and The Black* by drawing on official state and federal records and newspapers to trace the debate over the arming of black Southerners throughout the war, culminating in the raising of black troops by the Confederate government in March of 1865. Wesley's essay consciously compared the situation of blacks in various states. With one exception, no other scholarly essay of a generalized nature in a professional journal has appeared since 1919.

The next essay on black Confederates with a wide scope appeared 60 years later, in the *Smithsonian Magazine* in 1979. J. K. Obatala's "The Unlikely Story of Blacks who were loyal to Dixie" was not footnoted and thus we do not know where he got his information, but most of it is anecdotal in nature, stories of individuals and small groups of black Southerners who demonstrated their allegiance to the Confederacy. Obatala began by glancing back at the Confederacy to note that the severe antagonism and separation between the races in the South is a result of the Reconstruction period rather than the Civil War era. Thus he reminds us of the need to be sensitive to the historical figures we deal with in the context of the time they lived, rather than allow the ideological and intellectual assumptions of our own day to dictate what we have to say about the people of the Civil War era, both black and white.

Obatala noted that in 1861 black Southerners across the South displayed their support for secession. In widely separated places like Helena, Arkansas, and rural Georgia, black Southerners held fund-raising events such as dances and food sales. Despite their obviously limited financial resources, they felt strongly enough to take it upon themselves to help pay for uniforms and equipment for Confederate soldiers. For example, Obatala recounted the story of the all-black "Ethiopian Serenaders" in Richmond, a minstrel band that donated the profits from some of their shows to the Confederate cause. Obatala then proceeded to tell the story of laborers, cooks, etc., all of whom made a significant contributions to the Confederacy. In closing, Obatala speculated on the sources of motivation of these black Southerners. He noted their strong attachments to their local communities and their belief that freedom would come to them in the end.

Obatala came to an interesting conclusion, one that no other historian has dared to agree with. He linked the black Southerners in Confederate service to the ancestors of today's forward-looking, successful black businessmen. An individual black Southerner could have had

> at least a primitive, instinctive feeling that his fortunes were tied inextricably to those of the South. That he was a Southerner. In this regard, that black Confederate—far more than the Reconstruction politicians who were appendages of the Republican North—was the prototype of the modern, middle-class black of the 'New South.' In fact, it was a strong sense of regional pride that helped generate the Civil Rights movement of the 1950's and 60's.

Obatala closed with a vivid and striking thought: that contemporary black leaders like Andrew Young and Vernon Jordan, "who come from educated families, with deep roots in the South, may conjure up to us the ghosts of martyred Union soldiers and runaway slaves. But in fact their historical ancestors might just have worn the butternut of the Old South rather than the blue of the Union Army."

Jeff Carroll's essay on Primus Kelly, entitled "Dignity, Courage and Fidelity,' in the *Confederate Veteran* in 1990, is more representative of the genre. Kelly was born a slave in North Carolina, where his parents were the property of the John West family. Like many black and white Southerners, West's sons Robert, Richard and John, Jr., and slave children grew up in intimate familiarity with each other, despite being on opposite ends of an unequal social relationship. Yet their personal friendship and love obviously overcame, or flourished in spite of, the harsher aspects of slavery. When the West family moved to Texas, Kelly went with them. When the sons went of to war in 1861, they went to Houston to catch the train east with their regiment, the 8th Texas Cavalry, also known as Terry's Texas Rangers. When they got to the train station, there was Primus Kelly, prepared to go with them. Prohibited from enlisting because of his race, Kelly served the entire war with the West sons, apparently carrying a gun and fighting at such places as Shiloh and Chickamauga. One of the white West boys was wounded twice, and each time Kelly carried him home, nursed him back to health, and, when he recovered, rode back to the army with him. While he may have also filled the role of a servant, he was a Confederate soldier through and through. The author believed he was the only black Texan to serve in the army.

New Orleans possessed a large and vibrant black community in the 1860s, one that interacted extensively with the French community. This had far-ranging ramifications for the experiences of black Southerners in Confederate military service. A regiment of 1,300 men was raised in 1861, called the 1st Louisiana Native Guards, and included many of the leading individuals in the New Orleans black community. They provided their own weapons and uniforms and spent the greater part of their time in Confederate service as Provost Guards in the black sections of New Orleans. When the Federal forces captured the city in 1862 the Native Guards surrendered rather than evacuate the town. Later that year when Ben Butler began to raise black troops for his own use, some of these same men volunteered for duty in blue. Mary Berry's 1967 essay in *Louisiana History* on "Negro Troops in Blue and Gray: The Louisiana Native Guards, 1861-1863" concentrated most of its emphasis on Butler's men, with only a brief acknowledgement of the Confederate Native Guards. She did note that black Louisianans had played a significant part in Louisiana's military history ever since the beginning of settlement, having fought for and against the French, Spanish and English, as well as with Andrew Jackson in the Battle of New Orleans in 1815. She pointed out that by late 1861 about 3,000 black Louisianans were enrolled in state troops and militia organizations in the state, in service to the Confederate cause. Using newspapers accounts of their training and government records, Berry passed quickly over the Confederate Native Guards and spent her energy on the Federals.

Art Bergeron's 1985 essay in *Civil War History* on "Free Men of Color in Grey," a revised version of which is included in this volume, is easily the most accomplished work available to date. His research into census and population data, pension records and other materials turned up a number of specific individuals who found their way into Confederate service from Louisiana. It is a model of objective scholarship.

Scott Sallee's essay on Peter Vertrees in *Blue and Gray* in 1990 is similar to others in that Sallee saw Vertrees' experience as unique. On another level it is a story that is representative in that Vertrees was a body servant, a class of person rarely written about by historians. The majority of blacks in Confederate service were undoubtably in this category, yet almost nothing has been written concerning their lives and experiences. Born in Kentucky to a black mother and a white father, Vertrees spent 4 years working as a Surgeon's Assistant under his white uncle, who was a Surgeon for the 1st Kentucky Infantry, a part of the famous Orphan Brigade. They saw service in nearly all the major battles of the western theater.

Greg Tyler's two essays in *Civil War Times Illustrated* in 1989 and 1990 on Henry Brown fall into the familiar pattern. Henry Brown was a drummer in his hometown Darlington Guards, a militia unit in the years before the war. When they joined Confederate service in 1861 Brown went along, and stayed in the army for the entire war. He served in the 8th and 21st South Carolina Infantry regiments and participated in all their campaigns. Somewhere along the line he captured a pair of Yankee drumsticks, which he proudly displayed for the rest of his life.

Brown was well-liked and respected by black and white alike, and when he died the town built a monument in his honor in the middle of town. Tyler quotes a member of a local Round Table at the rededication of this monument as saying that "Private Brown was a unique soldier. He was one of a kind. He was, as far as we know, the only free black to serve as a genuine soldier from South Carolina in the Civil War." Yet seventeen years earlier Alexis Heisley had studied the pension records of South Carolinians and found at least one more. Her work appeared as "Black Confederates" in the *South Carolina Historical Magazine*.

Wayne Austerman's essay on "Virginia's Black Confederates" falls between those who saw their subjects as unique and a more general approach. Writing in the *Civil War Quarterly*, which later became *Civil War Magazine*, Austerman surveyed the experience of black Virginians in the Confederacy, from laborers to servants to those who engaged in combat. Anecdotal in style, Austerman seems to have based most of his work on newspaper accounts of various activities. He also noted that such stalwart Confederates as Stonewall Jackson and Henry Kyd Douglas had strong relationships with blacks.

When Ed Smith wrote his essay in 1990, it was much like the proverbial voice in the wilderness. Few others had written about black Confederates before him, and only one or two had realized, as Smith clearly did, that an examination of the real lives of black Southerners would lead to a story quite different from the one usually told by historians.

Epilogue: The Story of Andrew and Silas Chandler

The photograph on the cover is of Lt. Andrew Chandler, 44th Mississippi, and his servant, Silas Chandler. The original is in the possession of the Chandler family, and was given to us with permission to publish it by Mr. Andrew Chandler Battaile, of Belden, Mississippi.

At age sixteen my great grandfather, Andrew Martin Chandler, pictured on left, volunteered for service with Company F, 44th Mississippi Regiment on August 8, 1861. He took with him his body servant Silas Chandler, pictured on right. They were both of the same approximate age at the time of enlistment.

On 12 September their unit was transferred into Confederate service. They participated together in several campaigns to include: The Battle of Belmont, Missouri on November 7, 1861; Shiloh, Tennessee, April 6 and 7, 1862; Murfreesboro, Tennessee, December 30, 1862 and January 1,1863; and Chicamauga, Georgia, September 19 and 20, 1863.

At the Battle of Shiloh Andrew Martin Chandler was captured and sent to a Union prisoner of war camp at Camp Chase, Ohio. In August of 1862 he was released in a prisoner exchange. It is unknown whether Silas was also captured and accompanied him to Ohio.

Upon his release, Andrew and Silas returned to Confederate Service. Andrew M. Chandler was seriously wounded in the leg and foot at the Battle of Chicamauga in September 1863. Silas faithfully stayed by Andrew Martin and accompanied him to a hospital in Atlanta where he assisted in his nursing and care until his family was able to come from Mississippi and assist them both in returning home. It is very likely that without Silas' help and assistance, his master's life would have been in jeopardy.

After the war they returned to Mississippi. Silas received a pension from the State of Mississippi which was paid by the state to Confederate Veterans. Andrew gave him some land and the money to build a Church, which still stands.

These two Mississippians were likely childhood playmates. They were prematurely thrust into adult roles and went off together to experience the adventure and horror of war. It is not difficult to speculate that as a result of sharing these very trying life experiences that a special bond existed between them.

Over the generations Andrew Martin's family has lost touch with Silas' family. A couples of years ago my wife and son and I had a moving and emotional experience. we had the pleasure of visiting by phone with Silas' great grandson, Bobbie Chandler, who now resides in Washington D.C. For us, it was truly as if we had been reunited with a missing part of our family. Bobbie Chandler still returns to Mississippi to visit relatives and it is our hope that we will be able to meet with him and his relatives and renew the bonds that existed between our ancestors.